Strategic and Tactical Asset Allocation

Henrik Lumholdt

Strategic and Tactical Asset Allocation

An Integrated Approach

palgrave
macmillan

Henrik Lumholdt
Instituto de Empresa Business School
Madrid, Spain

ISBN 978-3-030-07802-7 ISBN 978-3-319-89554-3 (eBook)
https://doi.org/10.1007/978-3-319-89554-3

Cover credit: Getty/Colin Anderson

Printed on acid-free paper

This Palgrave Macmillan imprint is published by the registered company Springer Nature Switzerland AG
The registered company address is: Gewerbestrasse 11, 6330 Cham, Switzerland

Preface

Decisions, decisions, decisions. Wouldn't it be great if we could leave our investments to take care of themselves, in some kind of passive or neutral approach? The term "passive" is a straightforward concept when it comes to a specific asset class, such as stocks or bonds. We can choose an active manager who tries to outperform the overall market by picking the right securities at the right time. Or we can choose a low-cost index fund or Exchange Traded Fund (ETF) and passively track the overall market.

But "passive" is a more ambiguous concept when it comes to asset allocation. We could compose a portfolio of assets with given relative weights and then stick to that. This would be passive in the sense that we would make no subsequent adjustments apart from rebalancing. But it wouldn't be passive in the sense that we had made no decision. We would simply have shifted the decision to a more strategic level, allowing the final outcome to depend entirely on our assumptions about returns over the investment horizon. These assumptions would be tested again and again, sometimes severely as during the crises of 2001–2003 and 2008–2009. Will we hold up or will we bail out at precisely the wrong moment and lose faith in our long-term strategy? Is there no alternative to such a one-sided approach? The view expressed in this book is that there is.

In some respects asset allocation resembles navigation at sea in the old days when most ships had sails. We need an overall map to indicate general directions to our destiny. That is our strategy. But we also need to be able to temporarily divert from the general route when changes in winds or currents make this necessary. That is where tactics enter the picture.

The tactics do not contradict the strategy but are meant to reinforce it and make it viable. The central idea of this book is that for most investors an integrated approach between strategic and tactical asset allocation makes the most sense.

Asset allocation is almost by definition a top-down exercise. Stock-pickers, arbitrageurs or portfolio managers specializing in a given asset class are naturally focused on company, market or instrument specifics. The asset allocator, by contrast, must think big-picture in order to generate views about asset classes as a whole and the interaction between them under different scenarios. Top-down factors are therefore at the forefront of asset allocation decisions.

This book is aimed at finance practitioners looking for a coherent framework for decision-making in asset allocation. It therefore covers each step in the asset allocation process, from the strategic to the tactical level. It is ideally suited for portfolio or wealth managers, financial analysts, strategists, chief investment officers and other finance professionals engaged in either making or recommending investment decisions.

The field of asset allocation has never been more exciting. Frontiers are constantly being moved and the asset management industry is undergoing a minor revolution. This is reflected in academic finance as well where old ideas are being revised and new ideas are being tested empirically as never before. Inevitably, the literature in the field has also grown by leaps and bounds.

Before writing this book, I set myself the following goals:

- It should be self-contained.
- It should be concise rather than encyclopedic and focus exclusively on asset allocation.
- It should include the most relevant empirical evidence and strike the right balance between theoretical principles and the often fuzzier real environment in which market practitioners must operate.
- It should express an opinion about the subject and offer a concrete approach to asset allocation.

I leave it to you to decide whether I have managed to meet these goals or not. The structure of the book is as illustrated below:

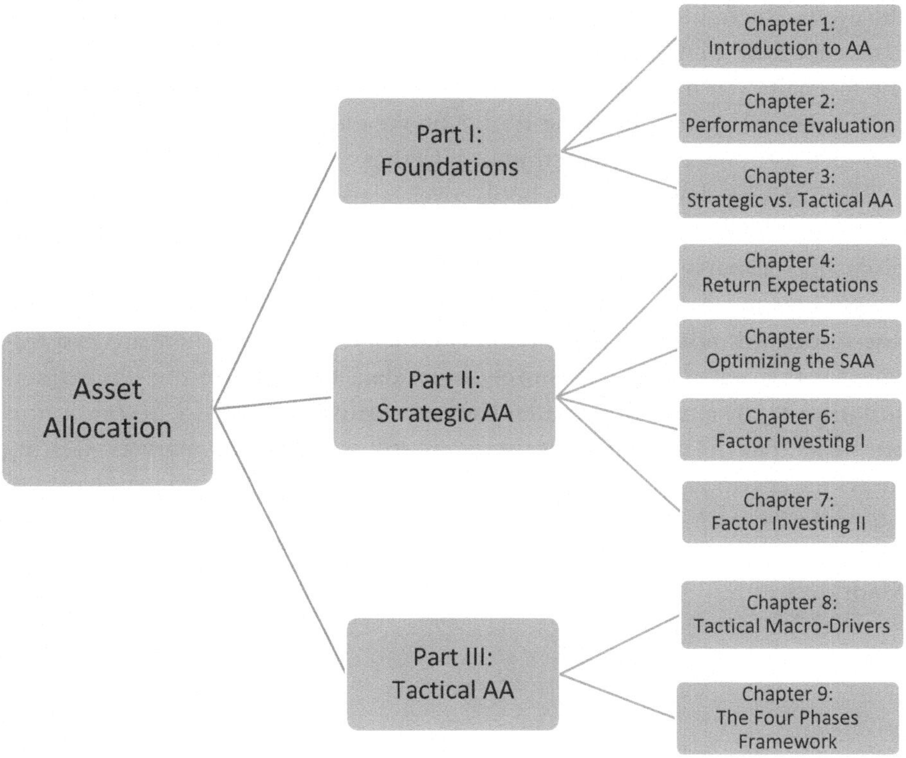

Part I sets out the practical backdrop to asset allocation, emphasizing how the different levels of decision interact and how performance is subsequently evaluated. It rounds off with a preliminary discussion of why the strategic and tactical approaches should be integrated.

Part II goes through each element in the strategic asset allocation process. It takes a close look at which factors determine long-term asset returns and discusses the challenges of forming expectations. This is followed by a discussion of the pitfalls of optimizing the strategic asset allocation, possible remedies and alternative approaches. Part II finishes with two chapters on factor investing, a subject of growing relevance to modern investors. It looks at the theory behind factors, their empirical record and issues of implementation.

Part III zooms in on the tactical level. It discusses the relevance of the business cycle and how it relates to fluctuations in corporate earnings and the policy decisions made by the central bank. It shows how using the concept of the output gap can provide useful information on where are in the cycle at any given moment. The key idea here is the business cycle is of crucial importance, and we show how different asset classes tend to perform in different phases of the cycle. The framework used is suggested as a useful background for tactical asset allocation (TAA) decisions. An appendix at the end of the book outlines the mechanics of mean-variance optimization (MVO). We make reference to MVO several times throughout the book and the appendix is therefore included as a concise introduction or refresher.

The first two chapters of the book cover relatively standard topics and may be skipped by readers who are already familiar with this. From there on, the discussion departs from standard textbook material, reflecting the many assessments to be made and the challenges facing the practical asset allocator. The reader will notice that the book is rather US-centric. There are two reasons for this. Firstly, there is simply more data available on the US markets and most of the empirical research has been focused on the US. Secondly, it is our belief that the main market trends are still set in the US markets. Getting the US scenario right is therefore a crucial starting point, independently of where the investor is based.

Madrid, Spain Henrik Lumholdt

Acknowledgments

You know that you have friends in life when someone offers to help—and then actually does so. The following people have provided unique input and invaluable advice.

Ignacio Montejo, Founding Partner and Director of International Capital Research (ICR) said to me that he "wouldn't mind having a look at the book". What followed was much more detailed and valuable feedback than I could possibly have expected. Direct errors were spotted, be it in a formula or a sentence, inconsistencies were pointed out, new ideas were suggested, I could go on.

Ignacio Chacon de la Rosa, Quantitative Multi-Asset Portfolio Manager at Fonditel, said he didn't really have much time, but that I was welcome to send him the manuscript. When we would subsequently meet for lunch, Ignacio always brought printed copies of the Word documents with underlinings in several colors. No details missed. Getting close to the deadline for the book, Ignacio helped me to remember some of the specifics of the study of the Four Phases framework which we developed together, but which ultimately relied on Ignacio's meticulous number crunching.

Teis Knuthsen, Chief Investment Officer of Kirk Kapital, and transitioning to his current position when we got in touch, offered to have a look at the manuscript. How he found the time is still a puzzle to me. But he did. Indeed, in one of our conversations about Factor Investing, he offered to send me his research on factor cyclicality. In the end, he wrote the appendix to Chap. 7 on this topic instead.

Jan Loeys, Managing Director and Senior Advisor, Long-Term Strategy, at J.P. Morgan, and also transitioning to a new role at his firm, found time to offer feedback in the early stages of the book. Jan reminded me that this should be a book for decision-makers. "Avoid too much on the one hand, and on the other hand—state your views!" said Jan. Good advice.

Ignacio Muñoz Alonso, fellow adjunct professor at the IE and well-honed finance professional, read the book toward the end and offered several useful suggestions.

Ignacio de la Torre is the academic director of the IE Business School apart from being a partner at Arcano Partners. He is the principal reason why the finance program at the business school has prospered the way it has, which brings me to the next group to mention: all my present and former students. In many ways they are really the reason I undertook this project in the first place. At the IE we talk theory, but we certainly also talk real markets. Young people full of appetite on life, and unafraid to ask relevant questions, keep you on your toes. They keep reminding me that finance is anything but dull.

Steven Zitzer took up the role of editing the manuscript. He looked at the text with a magnifying glass and eliminated as many direct errors as possible. But Steven also gave excellent advice on writing style.

Finally, and most importantly, my thanks to Maria, my partner in life to whom I dedicate this book. Maria joked that I had a not-so-secret mistress, also known as "El libro". So true. But she put up with it and encouraged me all the way. Lucky me!

The usual disclaimer applies: I retain full rights to all remaining errors.

Contents

About the Author

Henrik Lumholdt is a seasoned finance professional with more than 30 years of capital markets experience. He is the founding partner of Inside Economics, a consultancy, which advises international investors and multinational corporations. Henrik was until recently the Chief Investment Strategist for Spain's largest asset management company, BBVA AM. Previous positions include Chief Economist for Bank of America, Spain, Head of Fixed Income Research at FG/Merrill Lynch, and Senior Economist at Nordea Bank. A member of the work group for international economics at Spain's think tank, El Real Instituto Elcano, he spends a considerable part of his professional time focused on international economies and markets. Henrik has been an adjunct professor of finance and economics at IE Business School since 2001 and has won numerous prizes for outstanding teaching.

List of Figures

List of Tables

Part I

Foundations

1

Introduction to Asset Allocation

"More people should learn to tell their dollars where to go instead of asking them where they went."
—Roger Bacon

This is the first of the three foundational chapters of the book. We start off by defining *asset allocation* and *asset classes* in Sect. 1.1. We then move on to examine the *asset allocation process* in Sect. 1.2, the division between *strategic asset allocation* (SAA) and *tactical asset allocation* (TAA) in Sect. 1.3, and the investment process in Sect. 1.4. We finish with an analysis of *rebalancing strategies* and their implications in Sect. 1.5.

1.1 Asset Allocation and Asset Classes

The term asset allocation refers to the composition of an investor's portfolio on different *asset classes*. A central tenet of asset allocation is that this composition is the main determinant of the risk and expected return of the portfolio, while the exposure to different asset classes constitutes the main source of diversification. From the perspective of modern portfolio theory, asset allocation represents the investor's exposure to *systematic risk* which highlights its importance.[1]

[1] See also Sharpe et al. (2007). In modern portfolio theory (MPT), systematic risk affects all assets and is "macro" in nature. The appendix at the end of the book provides a brief review of MPT.

H. Lumholdt, *Strategic and Tactical Asset Allocation*,
https://doi.org/10.1007/978-3-319-89554-3_1

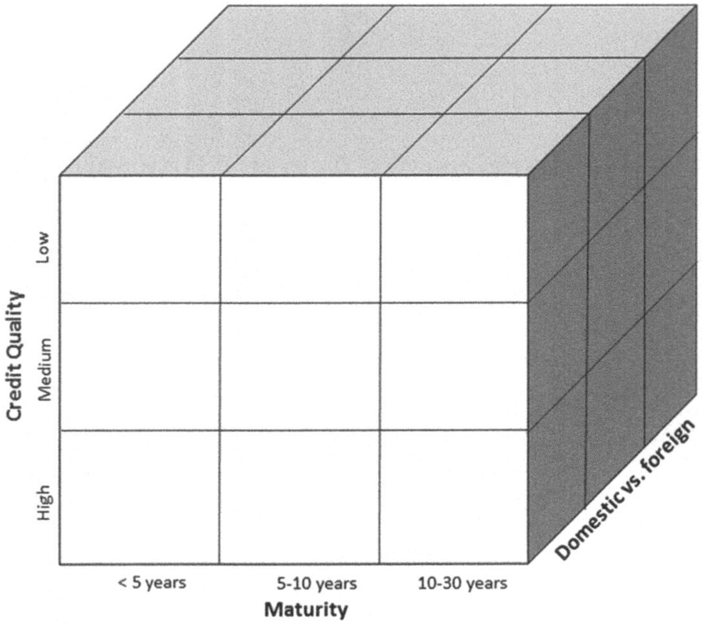

Fig. 1.1 A bond universe

What constitutes an asset class? A general criterion is that assets within an asset class share the same risk and return characteristics and react to similar factors. The return on assets within an asset class should therefore have a *high correlation*, whereas the correlation between one asset class and another should be significantly lower (giving rise to the diversification effect). It follows that if the correlation between assets within a defined asset class is too low, there is a case for changing the definition and treating them like two or more asset classes. Conversely, a high correlation between two asset classes constitutes a reason for treating them as one. Figure 1.1 provides an illustration of the *bond universe*.

Bonds have different *maturities*, different *credit quality* and can be *domestic* (from the investor's point of view) or *foreign*. This classification clearly does not encompass all types of bond instruments. But more importantly, we might equally be interested in distinctions such as "*government paper vs. credit*" and "*developed market vs. emerging market paper*". Government paper is generally considered "risk-free", even if there are some exceptions to this rule,[2] whereas, for example, high yield bonds with a low credit rating often exhibit

[2] Countries which have their own currency can always opt for some form of monetization of their local currency debt. For this reason, defaults mostly affect foreign currency denominated debt.

behavior more similar to that of equities than to government bonds. Similarly, developed market bonds are typically analyzed differently from emerging market bonds because their sensitivities to general factors differ substantially. All of this highlights the need for relatively specific definitions of asset classes for the purposes of asset allocation.

Figure 1.2 illustrates three dimensions for the *equity universe*. Here we have employed the *Morningstar Style Box* classification,[3] adding the "domestic vs. foreign" dimension. Again, other distinctions may be equally relevant, such as sector and degree of interest rate sensitivity.

One asset class definition in particular does not seem to live up to our criterion of homogeneity of the constituent assets: *alternative assets*. Firstly, this asset class includes categories as different as real estate, direct equity and hedge funds which exhibit low or even negative correlations. Secondly, it fails to distinguish between what are truly "assets" (such as real estate) and what are managed investments such as private equity and hedge funds. For the purposes of asset allocation, this general grouping is clearly not effective.

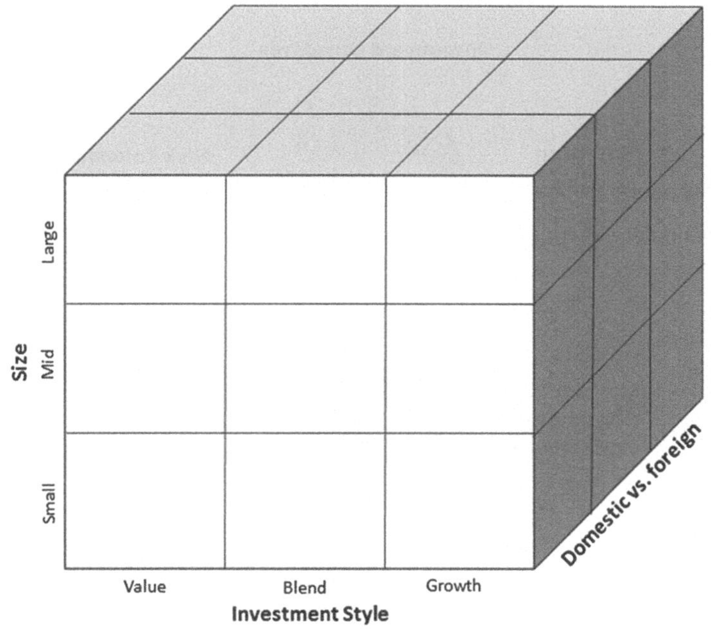

Fig. 1.2 An equity universe

[3] See also http://www.morningstar.com/InvGlossary/morningstar_style_box.aspx.

1.2 The Asset Allocation Process

To illustrate the different elements in the process, consider an investor ("the sponsor") who has given a mandate to an investment manager ("the manager") to manage a given capital which is initially in the form of cash. The sponsor can be a private individual or an institutional investor such as an insurance company, a pension plan, a foundation or a university endowment. The *Asset Allocation Process* will then essentially consist of three elements, as illustrated in Fig. 1.3.

The *Investment Policy* is formulated either exclusively by the sponsor or in conjunction with the investment manager, and provides overall guidelines for the manager. Its elements will typically include:

1. ***Investment objectives.*** While these can vary considerably, a basic distinction can be made between an objective of *capital preservation* and one of *capital appreciation*. While the former is associated with a conservative investment profile, even this type of investor must aim for a return which is high enough to match inflation in order to conserve the purchasing

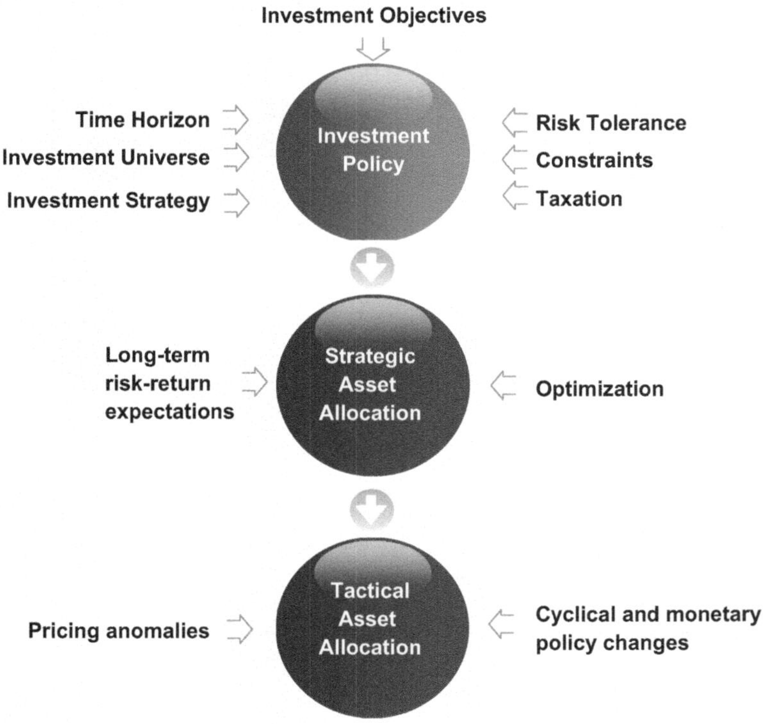

Fig. 1.3 The asset allocation process

power of the capital. A pure capital appreciation objective, on the other hand, would aim at growing the value of the capital in *real terms*. The so-called *total return* approach, used by some university endowments and foundations, seeks a high capital growth over time by reinvesting income, having an equity bias and paying out a proportion of this on an ongoing basis which is sufficiently below the average expected return to be deemed sustainable.[4]

2. ***Time horizon.*** All other things being equal, a longer time horizon will normally imply a greater willingness to accept short-term volatility since the long-term investor has the opportunity to match bad years with subsequent good years.[5] A longer-term investor, on the other hand, is more susceptible to the eroding effects of inflation. Knowledge of the investor's time horizon is relevant to other issues than risk in a narrow sense, however, such as the maturity of fixed income securities in the portfolio and the degree of liquidity of the financial instruments employed in general. To illustrate, even AAA-rated long-dated bonds might be considered relatively risky for an investor whose time horizon is much shorter than the term to maturity, since price declines from upward pressure on long-term yields over the holding period might overshadow the income from coupon payments. For the long-term investor, on the other hand, the long-dated bond, if held to maturity, offers an ex ante certain nominal return, even if the real return remains uncertain. Similarly, a low degree of liquidity of a given instrument might constitute an unwelcome complication for the short-term investor but no obstacle to the long-term investor.
3. ***Investment universe***. The choice of which asset classes to allow in the portfolio is a function of a list of factors including the investor's *time horizon*, requirements for *liquidity*, *attitude to risk* (including currency risk) and general *financial experience*. In this book we will concentrate on liquid financial assets, such as:

   - *Cash or cash equivalents* (such as CDs, Treasury bills [T-bills] or commercial paper with a maturity of 90 days or less).
   - *Currency* other than the investor's reference currency.
   - *Bonds:* domestic or foreign; developed or emerging markets; government or corporate paper; investment grade or lower rating; short term, intermediate or long term.

[4] See also Swensen (2009).

[5] On the assumption of mean-reversion of returns over time.

- *Stocks:* domestic or foreign; developed or emerging markets; value or growth; large-cap, mid-cap or small-cap.
- *Commodities.*

4. ***Investment strategy*** in this context refers to what type of *investment management approach* will be employed to meet the investment objectives. Relevant distinctions in this connection include:

   - *Passive*: minor and/or infrequent adjustments of the portfolio to market conditions.
   - *Active*: major and/or more frequent adjustments to market conditions.
   - *Directional*: high positive correlation with the underlying markets.
   - *Contrarian*: high negative correlation with the underlying markets.
   - *Market-neutral/arbitrage*: low or no correlation with any one market; depending on relative value between instruments.

5. ***Risk tolerance*** can be formulated in various ways, such as a *maximum volatility* of the overall portfolio (or of individual elements), measured over a given period or a *maximum drawdown* within, say, any given month, quarter or year.
6. ***Constraints*** on the portfolio management include requirements like a minimum *income generation* from the portfolio, a minimum level of *cash-holding* at any given time or a *maximum holding(s)* of individual securities (typically because of regulatory restrictions).
7. ***Tax status and other unique circumstances*** can often exclude certain investments or concentrate the portfolio on certain investment instruments.

1.3 Strategic and Tactical Asset Allocation

Once the parameters of the investment policy have been laid down, the SAA can be formulated. This asset allocation has a long time horizon (5–10 years or more) and is based on expectations regarding long-term risk and return of the different asset classes and the correlation between them. Optimization techniques from modern portfolio theory are often employed at this stage.

The SAA constitutes a *policy* asset allocation which is typically stated as a target weight for each asset class with some permitted variation around the target. To illustrate, the investor's SAA might stipulate that large company stocks shall take up 30% of the portfolio, small and mid-cap stocks 20%, medium-term government bonds 25%, high-grade corporate bonds 15% and cash 10%, but that the manager is allowed to deviate from this within given ranges. The central weight in this policy asset allocation is henceforth the investment manager's *benchmark:*

- Large company stocks: 35% +/− 15 percentage points
- Small- and mid-caps: 20% +/− 10 percentage points
- Medium-term government bonds: 25% +/− 15 percentage points
- High-grade corporate bonds: 15% +/− 10 percentage points
- Cash: 5% +/− 5 percentage points

Even though the SAA is static in nature, the longer-term assumptions underlying it must be periodically revised and modified which can give rise to changes to the SAA itself. This revision is typically done once a year.

TAA constitutes an *active* complement to the SAA which is essentially passive. In TAA, deviations from the target weights in the SAA, but within the permitted ranges, are made deliberately, on a discretionary basis. The central tenet of TAA is that such deviations of portfolio weights, carried out over shorter periods (say three months to a year) can add value to the portfolio. The deviations may be prompted by apparent pricing anomalies (inefficiencies) in the market or by changes in economic fundamentals and monetary policy, which are of such importance that they make short-term return forecasts differ significantly from those estimated for the purposes of the SAA. The short-term view is expressed by going *overweight* against the central target of those assets that are expected to outperform and going *underweight* those assets which are expected to underperform, with a view to returning to benchmark levels once the out- or underperformance has materialized.

Any deviation in the weight of one asset class obviously has implications for the weight of the others. If the manager, for instance, feels particularly bullish about stocks in general at any given time, given the ranges for each asset class in our example, she could take the overall weighting of equities all the way up to 80% and would then have to decide how to "pay" for this through a reduction in the non-equity components. Or the manager might feel particularly bullish about small and mid-capitalization stocks and go all the way up to a 30% weighting of this asset class while reducing large caps to 25%, thus leaving the overall weighting of equities unchanged. This highlights that Asset Allocation requires an integral view of the portfolio, where the interaction between the different asset classes is taken into account. TAA is examined in depth in Part III of the book.

1.4 The Investment Process

When the investment policy has been formulated, and the parameters of the SAA and the TAA have been fixed, the investment manager can begin the actual investment process. This is illustrated in Fig. 1.4. The first step is to decide on the specific securities that will constitute the portfolio and then to execute the relevant trades. At professional asset management firms, the execution desk will typically provide useful information about flows and market liquidity to help the portfolio manager optimize the timing and size of each trade until the full portfolio has been constructed.

Deviations from the Target Weights of the SAA

It is important to distinguish two types of variations around the SAA:

1. Decisions on TAA which, as discussed previously, are discretionary and based on shorter-term expectations that differ from those of the SAA.
2. Variations rising from different performance between the asset classes giving rise to "portfolio drift" away from the target weights in the SAA.

We will look at the second category in the following, the topic of *rebalancing*.

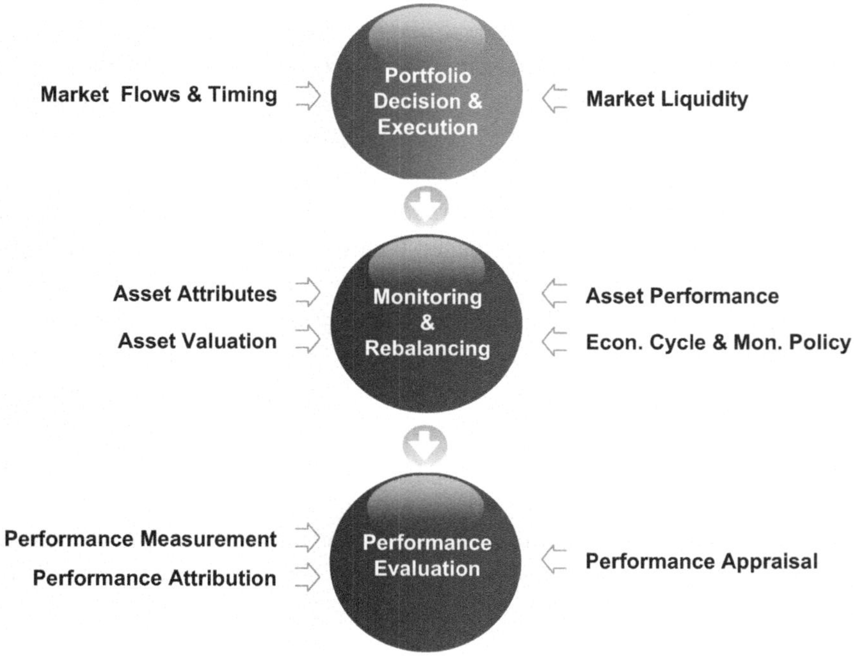

Fig. 1.4 The investment process

1.5 Rebalancing

A different performance among the different asset classes in the portfolio will automatically imply a shift away from the central targets in the SAA. In our example, if stocks in the portfolio yielded 10% over a given period while bonds yielded 2%, the weight of stocks would increase from 55% to around 57%, while the weight of bonds would decline to around 43% from 45%.[6] Whether or not this will prompt a portfolio adjustment from the manager depends on the *rebalancing strategy* followed. We will start by reviewing a study which outlines the profiles of three different rebalancing strategies. As we will see, which strategy is preferable in principle depends on our assumptions about future market behavior. In practice, however, the historical market record is clearly relevant, and we will round off with an empirical study of rebalancing strategies which provides some useful guidelines.

Perold and Sharpe (1988) examine three basic rebalancing strategies:

- Buy-and-Hold
- Constant Mix
- Constant Proportion Portfolio Insurance (CPPI)

They assume a simple portfolio of two assets one of which is risky (stocks), while the other is risk-free (T-bills, *with a zero yield*) and ask (a) which strategy is preferable for what market dynamics and (b) what risk tolerance the investor should have for each strategy to be appropriate.

Buy-and-Hold

Our example above corresponds to the *Buy-and-Hold* strategy. A weighting of each portfolio component is made initially and no subsequent adjustments are made. As we saw, an outperformance by stocks versus bonds, with no subsequent adjustment, would imply a higher weighting of stocks going forward, and vice versa. Generally, this strategy implies that the asset weights *drift* with the market. In Perold and Sharpe's two-asset example, the investment in T-bills constitutes a *floor* for the portfolio. Assuming an investment of $100 and a 60/40% allocation to stocks and bills respectively, under the Buy-and-Hold strategy the value of the portfolio could,

[6] For each dollar invested, the value of stocks would increase from $0.55 to 0.55 × 1.10 = $0.605, while the value of bonds would increase from $0.45 to $0.45 × 1.02 = $0.459, and the value of the overall portfolio would increase to $0.605 + $0.459 = $1.064. The weight of stocks would then be $0.605 / $1.064 ≈ 0.57 or 57%, while the weight of bonds would be $0.459 / $1.064 ≈ 0.43 or 43%.

in principle, fall to $40 (in the unlikely event that stocks went to zero) but never below this value.

- *The value of the portfolio is a linear function of the value of the stocks in the portfolio.*
- *The Buy-and-Hold strategy therefore implies that the investor's risk tolerance varies positively with wealth and stock market returns.*

Constant Mix

Investors following the *Constant Mix* strategy will decide on the initial weight of each portfolio component and rebalance the portfolio to bring weights back to their initial level after market movements have taken place. This implies that the proportion of the risky assets is independent of the level of wealth and that investors will hold risky assets at all wealth levels. In our two-asset example, the target investment in stocks is a constant, that is

$$\text{Target Investment in Stocks} = \text{m} \times \text{Portfolio Value}$$

where $0 \leq \text{m} \leq 1$.

Returning to our $100, 60/40% stock/T-bill investment, if the stock market drops 10% the value of stocks in the portfolio will have dropped to $54 and the overall portfolio to $94. Stocks now assume a weight of $54/$94 = 57.4% which is below the target of 60% and therefore prompts rebalancing. After the market move, the 60% corresponds to 0.6 × $94 = $56.4, so the manager will buy $2.40 of stocks, funding the purchase through the sale of bills of that amount. What would happen in the opposite example? If the stock market rose by 10%, the value of the stocks in the portfolio would increase to $66 and the value of the overall portfolio to $106. Stocks would now take up $66 / $106 = 62.3%. After the market move, the 60% would correspond to 0.6 × $106 = $63.6, so the manager would sell $2.4 of stocks to bring the weight back to the target 60% using the proceeds from this sale to add to the T-bills.

In summary, the Constant Mix strategy implies that:

- *A fall in the value of stocks (or the risky asset) => a purchase of stocks*
- *A rise in the value of stocks (or the risky asset) => a sale of stocks*

Because the Constant Mix strategy is essentially *contrarian*, it will underperform the Buy-and-Hold strategy in markets with a strong up- or downtrend. In the bull market case, the investor following this strategy is effectively selling into the uptrend in order to keep target weights, whereas the Buy-and-Hold investor benefits from the increasing weight of stocks as the stock market goes up. In the bear market case, this investor is effectively buying into the downtrend, whereas the percentage weight of stocks for the Buy-and-Hold investor is automatically decreased as stocks move lower. Whereas the payoff of the Buy-and-Hold strategy is *linear*, that of the Constant Mix strategy is *concave*, underperforming both in up- and downtrends.

Markets, of course, rarely move in straight lines for more than short periods of time. Going back to our previous example, consider the situation in which the stock market corrects 10% but then subsequently moves back to where it was previously. What happens in the Buy-and-Hold case is obviously that the value of the portfolio is simply returned to where it started. The Constant Mix strategy would beg to differ, however. If the value of stocks goes from $60 to $54, the weight of stocks moves from 60% to 57.4% as we saw. The Buy-and-Hold investor will do nothing, but as we saw the Constant Mix investor will now buy $2.40 worth of stocks to rebalance the weight of stocks back to 60%. Consider now the subsequent 10% market move back up. The Constant Mix investor is now holding $56.4 in stocks against $54 of the Buy-and-Hold investor, and gains $0.24 relative to the other strategy. The more frequently such reversals are repeated the greater the advantage of the Constant Mix strategy.

In summary, the Buy-and-Hold strategy will tend to do best in markets with a strong trend (up or down), whereas market volatility, especially if in a relatively trend-less market, will tend to benefit the Constant Mix strategy.

Another essential difference between the two strategies concerns the question of the *floor*. As mentioned, in the Buy-and-Hold strategy the T-bill component (or the risk-free component) constitutes a minimum value of the portfolio. The Constant Mix strategy has no such floor and could, in principle, see the value of the portfolio go all the way to zero—or close to. In a continuous down market the Constant Mix investor would keep shifting money away from T-bills to stocks which in turn would see ever lower values.

Constant Proportion Portfolio Insurance

The *Constant Proportion Portfolio Insurance* (CPPI) is a dynamic strategy designed to provide access to upward trends in stock markets (or risk assets in general) while protecting the capital in downward trends. It does this by ensuring that the value of the portfolio does not fall below a *floor* level which must initially be lower than the value of the total assets. A different way to achieve both the exposure and the portfolio insurance would be to combine an investment in zero-coupon bonds, (providing the floor) with the purchase of call options (providing the upside potential from the stocks or risky assets).

The key difference from this strategy is that in the CPPI rebalancing takes place continuously, changing the weighting of the risky versus the risk-free asset according to market conditions.

The difference between the value of total assets and the floor is called the *cushion*. Exposure to equities (risky assets) is kept at a constant multiple of the cushion (hence the name), that is

$$\text{Dollars in stocks} = m\left(\text{Assets} - \text{Floor}\right)$$

m is called the *multiplier*. Continuing with our \$100 investment, suppose the floor is \$75 and the multiplier is 2. The investment in stocks will then be 2 × (\$100 – \$75) = \$50, while T-bills would take up the remaining \$50.

The maximum percentage loss on the stocks which is tolerable is inversely related to the size of the multiplier and equals *1/m*. In our example, the maximum tolerable drop in the stock market would be 50% (1/2) which would reduce the value of the stocks in the portfolio to \$25 and the value of the overall portfolio to \$75. Had the multiplier instead been 3, the investment in stocks would have been \$75 and the investment in T-bills \$25. The maximum tolerable loss would then be 33% (1/3). For a given level of the floor, the higher is *m*, the greater the exposure to the stock market or risky asset. But a higher *m* also increases the risk that the cushion will be wiped out in a sudden downturn. This is referred to as the *Gap Risk*. When the CPPI is issued as a product by a financial institution, this risk will typically be borne by that institution.

To examine the payoff profile of the CPPI, we continue with the example of a \$100 investment, a floor of \$75 and a multiplier a 2. Consider the situation if the stock market falls by 10%. The value of the stocks has now fallen to \$45 and that of the overall portfolio to \$95. Following our previous rule, the dollar amount in stocks should now amount to 2 × (\$95 – \$75) = \$40. To rebalance the portfolio, the manager will therefore sell \$5 worth of stocks and place the proceeds in T-bills. In the opposite example, with stocks rising 10% in value to \$55, the rule would instead dictate a 2 × (\$105 – \$75) = \$60 investment in stocks and prompt a \$5 purchase of stocks financed through a sale of bills.

To summarize, a CPPI strategy implies that:

- *A fall in the value of stocks (or the risky asset) => a sale of stocks*
- *A rise in the value of stocks (or the risky asset) => a purchase of stocks*

As can be seen, the rebalancing using the CPPI is the opposite of that required under the Constant Mix strategy. While that strategy benefits from oscillating but flat markets, and the Buy-and-Hold strategy is neutral to these circumstances, the CPPI would suffer. The manager would effectively be "whipsawed", increasing exposure to stocks in each upturn, which would then be followed by a downturn, and decreasing stock exposure in each downturn, which would then be followed by an upturn. The CPPI is effectively the mirror image of the Constant Mix strategy whereas a combination of the two would effectively amount to the Buy-and-Hold strategy. In terms of the multiplier, the Buy-and-Hold is a special case with $m = 1$, whereas in the Constant Mix strategy, $0 \leq m \leq 1$. In the CPPI, $m > 1$.

Because the CPPI gets progressively more aggressive in a bull market and progressively more defensive in a bear market its payoff profile is *convex*. In linear upward or downward markets, the CPPI strategy would always outperform both the Constant Mix strategy and the Buy-and-Hold strategy.

Why the Need for a Rebalancing Strategy?

While interesting from the point of view of comparison, the CPPI has been used mostly in structured products and less so in standard portfolio management. In the following we will therefore understand rebalancing as referring some variety of the Constant Mix strategy. To see its practical relevance, consider the empirical fact that risk assets, such as stocks, tend to outperform risk-free assets over the longer term. A consequence of this differential return is that the SAA will tend to drift away from its target weights, as risk assets assume a growing weight versus risk-free assets, as noted previously. If a severe bear market then follows a period of high positive returns (such as happened in 2001–2003 and 2007–2009), the investor will have a high level of risk exposure at precisely the worst time.

A simplified example will illustrate: A Buy-and-Hold investment of $100 is divided 50:50 between equities and long-dated government bonds. The investment is held for ten years, during which period equities yield a constant return of 10% per year and government bonds yield a constant return of 4% per year. After the ten years, the value of the portfolio and each of its components will be as follows:

- Equities: $\$50x(1 + 0.10)^{10} = \$129.69$
- Bonds: $\$50x(1 + 0.04)^{10} = \$74.01$
- Total Portfolio: $\$129.69 + \$74.01 = \$203.7$

Equities will now assume a weight of $\frac{\$129.69}{\$203.7} = 0.64$ or 64% as opposed to the 50% of a portfolio fully rebalanced according to the Constant Mix strategy, while the weight of government bonds has fallen to $\frac{\$74.01}{\$203.7} = 0.36$

or 36%. The Buy-and-Hold strategy has effectively shifted 14 percentage point of portfolio weight toward the risky asset, away from the risk-free asset, a significant increase in risk.[7]

Is there a cost attached to the rebalancing strategy? In this unrealistic example of constant returns every year (a perfectly trending market), there clearly is. Rebalancing the risk asset back to its 50% weight each year effectively eliminates part of the *compounding effect* of the return on the outperforming risky asset, while increasing that of the underperforming risk-free asset: a negative effect in net terms. Because real financial markets do not move in such straight lines, the net effect on return from using the rebalancing strategy would depend on market dynamics in any given period. Before looking at historical data, we can make the following general observations:

- *Market behavior:* mean-reverting markets will tend to favor rebalancing while trending markets will do the opposite (as discussed by Perold and Sharpe).
- *Time horizon:* a longer time horizon for investors implies a greater likelihood of portfolio drift and hence a greater benefit from rebalancing.
- *Transaction costs:* generally work against rebalancing. This is a larger problem the more illiquid are the assets in the portfolio, and the more frequent is the rebalancing. It will generally pose a larger problem to private than to institutional investors.
- *Taxation:* rebalancing can prompt capital gains tax reducing the incentive to adjust the portfolio.

The last two factors can to some extent be overcome by applying any coupon or dividend payments over the investment period to rebalancing. For institutional investors, such as pension funds, inflows of cash can be employed to increase the weight of underperforming assets, while outflows can be employed to decrease the weight of outperforming assets.

An Empirical Study

In a white paper, Ilmanen and Maloney (2015) offer an exhaustive empirical study of rebalancing strategies. Using monthly data for 43 years since 1972, the authors examine the performance of a portfolio with the following composition:

[7] This likely understates the increase in portfolio risk. As will be discussed in later chapters, government bonds typically rally during *flight-to-quality* periods, and have a negative correlation with stocks. In our example, market drift has not only increased the exposure to stocks, it has reduced the weight of the hedge asset as well.

- 30% *US equities*, represented by the MSCI US Index
- 20% *non-US equities*, represented by the MSCI World ex US Index
- 20% *US government bonds*, represented by the Barclays US Treasury Intermediate Index
- 20% *non-US government bonds*, represented by the Barclays Global ex US Treasury Hedged Index
- 10% *commodities*, represented by the GSCI Index

The authors note that the rebalancing process must include the following decisions:

- *When to rebalance*: the frequency of rebalancing and whether to use a fixed schedule (a "calendar approach") or a given deviation from the SAA targets (a "trigger approach").
- *How much to rebalance* ("degree of rebalancing"): full or partial adjustment back to the SAA targets.

Using these distinctions, the study presents data comparing a Buy-and-Hold strategy with:

a) Rebalancing strategies employing biennial, annual or monthly rebalancing and a trigger approach involving deviations of +/−30%, +/−20% and +/−10% from the SAA target weights.
b) Rebalancing strategies using annual and monthly adjustments of 100% of the deviation from the SAA target weight, and partial approaches where only 25% and 50% of the deviation is being adjusted.

Annual trade costs are assumed to be 0.5% for all asset classes in the case of full adjustment to the target SAA, and a proportion of that for the partial approaches.

The data generally support the idea of rebalancing.[8] All of the strategies examined outperformed the Buy-and-Hold strategy, both in terms of expected return, volatility and maximum drawdown. The data generally favor a relatively low *frequency of rebalancing* from a return point of view but indicates virtually no difference with respect to volatility whether high or low frequency is being used. The net return of the portfolio using the biennial, annual and monthly rebalancing strategies are 9.3%, 9.2% and 9.0%, respectively, compared to 8.7% for the Buy-and-Hold strategy, but the volatility of the return

[8] The authors also examine rebalancing with a more simplified portfolio. This varies the details, but leads to the same overall conclusion. See further Ilmanen and Maloney (2015).

is nearly identical across the three strategies (8.0–8.1%) vs. 9.0% for the Buy-and-Hold strategy.

As far as the *trigger-based strategies* are concerned, the range of returns for the +/−30%, +/−20% and +/−10% strategies is as low as 9.0–9.1%, whereas the volatility of the +/−10% strategy (8.1%) is somewhat lower than that of the +/−30% strategy (8.3%). The *degree of rebalancing* matters less than might be expected. While annual rebalancing generally outperforms monthly rebalancing in terms of return, volatility is in a range as narrow as 8.0–8.1%, independently of whether a 25%, 50% or 100% rebalancing is used.

On balance, the study therefore points to using a relatively *low frequency* of rebalancing and, taking cost into account, a *partial approach* as opposed to full rebalancing. Another observation is that the period used is relatively long which, as argued previously, should be expected to favor rebalancing. Shorter periods with a clearly trending risk market are likely to show a less favorable result from rebalancing from the point of view of portfolio return, while the advantage of lowering risk would likely be preserved. In such cases, a trade-off is clearly involved.

Even with such caveats regarding the investment period, the data clearly favor rebalancing from a *risk management* point of view. The maximum drawdown across all the rebalancing strategies examined is around 30% compared to around 40% for the Buy-and-Hold strategy. If investors "lose faith" during sharp downturns, or are forced to reduce portfolio risk for institutional reasons, they might sell out close to the bottom in a stock market downturn, and have a minimum exposure to a subsequent upswing. Rebalancing has the advantage of being a disciplined approach working against a tendency to "buy high and sell low" during severe market conditions.

1.6 Conclusion

Defining asset classes in a consistent way is crucial to both the management of the asset allocation portfolio and to the subsequent performance evaluation (more on this in Chap. 2). The constituents of an asset class should generally exhibit a high correlation, whereas the correlation between the asset classes should be as low as possible. Failing this, redefine.

The SAA is the anchor of the portfolio and serves as the subsequent benchmark for the TAA. The SAA should be based on long-term capital market expectations, including valuation (more on this in Chap. 4). It should be revised with regularity, say once a year, but modified only marginally unless truly important changes have taken place in the underlying long-term drivers of returns. Returns are also influenced by cyclical factors, changes in monetary policy or mispricings which are shorter term in nature. Adjusting to these factors is the role of the TAA which takes place in a band around the targets of the SAA. As we will argue persistently in this book, the TAA is a complement not an alternative to the SAA.

While the target weights of the SAA should be held mostly constant, deviations from these weights should be a consequence of *conscious decisions*. Unless you have truly changed your SAA view, adjust the portfolio back to the target weights but do so with a relatively low frequency to limit transaction costs.

Should rebalancing replace TAA? We believe it should not. It is clear that if the manager wishes to increase risk exposure during a bullish market trend, a way to do this would be to simply allow the portfolio to drift, thus suspending rebalancing for a time. Conversely, rebalancing to a lower risk exposure might go hand in hand with TAA decisions to do so. But in this case it is the TAA which dictates the decision, not the rebalancing.

In Chap. 6 we will examine Factor Investing which has grown considerably in importance in recent years. One of the strategies applied is so-called momentum which favors overweighting assets which have outperformed recently, and underweighting underperforming assets. Does this contradict the idea of rebalancing? We think not. Firstly, the momentum strategy is applied only to a part of the portfolio. Secondly, and more importantly, the strategies in Factor Investing work better together than on a stand-alone basis and, in our view, belong squarely in the category of SAA.

References

Ilmanen, Antti, and Thomas Maloney. 2015. "Portfolio Rebalancing, Part 1 of 2: Strategic Asset Allocation", AQR Portfolio Solutions Group.

Perold, André F., and William F. Sharpe. 1988. "Dynamic Strategies for Asset Allocation", *Financial Analyst Journal*, January, 16–27.

Sharpe, William F., Peng Chen, Jerald E. Pinto, and Dennis W. McLeavey. 2007. "Asset Allocation", in Managing Investment Portfolios: A Dynamic Approach, 3rd edition, ed. John Maginn, Donald Tuttle, Dennis McLeavey and Jerald Pinto. Hoboken, N.J.: John Wiley & Sons.

Swensen, David F. 2009. "Pioneering Portfolio Management: An Unconventional Approach to Institutional Investment". New York, NY: Free Press.

2

Performance Evaluation

"There are 3 types of accountant—those that can count and those that can't."
—Anon

In this chapter, we address the following questions. Which *benchmark* should be used to assess the performance of active managers? How can we measure the *risk-adjusted performance* of portfolio managers? Finally, how do we measure *how* an active manager achieved a given return?

2.1 Benchmarks

A benchmark is clearly necessary for assessing the skills of a manager. It also plays an important role in defining the sponsor's *investment universe* and *risk tolerance*. The choice of benchmarks is therefore an important initial part of the asset allocation process. But what constitutes an effective benchmark? The following criteria are generally accepted[1]:

- **Unambiguous.** Identities and weights of securities or investment styles are clearly defined.
- **Investable.** The benchmark represents a viable *passive* alternative to the active portfolio.
- **Measurable.** Returns can be calculated with a high frequency.

[1] See, for example, Bailey et al. (1990), Bailey (1992) and Bailey et al. (2007).

H. Lumholdt, *Strategic and Tactical Asset Allocation*,
https://doi.org/10.1007/978-3-319-89554-3_2

- **Appropriate.** The benchmark reflects the manager's investment style or area of expertise.
- **Reflective of current investment opinions.** The manager has current knowledge of the securities or factor exposures in the benchmark.
- **Specified in advance.** The benchmark is specified prior to the start of an evaluation period.
- **Owned.** The investment manager is aware of and accepts accountability for the constituents and performance of the benchmark.

Benchmark indices are normally *total return* indices (i.e. including any income received such as coupon payments for bonds and dividends for stocks). In the following, we will examine some of the categories most commonly used.

Broad Market Indices

In the equity space most general broad market indices are *capitalization-weighted*, where the weight of each company is calculated as:

$$w_i^m = \frac{q_i \, p_i}{\sum_j^n q_j \, p_j} \tag{2.1}$$

w_i^m is the *weight of stock i* in the index, the numerator is the *market cap of stock i* (number of outstanding shares, q_i, multiplied by the market price per share, p_i) and the denominator is the *market cap of all securities in the index* (market cap per stock summed over all stocks). The market cap is normally limited to the *free float*, that is, the publicly traded shares outstanding, excluding any shares held by founders, directors and so on.

There are clear advantages to market-cap indices, and they remain the most widely used benchmark for mutual funds. They are representative of a Buy-and-Hold investment strategy with no rebalancing required, beyond what is implied by constituents entering or leaving the index. The growth in index funds and Exchange Traded Funds (ETFs) based on these indices means that they constitute a relevant, and cheap, *passive alternative* to actively managed schemes. Only market-cap indices can be *macro-consistent*, meaning that if all investors held their components none would be left over. Moreover, these indices are the closest proxy to the *market portfolio* of the capital asset pricing model (CAPM), implying that they are more likely to be *mean-variance efficient*[2] than any other indices.

[2] Meaning that they offer the highest expected return for any level of risk. See further the Appendix to the book.

In spite of these characteristics, market-cap indices have been subject to criticism from the point of view of their representativeness of the market. In market cap-weighted indices, "overpriced stocks" will tend to assume an increasing weight in the index, while "underpriced stocks" will assume a declining weight. The net result is that the index can become unduly concentrated on a few issues and/or sectors, and be prone to "bubbles". To illustrate the issue of concentration, the weight of the top ten constituents of the Standard & Poor's 500 as of May 31, 2017, was 19.1%. Five out of the top ten were technology stocks, and information technology took up 23.2% of the total index.[3] Some researchers argue that indices should offer a more adequate measure of the *economic footprint* of stocks and propose so-called fundamentally based indices.

Fundamentally Based Indices

Arnott et al. (2005) constructed indices using *gross revenue*, *equity book value*, *gross sales*, *gross dividends*, *cash flow* and total *employment* as weights. They found that indices with such a weighting outperformed cap-weighted indices by 197 basis points on average per year over the 43-year period from 1962 to 2004. Moreover, the results were robust both across time, phases of the business cycle, bull and bear markets, and regimes of rising or falling interest rates.

In an article in the *Wall Street Journal*, Siegel (2006) validated these findings and offered what he called "The Noisy Market" Hypothesis. In his own words:

> *This new paradigm claims that the prices of securities are not always the best estimate of the true underlying value of the firm. It argues that prices can be influenced by speculators and momentum traders, as well as by insiders and institutions that often buy and sell stocks for reasons unrelated to fundamental value, such as for diversification, liquidity and taxes. In other words, prices of securities are subject to temporary shocks that I call "noise" that obscures their true value. These temporary shocks may last for days or for years, and their unpredictability makes it difficult to design a trading strategy that consistently produces superior returns. To distinguish this paradigm from the reigning efficient market hypothesis, I call it the "noisy market hypothesis".*

Siegel argues that fundamental indexation allows investors to capture such mispricings and achieve returns superior to those on capitalization-weighted indices, even though they do not know the fair value of securities.

[3] See further http://us.spindices.com/indices/equity/sp-500

Perold (2007) opposes this view on two counts. Firstly, he argues that since collective holdings must sum up to the market portfolio, investors who are overweight given stocks must necessarily be matched by others who are underweight the same stocks. In aggregate, it is therefore a zero-sum game, implying that the fundamentally based indices cannot constitute an alternative for *all investors* (put differently, they are macro-*in*consistent[4]). More importantly, securities might be assumed to move toward their underlying fair value, but there is no basis for knowing which stocks will do so and when. If investors do not know that fair value of stocks, the direction of the market will effectively be random and fundamental indexation will not allow investors to harvest superior gains compared to using market-cap indices.

Kaplan (2008) specifies that for a non-market-cap weighting to add value, the correlation between the fundamental values and the fair values must be higher than the correlation between market values and fair values. He sees no a priori reason to expect that this condition should be met. More importantly, since fair values are not observable, there is no basis for measuring it, and only the historical performance record of fundamentally based indices versus market-cap indices be used to evaluate this approach.

Note that this debate has taken mainly an investment point of view in which a fundamentally based approach is compared with a *passive* investment in a cap-weighted index (e.g. through an ETF).[5] Another matter is whether fundamentally based indices are appropriate in the performance evaluation of *active* managers. Returning to our criteria from above, we note that it may not apply with the criterion of being a truly passive index, while the last three criteria also look like a bit of a stretch. By comparison, broad-based indices seem to generally meet all criteria, except possibly for one: *appropriateness*. As specialization intensifies in asset management, a growing number of the investment styles employed in the industry differ so much from the broad-based indices that a different yardstick is called for. This takes us to the next benchmark category.

Style-Based Indices

In the previous chapter, we discussed dimensions of the bond market such as *credit quality* and *maturity*, and dimensions of the stock market such as *size* (small, mid, large) and *investment style* (value, blend, growth). Financial firms such as Barclays, J.P. Morgan Chase and Bank of America Merrill Lynch provide

---

[4] Robert Arnott's riposte to this has been that while this would apply if the entire investment universe switched to fundamentally based indices, vast sums of money would have to move in that direction first. See further Arnott (2006).

[5] This subject will be covered in depth in Chaps. 6 and 7.

detailed indices to track sub-divisions of the bond market, while equity index providers such as Standard & Poor's and the Frank Russell Company cover sub-groups of the overall market with different size and investment style. Such sub-indices can constitute benchmarks which are much closer to specific investment styles employed by the manager than the broader market.

We should take care, however, to ensure that the composition and the weightings of the index do not diverge excessively from what is realistic for the active portfolio. Moreover, different indices can vary significantly in performance. In a comparative study of the widely used Russell and S&P indices, Shankar (2007) notes that while the Russell indices are based solely on market capitalization, the S&P indices are constructed by an Index Committee. This turns out to matter relatively little in the case of large-caps covered by the S&P 500 and the Russell 1000, where the composition of the indices overlaps significantly; the S&P effectively constitutes a sub-set of the Russell index. Examining the period from January 1994 to December 2004, the study found an outperformance in cumulative return of the S&P 500 over the Russell 1000 of a modest 0.6%.

In contrast, for small-cap stocks, covered by the S&P 600 and the Russell 2000, the former outperformed the latter by as much as 69.5%, or more than a third, over the same period. Using three-year overlapping returns for the same period, the study found that the S&P 600 outperformed the Russell 2000 in eight out of the nine periods and by an average of 9.2% in each period. Using ETFs, so as to incorporate transaction costs, led to similar conclusions. Passive investors, it seems, would be rational to prefer index funds or ETFs based on the S&P 600 index, while active fund managers would be better off using the underperforming Russell 2000 as the benchmark for their performance.[6] All of this highlights the importance of ensuring that benchmarks are *unambiguous*, our first criterion on the list above.

Customized Indices

Broad market indices may contain more stocks than the manager will, or can, realistically invest in, and in different proportions. Moreover, the manager may on average have a more aggressive ("high beta") or more defensive ("low beta") risk profile than the overall market, or may have a permanent bias toward a particular investment style.

---

[6] Soe and Dash (2009) and Brzenk and Soe (2015) estimate that approximately half of the excess return of the S&P 600 over the Russell 2000 is due to recomposition effects of the Russell 2000 ("July Effect"), as outperforming small-caps are promoted to the Russell 1000 from the Russell 2000, while underperforming stocks are moved from the Russell 1000 to the Russell 2000. Chen et al. (2006) examines the impact of changes in index compositions for investors.

If this is not taken into account it may give rise to erroneous conclusions. As an example, a manager with a high-beta portfolio might be deemed to have beaten the market during a period of bullishness, even though little or no active management was actually carried out. Equivalently, a low-beta manager may be deemed inefficient during the same period despite successful security bets. A similar case could be applied to style biases which often give rise to a different performance from that of the general market. In essence, the benchmark should include any such static features so as to isolate what is the *truly active* part of the management of the portfolio. This will sometimes warrant a "tailor-made" approach. Customized benchmarks are based on the idea of a *normal portfolio*. The normal portfolio should be representative of the universe of securities in which the manager habitually operates and the style of investment employed.[7] This may be based on the historical investment record of the manager, or on a risk factor analysis.[8] A relevant measure of the appropriateness is the R^2 between the returns of the portfolio and the returns of the benchmark. Obviously, the higher this measure, the better the fit.

But how precise should the benchmark be? A highly granular approach will likely provide more precision in the assessment of the manager's performance, but this could come at the price of reducing her flexibility excessively. Consider the opposite case of that mentioned above: The manager might indeed vary from the benchmark in terms of risk or style, but these decisions are tactical rather than a static feature of the portfolio. If the benchmark is excessively "tight" this might reduce the manager's incentive to engage in any such deviations more than marginally. In the extreme case, the portfolio will resemble an index fund. Ultimately, the design of the benchmark must find a balance between the sponsor's appetite for active management and the needs for "room to maneuver" of the manager.[9]

Asset Allocation Benchmarks

In Chap. 1 we noted that once the central asset class weights of the SAA have been fixed, the SAA becomes the *benchmark* for the TAA. Exposure to several asset classes therefore necessitates the use of benchmarks for each asset class with a weighting dictated by the SAA. For individual assets, such as equities, investors can look up performance statistics for their benchmark with relative

[7] See also Kritzman (1987), Christopherson (1998), Kuenzi (2008) and Lo (2016).

[8] Sharpe suggests using quadratic programming to determine the exposure of a portfolio to different investment styles (or asset classes), represented by indices such as the one discussed previously. See further Sharpe (1988, 1992).

[9] All of this is related to the question of active risk vs. policy risk which we will discuss in the following chapter.

ease, unless a customized index is used. For asset allocation portfolios, additional calculations must be carried out to get the total picture. We'll look into this in the final section on *performance attribution.*

2.2 Risk-Adjusted Performance

How can sponsors rank portfolio managers? It is clear that even if the benchmark is chosen with care, this constitutes no guarantee that the risk of the portfolio and that of the benchmark will be identical. Indeed, if active management is about diverting from the benchmark, measures of the risk that this involves are called for. As we will see, this is not without its complications, however. We will look at five commonly used measures.[10]

The Treynor Ratio

How much risk has the manager undertaken in the portfolio in order to produce an excess return?

To determine the ex post relationship between the return on a specific portfolio and that of the market portfolio, Treynor (1965) introduced the *portfolio characteristic line*:

$$R_{it} = \alpha_i + \beta_i R_{Mt} + \varepsilon_{it} \tag{2.2}$$

The intercept in this regression, α_i, represents *unique returns* which will be smaller the more diversified is the portfolio; the slope, β_i, represents the portfolio's volatility relative to that of the market, while ε_{it} represents random residuals.

Treynor proposed the following performance measure:

$$T_p = \frac{\overline{R}_i - \overline{R}_f}{\beta_i} \tag{2.3}$$

The numerator of this ratio is the *excess return*, calculated as the difference between the average return on the active portfolio over the investment period, $\overline{R}_i$, and the average risk-free rate, R_f. The denominator is the *beta* of the portfolio. The Treynor ratio gives a measure of the *return obtained per unit of systematic risk*. It measures

[10] The review is not exhaustive. For a more extensive coverage, see, for example, Amene and Lesourd (2003) or Feibel (2003).

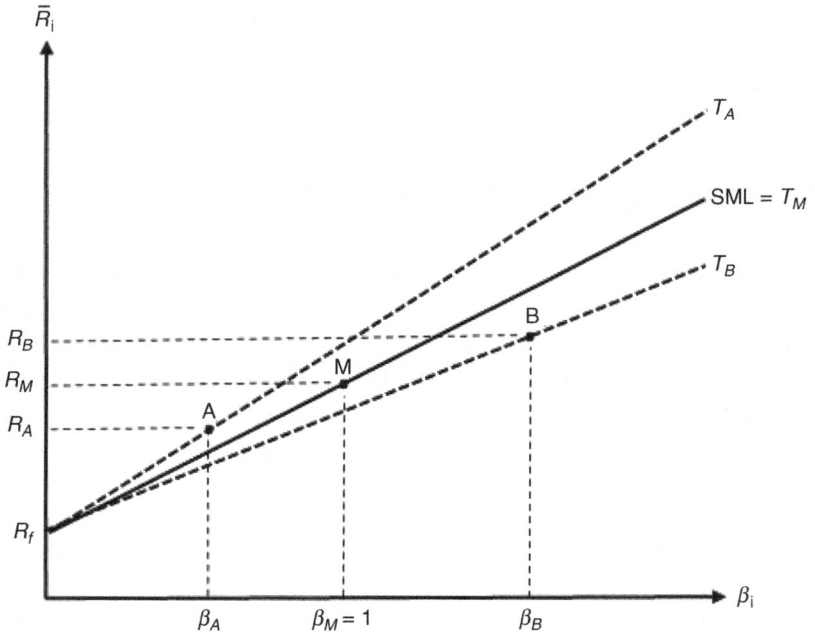

Fig. 2.1 Portfolio ranking on the Treynor ratio

the slope of a straight line in ($\beta_i, \bar{R}_i$) space, emanating from the risk-free rate, R_f, to the actual portfolio. In the case of the market portfolio, M, the Treynor ratio is represented by the ex post security market line (SML), as it is named in the context of the CAPM.[11] This is illustrated in Fig. 2.1 which pictures the two portfolios A and B and the market portfolio.

Which is the best performing portfolio? If we decided on the basis of return alone, it is clear that B is preferable, since $R_B > R_M > R_A$. In terms of the Treynor ratio, however, portfolio A is the best alternative, since $T_A > T_M > T_B$.

As an example, suppose that $R_f = 3\%$, and that the performance data in Table 2.1 correspond to the market portfolio, represented by the S&P 500 index, and the two portfolios A and B over a given period. While the return of 12% on portfolio B is the highest of the three alternatives, this portfolio delivered only 5.6% of return per unit of risk, well below both the benchmark and portfolio A. Clearly, returns should be risk-adjusted to be suitable for any ranking of portfolios or managers.

Is beta the appropriate measure of risk? The critique which has been raised is that this assumes that portfolios are (very) well diversified since this measure

[11] The Appendix to the book gives a brief review of the CAPM.

Table 2.1 The Treynor ratio: A numerical example

	Annualized return (%)	Beta	Treynor ratio
Portfolio A	8	0.6	(0.08–0.03)/0.6 = 0.083
S&P 500	10	1.0	(0.10–0.03)/1.0 = 0.070
Portfolio B	12	1.6	(0.12–0.03)/1.6 = 0.056

excludes any idiosyncratic risk. Failing appropriate diversification, beta will underestimate total risk and a poorly diversified portfolio might then score misleadingly well on Treynor's ratio. A more fundamental problem is the sensitivity of the result to the choice of benchmark. Roll (1977) famously criticized the CAPM on the grounds that the true market portfolio is unobservable. In a later paper,[12] he demonstrated that if the proxy for the SML fails to represent it correctly, investors might, for example, erroneously conclude that a given portfolio was outperforming (lying above the SML) when the opposite was actually the case. This takes us to the next measure, the Sharpe ratio.

The Sharpe Ratio

William Sharpe (1966) proposed what he originally termed the *reward-to-variability* ratio, but is now commonly referred to as the Sharpe ratio (SR):

$$S_p = \frac{\bar{R}_i - \bar{R}_f}{\sigma_i} \tag{2.4}$$

Like Treynor's measure, the SR relates the excess returns on a portfolio to its risk. The key difference is that the SR uses *total risk*, σ_i, rather than systematic risk, β_i. Note that the SR can also be understood as the excess return divided by the standard deviation of this excess return, $\sigma\left(\bar{R}_i - \bar{R}_f\right)$. Given that the standard deviation of the risk-free asset is assumed to be zero, the denominator reduces to σ_i.

The SR represents the slope of the ex post capital market line (CML) connecting the risk-free rate and the standard deviation of returns in $(\sigma_i, \bar{R}_i)$ space. The criterion for ranking portfolios is similar to that of the Treynor ratio. Portfolios lying above the ex post CML have outperformed the market portfolio while portfolios below it have underperformed it. The fact that the S_p includes idiosyncratic risk makes it more suitable for the ranking of less than perfectly diversified portfolios, and this ratio is more commonly used in

[12] See Roll (1978).

the investment industry. Still, using both ratios has the advantage of being able to separate the two types of risk which is sometimes relevant. For well-diversified portfolios, the two measures will give the same ranking.

One significant advantage of the SR is that it does not require a proxy for the market portfolio (or a benchmark). It therefore escapes Roll's critique.[13] But the validity of the SR does depend critically on the assumption that returns can be fully described by mean and variance, consistent with modern portfolio theory.[14]

Jensen's Alpha

Jensen (1968) proposes a different ex post formulation of the CAPM from the one we saw in Treynor's characteristic line. His regression of the relationship between the return on a specific portfolio and that of the market portfolio takes the following form:

$$\overline{R}_i - Rf = \alpha_i + \left(\overline{R}_M - R_f\right)\beta_i + \epsilon_i \tag{2.5}$$

which gives rise to *Jensen's alpha* measure:

$$\alpha_i = \overline{R}_i - \left[Rf + \left(\overline{R}_M - R_f\right)\beta_i\right] \tag{2.6}$$

Alpha is the difference between actual portfolio returns, $\overline{R}_i$, and expected returns based on the CAPM, $\left[Rf + \left(\overline{R}_M - R_f\right)\beta_i\right]$. Graphically, it measures the vertical distance to the SML, as illustrated in Fig. 2.2.

The CAPM in its pure theoretical form does not contemplate an alpha intercept. In the empirical context is therefore represents unique or abnormal returns above or below those predicted by the model. An index fund is likely to have an alpha close to zero. For an active fund, on the other hand, alpha expresses whether the manager was able to outperform the benchmark through decisions on market timing and security selection.

Jensen's alpha has the potential problem of leading to an incorrect ranking when comparing portfolios with significantly different risk levels. To illustrate, consider the portfolios outlined in Table 2.2. The risk-free rate, *Rf*, is assumed to be 3%, while the market risk premium, $\left(\overline{R}_M - R_f\right)$, is assumed to be 7%.

[13] Implicitly, the risk-free rate is the benchmark in the SR.

[14] We will return to this question in our discussion in Chap. 5.

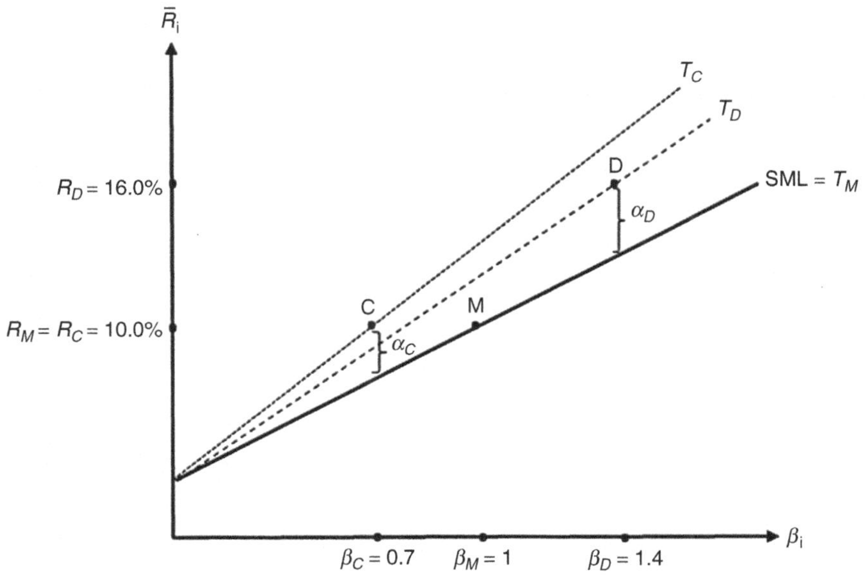

Fig. 2.2 Jensen's alpha versus the Treynor ratio

Table 2.2 Alpha versus the Treynor ratio: A numerical example

	Beta	Return (%)	(Jensen) Alpha	Treynor ratio
Portfolio C	0.7	10.0	10.0 – [3.0 + (10.0 – 3.0) × 0.7] = 2.1	(10.0 – 3.0)/0.7 = 10.0
Portfolio D	1.4	16.0	16.0 – [3.0 + (10.0 – 3.0) × 1.4] = 3.2	(16.0 – 3.0)/1.4 = 9.3
Benchmark	1.0	10.0	0.0	(10.0 – 3.0)/1.0 = 7.0

Ranking the investments according to their alpha clearly gives preference to portfolio D. Consider, however, the option of doubling the investment in portfolio C, financing the additional investment at the risk-free rate. This portfolio would have the same risk as D. Its return would be:

$$\begin{aligned} 2 \text{ times portfolio C} &= 2Rf + 2\left(\bar{R}_M - R_f\right)\beta_C + 2\alpha_C - Rf \\ &= Rf + 2\left(\bar{R}_M - R_f\right)\beta_C + 2\alpha_C \\ &= 3\% + 2\,x\left(10.0\% - 3.0\%\right)x\,0.7 + 2\,x\,2.1\% = 17\% \end{aligned}$$

On this measure, portfolio C actually deserves the highest ranking. This is illustrated in Fig. 2.2. Both portfolios clearly outperform the benchmark from the point of view of their T-lines which have a higher slope than the benchmark (SML or T_M). But the higher alpha of portfolio D derives from the fact that it has a higher beta, while it actually underperforms C from the point of view of its Treynor ratio. Jensen's alpha is therefore best applied to the ranking of portfolios belonging to a *peer group* with similar risk characteristics and the same benchmark.

The advantage of Jensen's alpha is that it offers an absolute measure of out- or underperformance against the benchmark. A t-test can subsequently be applied to see if the alpha is significantly different from zero. Because it is based on the CAPM, however, Jensen's alpha is subject to the same uncertainty over the choice of benchmark as the Treynor ratio.

The Information Ratio

The Information Ratio (IR), or *appraisal ratio*, has similarities with the SR and can be understood as a generalized version of this measure.[15] But whereas the SR uses excess return over the risk-free rate as the numerator, the IR uses *excess return over the benchmark*. And whereas the denominator of the SR is the standard deviation of the excess return over the risk-free, the denominator of the IR is the *standard deviation of the excess return over the benchmark*:

$$\mathrm{IR}_p = \frac{\bar{R}_i - \bar{R}_B}{\sigma\left(\bar{R}_i - \bar{R}_B\right)} \tag{2.7}$$

$\bar{R}_i - \bar{R}_B$ can be understood as the *active return* of the portfolio and $\sigma\left(\bar{R}_i - \bar{R}_B\right)$ as the *active risk*, also known as the *tracking error*.

This underscores the idea of the measure. Active managers will deviate from the benchmark to obtain a higher return. In doing so, they incur a risk relative to the benchmark. The higher is the excess return in relation to the relative risk incurred, or the higher is the reward from active management, the better the performance of the manager. Put differently, the IR is a measure of the quality of *information* held by the manager. The sponsor will often establish limits either for the tracking error or the IR for the portfolio which is going to be managed.

An alternative version of the IR uses Jensen's measure of risk-adjusted excess return, alpha, instead of the excess return in Eq. (2.3). The IR can then be expressed:

$$\mathrm{IR}_p = \frac{\alpha}{\omega} \tag{2.8}$$

where ω represents the standard deviation of the excess return.

[15] See also Treynor and Black (1973) and Sharpe (1994).

The financial logic of the IR is convincing, and the measure is commonly used in the investment industry. The choice of an appropriate benchmark is critical, however. Built-in biases in the portfolio can increase the tracking error, and thus reduce the IR, making even a skilled manager look like an underperformer. Aside from this, the IR depends as critically as the other measures on the assumption that portfolio returns are fully described by the two moments, mean and variance.

M²

A drawback of the Sharpe ratio is that unlike the Treynor measure or Jensen's Alpha, which are expressed in percentage terms, it has no *dimension*. If the portfolio in question registers an SR of 0.53 and its benchmark one of 0.49, we can conclude that our manager has outperformed her benchmark. But how much is an SR outperformance of 0.4?

Modigliani and Modigliani (1997) developed a measure which they originally termed *risk-adjusted performance* (RAP) but which has subsequently acquired the name of M^2 in reference to the surnames of its creators. M^2 gives a measure of the *differential return* of the portfolio adjusted to the same risk level as the benchmark:

$$M^2 = \overline{R}_{i^*} - \overline{R}_M \tag{2.9}$$

where $\overline{R}_{i^*}$ is the return on the risk-adjusted portfolio and $\overline{R}_M$ is the return on the market portfolio. The risk-adjustment is done assuming that the managed portfolio includes a position in a risk-free asset, such as T-bills. The position in the risk-free asset will be long if the portfolio is riskier than the market portfolio and short (corresponding to borrowing at the risk-free rate) if it is less risky. The respective weights of the managed portfolio and the risk-free asset are calculated as follows:

$$\text{Weight of the managed portfolio: } w_i = \frac{\sigma_M}{\sigma_i} \tag{2.10}$$

$$\text{Weight of the risk-free asset: } w_f = 1 - w_i \tag{2.11}$$

where σ_M is the standard deviation of the return on the market portfolio and σ_i is the standard deviation of the return on the managed portfolio. With this weighting, the risk of the managed portfolio will be equal to that of the benchmark:

$$\sigma_{i^*} = w_i \, x \, \sigma_i = \frac{\sigma_M}{\sigma_i} x \, \sigma_M = \sigma_M \tag{2.12}$$

The return on the risk-adjusted portfolio becomes:

$$\overline{R}_{i^*} = w_f \, x \, \overline{R}_f + w_i \, x \, \overline{R}_i \tag{2.13}$$

Insert Eq. (2.10) and (2.11) into (2.13) and (2.13) into (2.9). M^2 can now be expressed:

$$M^2 = \left[\left(1 - \frac{\sigma_M}{\sigma_i} \right) x \, \overline{R}_f + \frac{\sigma_M}{\sigma_i} x \, \overline{R}_i \right] - \overline{R}_M \tag{2.14}$$

Rearranging the terms of Eq. (2.10), we get:

$$M^2 = \overline{R}_f + \frac{\overline{R}_i - \overline{R}_f}{\sigma_i} x \, \sigma_M - \overline{R}_M \tag{2.15}$$

or

$$M^2 = \overline{R}_f + Sharpe\,ratio \; x \, \sigma_M - \overline{R}_M$$

In words, to calculate the M^2 of a portfolio multiply its Sharpe ratio by the standard deviation of the benchmark returns, add the risk-free rate and subtract the return on the benchmark.

To illustrate, suppose that the risk-free (rate) over a given period was 3%. We would like to compare the performance of portfolio A and portfolio B to their benchmark. Table 2.3 sets out the relevant data.

Portfolio A is the best choice on the basis of its Sharpe ratio which is 0.04 higher than that of the benchmark. But how much outperformance in terms of returns does this correspond to?

Table 2.3 Portfolio ranking on the Sharpe ratio: A numerical example

	Return (%)	Standard deviation (%)	Sharpe ratio
Benchmark	12	15	0.60
Portfolio A	10	11	0.64
Portfolio B	15	22	0.55

To answer the question, we need to establish the weight of each portfolio and the risk-adjusted return on each. Portfolio A has a lower standard deviation than the benchmark. Its weight > 100% therefore reflects leverage:

$$w_A = \frac{\sigma_M}{\sigma_A} = \frac{15}{11} = 1.3636 = 136.36\% \tag{2.16}$$

In contrast, portfolio B has a higher standard deviation than the benchmark and is therefore assigned a weight < 100% (the remaining part is placed at the risk-free rate):

$$w_B = \frac{\sigma_M}{\sigma_A} = \frac{15}{22} = 0.6818 = 68.18\% \tag{2.17}$$

The risk-adjusted returns become:

$$\overline{R}_{A^*} = w_f \; x \; \overline{R}_f + w_A \; x \; \overline{R}_A = -0.3636 \, x \, 3.0\% + 1.3636 \, x \, 10.0\% = 12.545\% \tag{2.18}$$

and

$$\overline{R}_{B^*} = w_f \; x \; \overline{R}_f + w_B \; x \; \overline{R}_B = 0.3182 \, x \, 3.0\% + 0.6818 \, x \, 15.0\% = 11.182\% \tag{2.19}$$

The results are summarized in Table 2.4. We see that the ranking of the two portfolios becomes the same irrespective of whether we use the Sharpe ratio or M^2. But the M^2 provides us with the useful information that portfolio A outperformed the benchmark by 0.5454% in risk-adjusted terms, while portfolio B underperformed it by 0.8182%.

Table 2.4 Portfolio ranking on M^2: A numerical example

	Weight of portfolio, w_i	Weight of risk-free asset, w_f	Risk-adjusted return (%), $\overline{R}_{i^*}$	M^2 (%)
Benchmark				
Portfolio A	1,3636	−0,3636	12,545	0,5455
Portfolio B	0,6818	0,3182	11,182	−0,8182

Practical Issues

Notwithstanding the virtues of the different of risk-adjusted performance, we will necessarily need to exercise judgment. These are some of the pertinent issues:

- **Period analyzed.** Risk-adjusted performance measures must necessarily be based on historical data. If too short a period is chosen, the result may not be sufficiently reliable; good or bad performance could be too dependent on good or bad luck. If too long a period is chosen, on the other hand, the sample may no longer be representative of the manager's investment style.
- **Sensitivity to new factors.** A change in "market regime",[16] for example, an increase in interest rate risk, may influence the portfolio and the benchmark differently. Risk-adjusted performance measures based on historical data may not capture this adequately.
- **Market correlations.** Inter-market correlations[17] are dynamic and give rise to changing strategies with respect to portfolio composition. The outcome might be a greater mismatch between the portfolio and its benchmark.

All in all, this highlights the importance of ongoing consultations between the sponsor and the manager. Qualitative factors can often assume an importance surpassing that of quantitative measures.

2.3 Performance Attribution

We have looked at risk-adjusted measures of how well a manager performs relative to a benchmark. But this still does not answer the question of *which decisions* gave rise to a given outperformance or underperformance. This is the topic of performance attribution. Since the benchmark represents the *passive* investment alternative, performance attribution is essentially an attempt to measure the value added (or subtracted) from engaging in *active portfolio management*, and identifying the sources of the differential returns versus the passive portfolio. Performance attribution can be carried out at the sponsor level and would then typically by part of an overall assessment of the performance and skills of third-party investment managers. Or it can be carried out at the level of the investment manager directly, as part of an ongoing effort to monitor and improve the portfolio process.

For the purposes of attribution analysis, a portfolio is partitioned into different *segments* with common characteristics. Segments could include, for

[16] We will look at this in greater depth in Chap. 9.

[17] More on this in Chap. 9.

example, international stocks or bonds, equity sectors or styles, and bonds with particular maturities and credit characteristics.[18] In the following, we will concentrate on segregating the tactical decisions regarding the weighting of the *asset class* from the *security selection*, which is central to performance attribution for TAA. Segment will therefore be synonymous with asset class.

Calculating Differential Returns

Suppose we were given the information that an asset allocation portfolio has returned 18% over a given year, while its benchmark has returned 15.7% over the same period. While this would allow us to conclude that the active management has produced a value added of 2.3% we still wouldn't know how this was produced.[19] In order to understand the *sources* of this outperformance we need more information on the composition of the benchmark and the return on the assets within it.

An investment manager can add value by selecting elements within each asset class with a superior performance relative to the benchmark while reducing or eliminating underperforming elements. We refer to this as the *security selection*. In addition to this, she can overweight asset classes which outperform the benchmark and underweight asset classes which underperform. Following our previous terminology, we refer to the latter as the decisions *on TAA*. This way of thinking is what underlies the framework developed in work by Brinson et al. (1986) and Brinson and Fachler (1985).

The Brinson, Hood and Beebower ("BHB") Model

We begin by defining the return on the overall portfolio as:

$$R^p = \sum_{i=1}^{n} w_i^p \times r_i^p \tag{2.20}$$

in which w_i^p is the weight of the i th asset in the portfolio and r_i^p is the return of the i th asset in the portfolio. $\sum_{i=1}^{n} w_i^p = 1$.

[18] See also, for example, Feibel (2003) and Amene and Lesourd (2003).

[19] Strictly speaking, we should refer to the outperformance as *percentage points* rather than %. Our manager has delivered an outperformance of 2.3% measured on the basis of the *initial capital* invested. But she has only outperformed the benchmark by ((1.18/1.157)−1) × 100 = 1.989%. We'll use % in the following for ease of exposition.

Similarly, the return on the overall benchmark is:

$$R^b = \sum_{i=1}^{n} w_i^b \times r_i^b \tag{2.21}$$

where w_i^b is the weight of the *i*th asset in the benchmark and r_i^b is the return of the *i* th asset in the benchmark. Again, $\sum_{i=1}^{n} w_i^p = 1$.

We would like to know how much the investment manager's decision on *TAA* and *security selection,* respectively, contributed to the performance of the portfolio versus the benchmark. To begin with the TAA, we define a ***notional portfolio*** in which the weights of each asset are those of the active portfolio, while the returns on each asset are those of the benchmark. This is our notional TAA portfolio. It is the equivalent of the performance of a manager who has no view on security selection within each asset class, and who therefore passively uses index funds, ETFs or the like for each asset class. This manager expresses her view exclusively by under- or overweighting each asset class at any given time.[20] The return on this notional TAA portfolio is then:

$$R^a = \sum_{i=1}^{n} w_i^p \times r_i^b \tag{2.22}$$

This allows us to calculate the contribution from the *TAA decisions* in isolation as the difference between the return on this notional portfolio and that of the overall benchmark, that is:

$$C^a = R^a - R^b = \sum_{i=1}^{n} w_i^p \times r_i^b - \sum_{i=1}^{n} w_i^b \times r_i^b = \sum_{i=1}^{n} \left(w_i^p - w_i^b\right) \times r_i^b \tag{2.23}$$

The contribution from the TAA decision in each segment is:

$$c_i^a = \left(w_i^p - w_i^b\right) \times r_i^b \text{ and } \sum_{i=1}^{n} c_i^a = R^a - R^b \tag{2.24}$$

The decision *on security selection* concerns the composition of assets (securities) within each asset class and hence the return on the portfolio per asset

[20] As far as she is concerned, r_i^p is an unbiased estimator of r_i^b.

class. We now define a second notional portfolio in which the weights are those of the benchmark but the returns are those of the portfolio in each asset class. The return on this portfolio, which expresses the decision on security selection exclusively, is:

$$R^s = \sum_{i=1}^{n} w_i^b \times r_i^p \tag{2.25}$$

The contribution from the security selection is then the difference between the return on this portfolio and the return on the overall benchmark:

$$C^s = R^s - R^b = \sum_{i=1}^{n} w_i^b \times r_i^p - \sum_{i=1}^{n} w_i^b \times r_i^b = \sum_{i=1}^{n} w_i^b \times \left(r_i^p - r_i^b\right) \tag{2.26}$$

The contribution from the security selection in each segment is:

$$c_i^s = w_i^b \left(r_i^p - r_i^b\right) \text{and} \sum_{i=1}^{n} c_i^s = R^s - R^b \tag{2.27}$$

The Interaction Effect

The TAA and the security selection decisions interact. For example, if the investment manager is overweight an asset class which outperforms the benchmark and her security selection *within* that asset class simultaneously outperforms the benchmark, we would need to include a cross-term to account for this. The interaction effect can be understood as any part of the difference between the performance of the portfolio and that of the benchmark which is not accounted for by the TAA and the security selection decisions, that is:

$$\begin{aligned} \text{Interaction Effect} &= R^p - R^b - \left(R^a - R^b\right) - \left(R^s - R^b\right) \\ &= R^p - R^a - R^s + R^b \end{aligned} \tag{2.28}$$

$$= \sum_{i=1}^{n} w_i^p \times r_i^p - \sum_{i=1}^{n} w_i^p \times r_i^b - \sum_{i=1}^{n} w_i^b \times r_i^p + \sum_{i=1}^{n} w_i^b \times r_i^b \tag{2.29}$$

which reduces to:

$$\sum_{i=1}^{n}\left(w_i^p - w_i^b\right)\times\left(r_i^p - r_i^b\right) \tag{2.30}$$

The contribution from interaction in the *i* th segment is:

$$I_i = \left(w_i^p - w_i^b\right)\times\left(r_i^p - r_i^b\right) \text{ and } \sum_{i=1}^{n} I_i = R^p - R^a - R^s + R^b.$$

By inspecting the formula, we derive the following rules for the interaction effect (Table 2.5).

An Example

We now go back to our previous example and complete the information in Table 2.6.

We begin by calculating the return on the portfolio and the benchmark respectively:

$$R^p = 0.50\times 12\% + 0.30\times 20\% + 0.20\times 30\% = 18\%$$

$$R^b = 0.60\times 10\% + 0.25\times 22\% + 0.15\times 28\% = 15.7\%$$

Table 2.5 Determinants of the interaction effect

Portfolio weight vs. BM	Asset class perf. vs. BM	Interaction effect
Overweight	Superior	Positive
Overweight	Inferior	Negative
Underweight	Superior	Negative
Underweight	Inferior	Positive

Table 2.6 Example: Portfolio versus benchmark returns

	Portfolio weight (%)	Benchmark weight (%)	Portfolio return (%)	Benchmark return (%)
US equities	50	60	12	10
European equities	30	25	20	22
Emerging Markets equities	20	15	30	28
Total	100	100		

Out of the 2.3% outperformance versus the benchmark, how much is due to TAA and how much to the security selection?

We start by calculating the return on the notional TAA portfolio:

$$R^a = 0.50 \times 10\% + 0.30 \times 22\% + 0.20 \times 28\% = 17.2\%$$

So the contribution from the TAA decisions is:

$$C^a = R^a - R^b = 17.2\% - 15.7\% = 1.5\%$$

We then calculate the return on the notional security selection portfolio:

$$R^s = 0.60 \times 12\% + 0.25 \times 20\% + 0.15 \times 30\% = 16.7\%$$

So the contribution from the security selection decision is:

$$C^s = R^s - R^b = 16.7\% - 15.7\% = 1\%$$

We note that the sum of the contribution from TAA and security selection is 2.5%, but the total contribution is 2.3%. So the interaction effect is actually a negative −0.2% in this case.

We can do these calculations separately for each segment. For US equities, for example, the TAA effect is (0.50 − 0.60) × 10% = −1%, whereas the security selection effect is 0.60 × (12% − 10%) = 1.2%. Similarly, the interaction effect for US equities is (0.50 − 0.60) × (12% − 10%) = − 0.2%. Doing this for all asset classes, we can create a complete portfolio as seen in Table 2.7.

The interaction element must be included to make the attribution figures add up, but it does not represent any investment decision per se. For this reason, most users will include it in either the TAA or the security selection component.

Table 2.7 Example: Portfolio attribution per asset class

Asset class	Portfolio weight (%)	BM weight (%)	Portfolio return (%)	BM return (%)	Asset allocation (%)	Security selection (%)	Interaction (%)
US equities	50	60	12.0	10.0	−1.0	1.2	−0.2
European equities	30	25	20.0	22.0	1.1	−0.5	−0.1
EM equities	20	15	30.0	28.0	1.4	0.3	0.1
Total	100	100	18.0	15.7	1.5	1.0	−0.2

The Brinson-Fachler ("BF") Model

Looking at the first element in the portfolio, US equities, we note that our performance attribution assigns a negative value to TAA in this segment. In the BHB framework, this will always be the case when we underweight a segment with a positive return (or overweight a segment with a negative return). But does this accurately reflect the investment manager's investment decisions?

If her job is to beat the overall benchmark (which, as we saw, yielded 15.7%), arguably she is doing a better job underweighting any asset class which yields less than that benchmark, even if that asset class produces a positive return.

The BF model takes this into account by calculating the contribution from the TAA decision against the *overall benchmark*, that is, as the excess weight times the excess return in each segment:

$$R^a - R^b = \sum_i^n \left(w_i^p - w_i^b\right) \times \left(r_i^b - R^b\right) \tag{2.31}$$

Because overweights and underweights in the portfolio versus the benchmark cancel out each other, they must sum to zero, hence

$$\sum_i^n \left(w_i^p - w_i^b\right) = 0$$

And

$$\sum_i^n \left(w_i^p - w_i^b\right) \times R^b = 0$$

Therefore

$$R^a - R^b = \sum_i^n \left(w_i^p - w_i^b\right) \times \left(r_i^b - R^b\right) = \sum_{i=1}^n \left(w_i^p - w_i^b\right) \times r_i^b$$

This means, that we will obtain the same overall TAA contribution to the differential return of the portfolio versus the benchmark as before. But *the distribution* of the return on the TAA decisions between each segment will be different. Redoing our performance attribution calculation in this way, we get:

Table 2.8 Example: TAA attribution with the BF model

Asset class	Portfolio Weight (%)	BM Weight (%)	Portfolio Return (%)	BM Return (%)	Asset Allocation (%)	Security Selection (%)	Inter-Action (%)
US equities	50	60	12.0	10.0	0.570	1.2	-0.2
European equities	30	25	20.0	22.0	0.315	-0.5	-0.1
EM equities	20	15	30.0	28.0	0.615	0.3	0.1
Total	100	100	18.0	15.7	1.500	1.0	-0.2

Looking at Table 2.8, TAA is now attributed a positive value in all three asset classes. This is a better representation of the TAA decisions, and the BF model is therefore the more widely used. Taking US equities first, the manager has been underweight by 10 percentage points and has thus kept 10% of the portfolio from underperforming the overall benchmark by 5.7% (10% – 15.7%) for a net gain of 0.57%. As far as European equities are concerned, our manager has outperformed the overall benchmark by 6.3% (22% – 15.7%) with 5% of the portfolio for a net gain of 0.315%, while in the EM equities segment her outperformance has been 12.3% (28% – 15.7%) for a net gain of 0.615. The attribution to security selection and interaction remain the same.

In practice, of course, the manager might well have changed both the TAA and the security selection several times during this investment period. In order for the performance attribution to be a good representation of the value added (by the manager), we would therefore have to assume that the weights and returns constitute some meaningful average.

2.4 Conclusion

The choice of benchmark for assessment of active managers warrants serious consideration. On the one hand, the criteria favoring neutrality and objectivity of the benchmark are generally best met using a market-cap index. This, however, may conflict so significantly with the investment approach employed by the manager that more specific indices are called for. Fundamentally based indices are one such alternative. While the debate this type of indices have given rise to is central to the question of Factor Investment (which we will discuss in Chaps. 6 and 7), this type of index is suitable only as a comparison with passive investments. Style-based indices become relevant when the investment manager employs a *systematic* tilt in the portfolio toward, for example, value or market cap for equities, where the objective is to isolate the contribution from the truly active part of the investment (which warrants a fee). But we emphasize the word systematic. Investment mandates with greater degrees of freedom or peculiarities prompt the need for more customized indices, in consultation between the sponsor and the manager. Here the important trade-off to be considered is between precision in performance measurement, arguing for a relatively tight benchmark, and the incentive of the manager to show initiate and be truly active, which argues for a less restrictive benchmark.

Performance must be seen in the light of the risk taken, and we outlined the most frequently used risk-adjusted performance measures. It is fair to say that there is no consensus on which measure is best and most practitioners employ more than one. All of the measures discusses rely on the assumption of modern portfolio theory that returns are normally distributed with the potential weaknesses this involves (we discuss this further in Chap. 5). Aside from this, practical considerations must be taken into account, such as the period analyzed and changes in market regimes and correlations between asset classes.

Finally, we looked at the question of how the manager produced a given return for asset allocation portfolios. We saw how returns can be decomposed into decisions on asset weights (TAA) and security selection. Asset allocation mandates frequently include both types of decisions, and segregating the two is clearly relevant both for self-assessment on the part of the manager and for the external assessment made by the sponsor.

References

Amene, Noël, and Veronique Lesourd. 2003. "Portfolio Theory and Performance Analysis", Hoboken, NJ: John Wiley & Sons.

Arnott, Robert D., Jason Hsu, and Philip Moore. 2005. "Fundamental Indexation", *Financial Analysts Journal*, March/April, 61(2), 83–99.

Arnott, Robert D. 2006. "An Overwrought Orthodoxy", *Institutional Investor*, 18 December, 36–41.

Bailey, J. V., T. M. Richards, and D. E. Tierney. 1990. "Benchmarks, Portfolios and the Manager/Plan Sponsor Relationship", in Current Topics in Investment Management, ed. Frank J. Fabozzi and T. Dessa Fabozzi, 349–363. New York: Harper Collins.

Bailey, J. V. 1992. "Are Manager Universes Acceptable Performance Benchmarks?", *Journal of Portfolio Management*, Spring, 9–13.

Bailey, Jeffery V., Thomas M. Richards, and David E. Tierney. 2007. "Evaluating Portfolio Performance", in Managing Investment Portfolios: A Dynamic Approach, 3rd edition, ed. John Maginn, Donald Tuttle, Dennis McLeavey and Jerald Pinto. Hoboken, NJ: John Wiley & Sons.

Brzenk, Phillip, and Aye Soe. 2015. "A Tale of Two Benchmarks: Five Years Later", S&P Dow Jones Indices, March.

Brinson, Gary P., and Nimrod Fachler. 1985. "Measuring Non-US Equity Portfolio Performance", *Journal of Portfolio Management*, Spring, 73–76.

Brinson, Gary P., L. Randolph Hood, and Gilbert L. Beebower. 1986. "Determinants of Portfolio Performance", *Financial Analysts Journal*, July/August, 42(4), 39–44.

Chen, Honghui, Greg Noronha, and Vijay Singal. 2006. "Index Changes and Losses to Investors in S&P 500 and Russell 2000 Index Funds", *Financial Analysts Journal*, July/August.

Christopherson, J. A. 1998. "Normal Portfolios: Construction of Customized Benchmarks", in Active Equity Portfolio Management, ed. F. J. Fabozzi. Frank J. Fabozzi Associates.

Feibel, Bruce J. 2003. "Investment Performance Analysis". Hoboken, NJ: John Wiley & Sons.

Jensen, Michael. 1968. "The Performance of Mutual Funds in the Period 1945–1964", *Journal of Finance*, 23(2), 389–416.

Kaplan, Paul D. 2008. "Why Fundamental Indexation Might—or Might Not—Work", *Financial Analysts Journal*, January/February, 64(1), 32–39.

Kritzman, Mark. 1987. "How to Build a Normal Portfolio in Three Easy Steps", *The Journal of Portfolio Management*, Summer, 13(21–23).

Kuenzi, David E. 2008. "Strategy Benchmarks", *Journal of Portfolio Management*, 29(2), 46–56.

Lo, Andrew W. 2016. "What Is an Index?", *The Journal of Portfolio Management*, 42(2), 21–36.

Modigliani, Franco, and Leah Modigliani. 1997. "Risk-Adjusted Performance", *Journal of Portfolio Management*, Winter, 23(2), 45–54.

Perold, André F. 2007. "Fundamentally Flawed Indexing", *Financial Analysts Journal*, November/December, 63(6), 31–37.

Roll, R. 1977. "A Critique of the Asset Pricing Theory's Tests", *Journal of Financial Economics*, March, 4(2), 129–176.

Roll, Richard. 1978. "Ambiguity When Performance Is Measured by the Securities Market Line", *Journal of Finance*, September, 33(4), 1051–1069.

Shankar, S. Gowri. 2007. "Active Versus Passive Index Management: A Performance Comparison of the S&P and the Russell Indexes", *The Journal of Investing*, 16-2, 85–95.

Sharpe, William F. 1966. "Mutual Fund Performance", *Journal of Business*, January, 39, 119–38.

Sharpe, William. 1988. "Determining a Fund's Effective Asset Mix", *Investment Management Review*, 2(6), 59–69.

Sharpe, William. 1992. "Asset Allocation, Management Style and Performance Measurement", *Journal of Portfolio Management*, 18(2), 7–19.
Sharpe, William F. 1994. "The Sharpe Ratio", *The Journal of Portfolio Management*, 21(1), 49–58.
Siegel, Jeremy. 2006. "The Noisy Market' Hypothesis", *Wall Street Journal*, June 14.
Soe, Aye, and Srikant Dash. 2009. "A Tale of Two Benchmarks". Standard & Poor's Occasional Paper, June.
Treynor, J. L. 1965. "How to Rate the Performance of Mutual Funds", *Harvard Business Review*, January/February, 43, 63–75.
Treynor, J. L., and F. Black. 1973. "How to Use Security Analysis to Improve Portfolio Selection", *Journal of Business*, January, 66–88.

3

Strategic Versus Tactical Asset Allocation

"The pessimist complains about the wind; the optimist expects it to change; the realist adjusts the sails."
—William Arthur Ward

In this chapter, we will evaluate the merits of using the SAA as a stand-alone approach versus combining it with TAA decisions. We will begin with a discussion of the nature of the *SAA as an investment decision*. This is followed by an examination of the concept of *macro-inefficiency* and how this relates to asset allocation and a review of some of the empirical research on the *importance of asset allocation*. We finalize with a discussion of the controversial concept of *time diversification*, the question of whether a longer time horizon warrants a greater exposure to risk assets, favoring the SAA alone approach.

3.1 Absolute Versus Relative Risk

The SAA as a Decision

As we have discussed previously, the *policy portfolio* or SAA constitutes the benchmark for any subsequent decisions on TAA. In the hierarchy of decisions, the TAA decisions therefore imply a *relative*, or active, *risk* vis-à-vis the SAA in the same vein as security selection implies a relative risk vis-à-vis the benchmark within each asset class.

H. Lumholdt, *Strategic and Tactical Asset Allocation*,
https://doi.org/10.1007/978-3-319-89554-3_3

Does the SAA itself have a benchmark? For some institutional investors, such as pension funds and life insurance companies, future liabilities can be clearly understood as the benchmark of the SAA; how well the SAA matches these liabilities is the yardstick for its success. Indeed, pension plans and investors with analogous liabilities will typically dictate relatively narrow margins for the SAA. For most other types of investors, however, any benchmark for the SAA is at best indirect. In the spirit of the CAPM, the benchmark should be the investable universe, and this is indeed used in empirical research (see below). In practice, this is rarely used in a performance evaluation of the SAA. Private investors might reasonably regard their needs for adequate means for retirement as a *quasi-liability*, and wealth planners will take all relevant information in this respect into account (such as age, health, current income and needs for future income) when recommending the SAA. But this hardly makes it a benchmark with the properties we analyzed in the previous chapter.

Does this make the SAA less subjective than the TAA? The answer is no. The fact that it is passive or static does not imply that it expresses no opinion. Indeed, since it concerns the *absolute risk* of the portfolio, it belongs at the highest level in the decision hierarchy of asset allocation. Its passive nature does not make it less uncertain either. As will be discussed in Chaps. 4 and 5, the SAA is determined by some optimization of long-term expectations of return, risk and the correlation between asset classes. The measurements and decisions that this gives rise to will inevitably be subject to uncertainties. These are some of the most important ones:

- **Uncertainly regarding long-term returns.** Estimates of long-term returns rest critically on factors such as macro-fundamentals and asset valuation. The forecaster often has the advantage of being able to assume mean-reversion for some variables. Still, estimates will in part need to be based on the historical record making them sensitive to the period chosen and to future changes in scenario. This is examined in Chap. 4.
- **Risk.** The standard approach to portfolio optimization implicitly assumes a constant level of risk throughout the investment period. The empirical fact is that risk is time-dependent. Moreover, traditional measures of portfolio risk are at best incomplete. When the assumption of normality does not hold, higher moments of returns distributions will need to be taken into account. This introduces complications for the pure Buy-and-Hold SAA approach. We will look at this in Chap. 5.
- **Asset class correlations.** The empirical observation is that correlations between the returns of the different asset classes vary considerably over

time, challenging the assumptions made for the purposes of portfolio optimization. We will look at the determinants of such changes and their implications in Chap. 9.

- **Dominance of macro-factors.** Recent years have seen an increase in the importance of macro-factors, often overshadowing asset-specific factors. Different *market regimes* give rise to the significantly different performance of the different asset classes. This is examined in Chaps. 8 and 9.
- **Cyclical dependencies.** The economy transitions through different phases, even though this is not always a smooth process. The performance of the main asset classes exhibits a dependency on such phases. This is examined in the final chapter of the book which offers an overall framework for TAA decisions.

3.2 Market Efficiency

Micro-Efficiency

The theory of *informational efficiency* is central to modern finance. When information is readily available to all market participants, the market price of an asset becomes an unbiased estimate of its true or "fair" value. By implication, only new information can move the price, and since new information cannot be predicted (except in the case of inside information), financial markets themselves become *unpredictable*. As long as deviations from true value are random, the true value of an asset in a sense becomes irrelevant to investors. If the probability of a move away from the true value equals that of a movement toward it, fundamental analysis of any kind becomes futile.

Efficiency, however, must be a matter of degree. Grossman and Stiglitz (1980) demonstrated the internal contradiction of perfectly efficient markets. If there is no benefit to be had from gathering information, no one would do so. But if no one produced information, prices would no longer be able to reflect all relevant information giving rise to inefficiencies. At the margin then, some equilibrium must exist between the costs and benefits of producing information. On a more practical level, there is clearly a difference in efficiency between heavily traded securities in liquid markets and less actively traded securities which attract less attention and research. In the first case, contrarian trades can remove anomalies at high speed and low cost. In the latter case, this might be both costly and difficult.

Macro-*In*efficiency

Of particular interest in the context of asset allocation is whether markets can be considered efficient in the *aggregate* or, put differently, whether *micro-efficiency* sums up to *macro-efficiency*. One of the fathers of the efficient market hypothesis, none other than Paul Samuelson,[1] suggested that it does not. To the extent that well-informed market participants are able to detect mispriced securities, such inefficiencies will be arbitraged away quickly. Their ability to *counter* a trend set by general market sentiment, however, is limited.

Focusing on the stock market, Jung and Shiller (2005) argue that investors are likely to possess good information about the earnings and dividends of well-known stocks. An active market between investors with different views will then make the efficient markets hypothesis a good approximation. This may not translate to the aggregate market, however, because such specific fundamentals tend to average out making overall trends more subtle and dependent on factors like economic growth, monetary policy and so on, which are harder to understand for the investing public.

To test these ideas, the authors identify 49 stocks that existed throughout the whole period from 1926 to 2001 and regress their dividend yield (dividend per share/share price) on the future changes in the dividends of these stocks. An efficient market should forecast a negative relationship between these two variables, because a low present dividend yield (meaning a high price of the stock relative to its dividend) should equate with a higher growth in future earnings, and vice versa (under perfect conditions with a correlation coefficient of −1). Their findings generally confirm the negative relationship. For ten-year periods within the sample, 42 out of the 49 companies showed a negative coefficient with an average of −0.440. The data thus support the efficient market hypothesis on the company level.

However, aggregating all the stocks into an index, and performing a single regression, produces the opposite result: a positive relationship with a coefficient above 0.3. The authors interpret these results as confirming Samuelson's idea that efficiency does *not* apply in the aggregate of the market.

More qualitative indicators of macro-inefficiency are the boom-bust dynamics seen in some speculative markets and the concept of market "bubbles" which are sometimes explained by "herd behavior". The central view expressed in this book is that the relationship between macroeconomic news and the performance of asset classes as a whole is generally less immediate

[1] See also Samuelson (1998).

than, for example, the impact of company news on the price of individual stocks. One reason is that incoming macro-information is more partial than company news and must be fitted into a general scenario or regime. Another reason is that market perceptions are influenced to a significant degree by the actions of central banks. We will return to these ideas later in the book.

3.3 The Importance of Asset Allocation

How important are decisions about strategic asset allocation? This seemingly straightforward question turns out to be more elusive than might be expected.

The founding study in this field is that of BHB (1986), who analyzed the performance of 91 pension plans in the SEI Large Plan Universe. The study covered a ten-year period from 1974 to 1983, comparing the performance of the funds with their policy portfolios (or SAA), using the ten-year average holding of each type of asset of all 91 plans as a proxy for the SAA.

The central question posed by BHB is what percentage of the *variation* over time in returns is due to the SAA. They answer this question by regressing each of the 91 funds' actual total return on their policy return and then averaging the R-squares of the regressions. The key result of this analysis was that the average policy return explained as much as 93.3% of the variation, with a minimum of 75.5% and a maximum of 98.6%. The remaining 6.7% of the average is then explained by active management (TAA and security selection). An update of the study (Brinson et al. 1991), using the period from 1977 to 1987, comes to the essentially same conclusion with the SAA explaining 91.5% of the variation in the return of the actual portfolio, with the lowest value being 67.7% and the highest being 98.2%.

This result has frequently been interpreted to mean that 93.7% of returns—rather than their variation—can be attributed to the SAA. Subsequent studies have demonstrated the problems with this interpretation. As an example, Statman (2000) creates a simulation of an average BHB manager with perfect foresight who beats the benchmark by 8.10% per year. The same regression as that used by BHB would still explain 89.4% of the variation, leading to the conclusion that TAA was unimportant despite this significant outperformance.

In an attempt at clarification, Ibbotson and Kaplan (2000) demonstrate that the answer to the question of "the importance of asset allocation" depends on what is being asked. This research uses ten years of monthly return data from 94 US balanced funds and five years of quarterly returns of 58 pension funds for a period ending March 31, 1998. Ibbotson and Kaplan offer three different angles:

1. *The time series approach*: how much of the variation in returns across time is explained by SAA?
2. *The cross-section approach*: how much of the variation in returns across funds' performance is explained by differences in SAA?
3. *The return levels approach*: how large a part of funds' actual returns is explained by the SAA?

With respect to the first question, the variability across time of fund returns, the study largely confirms the findings of BHB. For the median mutual fund, 87.6% of the return variation is explained by the SAA, against 90.7% of the median pension fund. Mutual funds appear to employ more active management than pension funds. With respect to the second question, the variation in returns across different funds, however, the resulting R^2 of 0.40 is considerably lower than in the case of the time series approach.

To answer the third question, the authors calculate the ratio between the compound annual policy return and the compound annual total return of the funds, a measure of performance. The ratio varies from 82% for the best 5% percentile of the mutual funds to 132% for the worst performing 95 percentile of the funds. For the pension funds, the corresponding percentages are 86% and 113%, respectively. On average, both types of funds underperform the policy return, meaning that the policy return explains more than 100%. Ibbotson and Kaplan make the point that the returns of the funds are mostly driven by their participation in the markets in general. The average underperformance should be expected since the funds incur transaction costs which are not included in the policy return.

Xiong et al. (2010) account for the *market effect* explicitly. Using monthly data for 4641 US equity funds, 587 balanced funds and 400 international equity funds for the period from May 1999 to April 2009, they decompose total portfolio returns into (1) the market return, (2) the return from the asset allocation policy and (3) active management (TAA and security selection) as follows:

$$R_{i,t} = M_t + \left(P_{i,t} - M_t\right) + \left(R_{i,t} - P_{i,t}\right) \tag{3.1}$$

where $R_{i,t}$ is the total return for fund i in period t, M_t is the market return of an equally weighted peer group of funds and $P_{i,t}$ is the total policy return for fund i in period t. A time series regression shows that market returns, M_t, account for as much as 83%, 88% and 74% of the total return in the three categories of funds, respectively, with the rest accounted for by the asset allocation policy, $(P_{i,t} - M_t)$, and active management, $(R_{i,t} - P_{i,t})$.

The authors then *remove* the market effect, to focus on excess return, defined as follows:

$$R_{i,t} - M_t = \left(P_{i,t} - M_t\right) + \left(R_{i,t} - P_{i,t}\right) \tag{3.2}$$

When regressing excess market return, $R_{i,t} - M_t$, on policy excess return, $(P_{i,t} - M_t)$, and active return, $(R_{i,t} - P_{i,t})$, they find that approximately half of the return variation comes from the asset allocation decision and the other half comes from active management. The authors point out that when using a cross-section approach the market effect is eliminated which makes it equivalent to the time series approach using excess returns. When using this approach, the authors consequently get to a similar conclusion to that of the time series approach, even though the dispersion of data becomes considerably higher. In a separate paper, Ibbotson (2010) concludes that while asset allocation is important, the idea that it accounts for more than 90% of the return variation is clearly misleading.

What is the takeaway from this research? Obviously, there is a difference between measuring what the industry does as a whole and what room for maneuver specific investors have. For example, the pension funds in the BHB study clearly engaged in very little active management making the SAA more important by implication rather than by design. But this also highlights the need for a very conscious approach. Some commentators stress that most of the effort is often focused on manager selection, treating the SAA as a given. Our view is that its importance warrants much more than that, and that the TAA can constitute an important complement which can compensate for some of the uncertainties of the SAA. Unlike the approach in the empirical studies, we therefore do not consider the two decision levels as entirely independent.

3.4 Time Diversification

The Importance of Time Horizon

Does a longer time horizon reduce risk the same way that diversification across asset classes will? If so, this would suggest that investors should vary their risk exposure over their lifetime. It would also appear to favor the SAA as a stand-alone approach. As we will see, the first conclusion holds up reasonably well while the second is at best debatable.

How is risk empirically related to time horizon? The data of Ibbotson et al. (2017) describe rolling returns of different asset classes. Large-cap stocks have seen a return as high as 53.99% in a given year (1933) and as low as −43.34% (1931). Expanding the time horizon to five years, the highest compound annual return was 20.06% (1995–99) and the lowest was −12.47% (1928–32). The range of variation between positive return periods and negative periods narrows further with a ten-year time horizon. Investment periods as long as 20 years see no returns on stocks in negative territory. Siegel (2014) offers similar calculations adjusted for inflation. He documents that stocks outperform bonds in real terms 80% of the time when the investment horizon is ten years, about 90% of the time when it is 20 years and close to 100% of the time when it is 30 years or more. Analyzing 19 countries over the period from 1990 to 2009, Estrada (2013) finds similar patterns in markets outside of the US. Given these empirical data, can there be any doubt that time diversifies risk?

The problem with this conclusion is that it focuses exclusively on one measure of risk. As a matter of principle, the volatility of the *average annual return* should in principle fall by the square root of the number of years invested, as indeed confirmed by the empirical data. The volatility of the *total holding period return*, however, will increase by the square root of the number of years invested.

This is expressed in Eqs. (3.3) and (3.4)[2]:

$$\sigma_{r1} = \frac{\sigma_n}{\sqrt{n}} \tag{3.3}$$

where σ_{r1} denotes the annualized standard deviation of returns, σ_n denotes the standard deviation of the total return over the period and n represents the number of years. Conversely:

$$\sigma_n = \sigma_{r1}\sqrt{n} \tag{3.4}$$

[2] Strictly speaking, this requires that returns are independent and identically distributed (i.i.d.) as in a random walk process. In discrete time we can express the holding period return over a given number of years as $(1 + HPR) = (1 + R_1)(1 + R_2)\ldots(1 + R_n)$, where R is the percent return per year and n is the number of years. Converting this to continuous time we use the log form: $ln(1 + HPR) = ln(1 + r_1) + ln(1 + r_2) + \ldots + ln(1 + r_n) = r_1 + r_2 + \ldots r_n$. If returns are i.i.d., the variance of the total return becomes $Var(r_1 + r_2 + \ldots + r_n) = Var(r_1) + Var(r_1) + \ldots + Var(r_n) = NVar(r_1)$. The standard deviation is then $\sigma_n = \sqrt{Var\left(r_1 + r_2 + \ldots + r_n\right)} = \sqrt{n}\sqrt{Var(r_1)} = \sigma_{r1}\sqrt{n}$. Hence, $\sigma_{r1} = \frac{\sigma_n}{\sqrt{n}}$.

Terminal Wealth

To illustrate this, Kritzman (1994) simulates a $100,000 investment in the S&P 500 assuming a lognormal distribution of returns, an expected return of 10% and a standard deviation of returns of 15%. Using a 95% confidence interval he computes the range variation in *terminal wealth* over different periods. He compares this with a risk-free investment with an annual return of 3%. The results are shown in Table 3.1. As can be seen, the dispersion in terminal wealth is considerable and grows over time. Even so, when the holding period is as long as 20 years, the worst case for stocks more or less breaks even with the risk-free investment.

The author then asks what would happen if we demanded a 99% confidence interval. The answer is that in that case the lower boundary of the terminal wealth does fall below the risk-free alternative. This is even more so with a 99.9% confidence interval. This highlights one of the problems with the notion that a longer time horizon warrants a greater weighting of stocks: while the *probability* of a loss falls the longer is the investment period, this is offset by the *magnitude* of the loss.

This is related to the question of the investor's attitude to risk. Kritzman expresses utility as the logarithm of wealth which is commonly used in financial economics. This utility function is such that the investor's satisfaction increases with wealth but at a decreasing rate. It therefore implies more disutility for a given decrease in wealth than the utility associated with an increase in wealth of the same size.

Given this utility function, consider the case of an investment of $100 which has a 50% chance of a one-third gain and a 50% chance of a one-fourth loss. The investor can choose between staying put or engaging in the investment in up to three periods. Given this distribution of returns, Kritzman calculates the expected value of the investment as:

Table 3.1 Simulations of Terminal Wealth

Terminal wealth ($)			
	S&P 500, with a 95% confidence interval		Risk-free investment
	Lower boundary	Upper boundary	
1 year	81,980	147,596	103,000
5 years	83,456	310,792	115,927
10 years	102,367	657,196	134,392
15 years	133,776	1,304,376	155,797
20 years	180,651	2,565,345	180,611

Source: Based on Kritzman (1994)

- 100 (starting wealth)
- 104.17 (after one period)
- 108.51 (after two periods)
- 113.03 (after three periods)

The utility of the investor's wealth after each period is calculated as the weighted average of the natural log of the wealth given all the possible outcomes in each period. It turns out that, given these assumptions, utility is invariant to investing or not and to investing for one, two or three periods. By implication, time diversification loses its relevance.

Within-Horizon Risk

Kritzman and Rich (2002) add another dimension to the question. They argue that investors are exposed not just to the risk of a loss at the end of their investment horizon but also to the risk of a loss *throughout* their investment horizon. This issue is particularly relevant for leveraged investors who risk breaching thresholds before the end of the investment period. More generally, investors tend to care about this risk because it causes them to worry about the result at the end of the investment horizon. The authors demonstrate how to estimate this risk.[3] Using a similar methodology on monthly data, Trainor (2005) shows a comparison between the "end-of-horizon risk" (what we referred previously as risk to terminal wealth) and the "within-horizon risk", as defined by Kritzman and Rich. The author shows that these two types of risk move in opposite direction over the time horizon. As an example, while the end-of-horizon risk of losing 25% or more falls from 2.1% for a one-year horizon to 1.0% for a 20-year horizon, the within-horizon risk grows from 5.2% for a one-year horizon to as much as 24.4% for a 20-year horizon.

Duval (2006) highlights some observable practical problems which conflict with the notion of time diversification. Private investors often do not think in terms of *percentage* gains or losses but rather in terms of *absolute* gains or losses. Time diversification assumes that the investor's asset composition is left untouched over the investment horizon. In the successful case, this implies a significant increase in wealth. But the investor is unlikely to have the same attitude to a $200,000 loss on $1,000,000 retirement money in year 30 as to a 20% loss on a $2000 Individual Retirement Account (IRA) account in year one. He cites a US survey for the period from 1984 to 2004 which demonstrates that the average mutual fund investor held their investment for only 2.5 years and had average returns of

[3] The authors use a statistic called "first-passage time probability". See further Kritzman and Rich (2002).

only 4% over the period against average 20-year market returns of 12%. Even if the principle of time diversification worked in principle, few investors seem to have the necessary discipline to benefit from it.

More recent work by Pástor and Stambaugh (2012) stresses yet another uncertainty factor. Expectations about the standard deviation of returns must be based on some true mean. But since this true mean is in fact unknown, this creates an additional uncertainty over future realized returns. The authors show that this uncertainty will grow over the investment horizon, making long-term returns more uncertain than short-term returns.

The Price of Options

Bodie (1995) approaches the question of time diversification from the point of view of option pricing. He argues that if time diversification worked, the cost of insuring against the risk that stock returns should fall below the risk-free should decrease the longer is the time horizon. This insurance against a shortfall can be approximated by buying a put option. The author argues that the higher price on longer-dated options compared to shorter-dated options argues directly against the central idea of time diversification.

Human Capital

One argument in favor of time diversification is the importance of *human capital*. Older investors close to retirement per definition possess little or no human capital, while they generally have more investment capital than younger investors. Younger investors, on the other hand, generally possess plenty of human capital and less investment capital. The latter group therefore has the possibility of compensating for any losses on their portfolio through harder work going forward, whereas the first group has no such flexibility. On this basis, the common practice of recommending a larger proportion of stocks for younger investors than for older investors, and using a gradually decreasing proportion over a lifetime seems quite reasonable.

3.5 Conclusion

As we will see in Chap. 4, the longer-term outperformance of risky assets over risk-free assets is well documented. This and the fact that stock market returns can be seen to mean-revert are the key reasons to accept short-term volatility to get access to higher longer-term returns. So why not put all the emphasis on SAA and exclude TAA decisions entirely? In this chapter, we have discussed some of the reasons.

The first reason is more conceptual. The SAA is not normally subjected to a benchmark the way TAA is. This makes it easy to overlook the *absolute portfolio risk* it implies and focus exclusively on *relative risk*, as expressed in the tracking error. But a higher tracking error can indicate a lower overall portfolio risk as well a higher overall risk.

More specifically, and as we shall explore in more depth in Chaps. 4 and 5, estimated future returns and the volatility of those returns are subject to considerable uncertainties as is the process of optimizing the SAA given the inputs. Empirical research on the importance of asset allocation has often been misinterpreted to imply that returns are practically only explained by the SAA. As we saw, recent studies have highlighted that the *market factor* accounts for a more significant part than was appreciated previously, which begs the question of whether that part can be managed more actively.

We also examined the question of whether time somehow diversifies risk. As discussed, this appears to hold both theoretically and empirically with respect to the volatility of average annual returns. But time diversification can easily be overstated. In return for this lower annual volatility, the adherence to fixed portfolio weights throughout a long period increases the risk attached to terminal wealth. More importantly, time offers no protection against *within-horizon risk* which is ultimately the way investors will experience the manifestation of risk over time.

The role of TAA is not to substitute the SAA but to remedy some of its inherent weaknesses. Opponents of TAA argue that tactical investment decisions require perfect foresight. We believe less than that will suffice. As will be discussed in Part III of the book, identifying *regimes* and *phases of the economy* requires less than perfect foresight and provides useful input for TAA decisions which can be modified dynamically. The uncertainties of the SAA and the TAA need not be additive. The passive risk of the SAA and the active risk of the TAA should ultimately be managed together.

References

Bodie, Zvi. 1995. "On the Risk of Stocks in the Long Run", *Financial Analysts Journal*, 51, 18–22.

Brinson, Gary P., L. Randolph Hood, and Gilbert L. Beebower. 1986. "Determinants of Portfolio Performance", *Financial Analysts Journal*, July/August, 42(4), 39–44.

Brinson, Gary P., Brian D. Singer, and Gilbert L. Beebower. 1991. "Determinants of Portfolio Performance II: An Update", *Financial Analysts Journal*, 47(3), 40–8.
Duval, Jack. 2006. "The Myth of Time Diversification: Analysis, Application, and Incorrect New Account Forms", *PIABA Bar Journal*, Spring edition.
Estrada J. 2013. "Stocks, Bonds, Risk, and the Holding Period: An International Perspective", *The Journal of Wealth Management*, Fall, 2013a, 25–44.
Grossman, S. J., and J. E. Stiglitz. 1980. "On the Impossibility of Informationally Efficient Markets", *American Economic Review*, 70(3), 393–408.
Ibbotson, Roger G., and Paul D. Kaplan. 2000. "Does Asset Allocation Policy Explain 40, 90, or 100 Percent of Performance?", *Financial Analysts Journal*, January/February, 56(1), 26–33.
Ibbotson, Roger G. 2010. "The Importance of Asset Allocation", *Financial Analysts Journal*, March/April, 66, 18–20.
Ibbotson, Roger, Roger J. Harrington, and James P. Harrington. 2017. "Stocks, Bonds, Bills and Inflation (SBBI) Yearbook". Wiley.
Jung, Jeeman, and Robert Shiller. 2005. "Samuelson's Dictum and the Stock Market", *Economic Inquiry*, 43(2), 221–228.
Kritzman, Mark. 1994. "What Practitioners Need to Know … About Time Diversification", *Financial Analysts Journal*, January/February, 14–18.
Kritzman, M., and D. Rich. 2002. "The Mismeasurement of Risk", *Financial Analysts Journal*, 58, 91–99.
Pástor, Ľuboš, and Robert Stambaugh. 2012. "Are Stocks Really Less Volatile in the Long Run?" *Journal of Finance*, 67, 431–477.
Samuelson, Paul. 1998. "Summing Up on Business Cycles: Opening Address", in Beyond Shocks: What Causes Business Cycles, Conference Series 42, ed. J. Fuhrer and S. Schuh, 33–36. Boston: Federal Reserve Bank of Boston.
Siegel, Jeremy. 2014. "Stocks for the Long Run", 5th edition. New York: McGraw Hill.
Statman, M. 2000. "The 93.6 Per cent Question of Financial Advisors", *Journal of Investing*, Spring, 9(1), 16–20.
Trainor, W. J. 2005. "Within Horizon Exposure to Loss for Dollar Cost Averaging and Lump Sum Investing", *Financial Services Review*, 14, 319–330.
Xiong, James X., Roger G. Ibbotson, Thomas M. Idzorek, and Peng Chen. 2010. "The Equal Importance of Asset Allocation and Active Management", *Financial Analysts Journal*, March/April, 22–30.

Part II

Strategic Asset Allocation

4

Long-Term Return Expectations

"If you don't know where you are going, you might wind up someplace else."
—Yogi Berra

How do we formulate expectations for long-term returns on the asset classes involved in the SAA? One approach would be to rely exclusively on the *historical record*. We will look at this in the first section. Another approach is to base our expectations on more *forward-looking indicators* such as longer-term macro-fundamentals, models of return and valuations. We will look at how this applies to risk-free government bonds, credit and equities in the subsequent sections.

How long is long-term? Expectations for longer-term returns are generally seen as more reliable than shorter-term forecasts due to *mean reversion* of the factors driving returns. Specifically, a sufficiently long-term view can "see through" the business cycle, might assume imbalances in terms of over- or under-valuations to have been corrected and all manner of market "noise" to have been eliminated. Still, a balance must be struck. If we choose too long a time horizon, we invite the risk that new imbalances, possibly different from any current ones, might have been created over the period. If our time horizon is too short, on the other hand, we may not be able to rely fully on mean reversion. In practice, most market projections focus on a ten-year horizon.

H. Lumholdt, *Strategic and Tactical Asset Allocation*,
https://doi.org/10.1007/978-3-319-89554-3_4

4.1 The Record

The Very Long Term

Jeremy Siegel[1] has documented over 200 years of US market history. The evidence points to a very clear long-term outperformance of stocks over other main asset classes. Siegel calculates the accumulated value of a $1 investment made in 1802 and kept until 2012 in stocks, bonds, T-bills and gold, respectively, assuming that all interest and dividends are reinvested:

- *Stocks*: $13.48 million
- *Government bonds*: $33,922
- *T-bills:* $5379
- *Gold:* $86.40

Clearly, this must be adjusted for inflation, which gives a much lower accumulated value. Returns are easier to relate to. Table 4.1 shows the compound annual returns over the whole period of 1802–2012, calculated in both nominal and real terms.

As can be seen, adjusting for inflation clearly changes the result. But the performance ranking of the asset classes remains the same.

Ibbotson et al. (2017)[2] provide detailed data for the US markets since 1926. A summary of their findings for the main asset classes is set out in Table 4.2.

Looking at the full period from 1926 to 2016, the data confirm the general pattern found by Siegel specifically:

Table 4.1 Asset class returns: 1802–2012

	Compound annual nominal return (%)	Compound annual real return (%)
Stocks	8.1	6.6
Govt. bonds	5.1	3.6
T-bills	4.2	2.7
Gold	2.1	0.7

Source: Siegel (2014)

[1] See also Siegel (2014) and earlier editions.

[2] The data material is updated yearly.

Table 4.2 Asset class returns: 1926–2016

	Annual total compound returns (%)	
	1926–2016	2007–2016
Large-cap stocks	10.0	6.9
Small-cap stocks	12.1	7.6
Long-term corp. bonds	6.0	6.9
Long-term govt. bonds	5.5	6.5
Inter-term govt. bonds	5.1	4.0
US treasury bills	3.4	0.7
Inflation	2.9	1.8

Source: Ibbotson (2017)

- *Stocks outperform bonds.* This conclusion holds for both large-cap and small-cap stocks compared to both long-term corporate and government bonds.
- *The size premium is positive.* Small-cap stocks outperform large-cap stocks.
- *Credit risk is rewarded.* Long-term corporate bonds outperform long-term government bonds, albeit not significantly.
- *Duration risk is rewarded.* Long-term government bonds outperform intermediate-term government bonds and T-bills.

Dimson et al. (2002) study 101 years of evidence, expanding the scope to 4 continents and 16 countries. The study highlights that the US experience stands out as particularly successful and does not apply to other countries to the same degree. In spite of these differences, the study confirms the long-term outperformance of stocks over bonds and bonds over T-bills.

The Recent Past

Comparing the last column in Table 4.2 covering the last ten years with the first one covering the whole 91-year period, we see notable differences. In particular, stocks barely outperformed long-term bonds while duration risk was even better rewarded than in the full 91-year period. This period, of course, included the Great Financial Crisis which implied a sizeable correction to the stock market. It also includes an important recovery from 2009 to 2016, however.

Ilmanen (2011) provides data for the 20-year period ending 2009 with a somewhat different breakdown. Table 4.3 summarizes some of the key data.

Again, we note a significant variation from the longer-term performance statistics. Importantly, the outperformance of stocks versus bonds is much

Table 4.3 Asset class returns: 1990–2009

	Performance statistics, 1990–2009		
	Annual comp. return	Annual volatility	Sharpe ratio
US equity market	8.5	15.5	0.34
US small-cap growth stocks	5.0	24.6	0.15
US small-cap value stocks	14.0	18.8	0.62
US treasuries	6.8	4.7	0.53
US investment-grade debt	7.0	3.9	0.67
US treasury bills	3.8	0.6	−1.17
US inflation	2.8	0.9	–

Source: Ilmanen (2010)

less pronounced. Given this modest outperformance, the higher volatility of stocks implied a much lower Sharpe ratio than that on both US Treasuries and investment-grade debt. Small-cap value stocks are the exception, however, outperforming the general stock market significantly both in terms of compound return and in terms of Sharpe ratio. Finally, duration risk is again very well rewarded with US Treasuries outperforming T-bills significantly.

This period excludes the general stock market recovery seen since 2009, but it *in*cludes both the bull market in the late 1990s and the bear market from 2001 to 2003 on the back of the collapse in tech stocks. The period also includes a significant downtrend in bond yields.

Time Variation

In Fig. 4.1 we have calculated ten-year rolling annualized nominal and real total returns on the S&P500 since 1900. As can be seen, a ten-year time horizon has implied very different returns in different periods. This begs the question of which is more representative going forward: the very long-term record, the more recent past, or some other 10- or 20-year period? The 2000s have been referred to as the Lost Decade for stocks. Does that mean we can safely disregard this decade and focus on the longer-term record? Put differently, can all the trends of the recent decade be considered *cyclical* or are some of them of more *secular* in nature? While the historical record is clearly useful as a point of reference, it offers little guidance in this respect and is hardly unambiguous as a basis for expected future returns. This is the key justification for an attempt at a more forward-looking analysis.

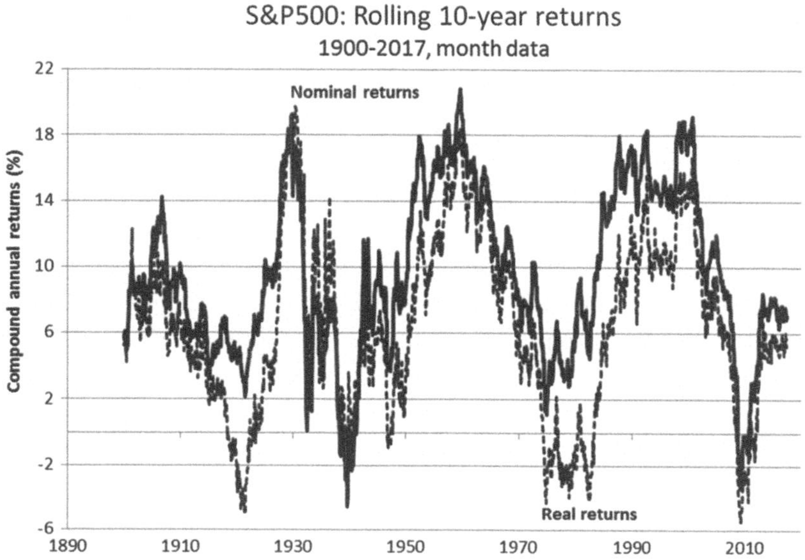

Fig. 4.1 Rolling ten-year nominal and real returns. (Source: Robert Shiller's data base, http://www.econ.yale.edu/~shiller/data.htm)

4.2 Macro-Fundamentals

From the point of view of investment returns, the key macro-fundamentals are longer-term *real GDP growth* and *inflation*. Over the shorter term, economies tend to exhibit cycles[3] of expansion and contraction which are driven primarily by the components of *aggregate demand*. Longer-term growth trends, however, are driven primarily by the *supply side* of the economy which determines its *potential output* or, put differently, its productive capacity. This in turn depends on *growth in employment* and *growth in labor productivity*. The growth in employment can be decomposed into the growth in the labor force and the growth in the labor participation rate (both driven by demographic factors). Productivity, on the other hand, can be decomposed into the contribution from new investment in physical capital (machines, equipment, plants, etc.) and a catch-all residual called total factor productivity (normally associated with technological progress, improvements in efficiency, etc.).

The general observation is that economies move toward a lower trend growth as they mature. This is seen most obviously in the case of developed economies like the US, Europe and Japan. The increase in productivity from new capital investment has diminished and, more importantly, technological breakthroughs of the past in areas like transportation and communications,

[3] We will look at cycles in more depth in the chapters on TAA.

which led to major improvements in productivity, are not matched in importance by modern-day innovations like the internet or the mobile phone. Another reason is that aging populations imply a gradually lower growth in the labor force. Emerging market economies have an inherent *potential* for higher growth. In some cases, their capital-to-labor ratio is still low and generally they can *catch up* by investing in known technologies already implemented in the developed economies. A further reason is that their underlying demographics are generally more favorable.[4]

While positive or negative future shocks to economic growth cannot be predicted, longer-term trends in demographics and productivity are relatively stable and therefore do lend themselves to forecasting. As we shall see, the link between the longer-term macro-fundamentals and market returns is clearest for bonds but more uncertain in the case of equities. The fundamental approach therefore cannot stand alone.

4.3 Default-Free Government Bonds

In this first part, we will examine government bonds which are presumed to be free of default risk. We begin our analysis with the concept of *forward rates*. To this end, we assume a *zero-coupon bond*[5] with a time to maturity of n periods and refer to the yield on this bond as the *spot rate* to distinguish it from the yield-to-maturity (YTM) on a regular coupon bond. We can decompose this spot rate into a known short-term rate and a series of *implied forward rates*:

$$(1+y_n)^n = (1+y_1)(1+f_{1,2})(1+f_{2,3})\ldots(1+f_{n-1,n}) \quad (4.1)$$

where

y_n = the spot rate on an n-period zero-coupon bond
y_1= the known one-period spot rate
$f_{1,2}$= the one-period forward rate from the end of period 1 to the end of period 2
$f_{2,3}$= the one-period forward rate from the end of period 2 to the end of period 3

[4] This general observation is not without its exceptions. As an example, India still has a very young population while China will face longer-term economic headwinds from aging due, in part, to the previous one-child policy which has now been abolished.

[5] A zero-coupon bond makes a single payment when it matures, unlike a coupon bond which makes payments at regular intervals, for example, semi-annually or annually. This makes it free of any bias. The yield-to-maturity on a regular coupon bond implicitly assumes that coupons will be reinvested at the same rate as its YTM which will apply only when the yield curve is flat.

$f_{n-1,n}$= the one-period forward rate from the end of period $n-1$ to the end of period n

A complete series of zero-coupon bonds allows us to construct a *spot curve,* depicting zero-coupon rates for maturities from 1 to n periods. Given these data we can find the *forward rate* between any two maturities, m and n, as follows:

$$\left(1+f_{m,n}\right)^{n-m}=\frac{\left(1+y_n\right)^n}{\left(1+y_m\right)^m} \tag{4.2}$$

As an example, suppose that the yields on one-, two- and three-year zero-coupon bonds (y_1, y_2 and y_3) are 3%, 4% and 5%, respectively. Since $y_3 > y_2 > y_1$ we have a *positively sloped* spot curve. Using Eq. (4.2) we calculate the implied forward rates from years 1 to 2 and 2 to 3, that is, $f_{1,2}$ and $f_{2,3}$, as follows[6]:

$$\left(1+f_{1,2}\right)=\frac{\left(1+0.04\right)^2}{\left(1+0.03\right)}=1.05009709 \Rightarrow f_{1,2}=5.009709\%$$

$$\left(1+f_{2,3}\right)=\frac{\left(1+0.05\right)^3}{\left(1+0.04\right)^2}=1.07028939 \Rightarrow f_{2,3}=7.028939\%$$

An investor with \$100 to invest and a three-year time horizon could choose to place the money in the three-year bond and hold it to maturity. The \$100 would then grow to \$100 $(1 + 0.05)^3$ = \$115.7625, after the three years. Alternatively, she would place the money in the two-year bond which would then grow to \$100 $(1 + 0.04)^2$ = \$108.16 after two years and reinvest this amount at the forward rate ($f_{2,3}$) for one year, implying a capital of \$108.16 (1 + 0.07028939) = \$115.762 at the end of the three years. Finally, she could go for the one-year bond for the first year, rolling it over at $f_{1,2}$ and $f_{2,3}$ after 1 and 2 years. Her capital would then grow to 100 (1 + 0.03)(1 + 0.05009709) (1 + 0.07028939) = \$115.7625. The three alternatives give the same investment result. We note that the positively sloped spot curve implies an even more positively sloped forward curve.

What do the forward rates express? The *expectations hypothesis* holds that implied forward rates represent *expected future short-term rates.* In our first example, the positively sloped spot curve would emanate from expectations of higher future short-term rates. Suppose now that the market gets to expect

[6] Note that the exponent n-m on the left side of Eq. (4.2) in our two calculations is simply 1.

even higher future short-term rates than previously. To stay with our example, if $f_{1,2}$ were predicted to be 6% rather than approx. 5%, the market would prefer to buy the one-year bond today and roll it over after one year to buying the two-year bond today and holding it to maturity. In this example, \$100 would be expected to grow to \$100 (1 + 0.03)(1 + 0.06) = \$109.18 after the two years using the first strategy as opposed to \$100 $(1 + 0.04)^2$ = \$108.16 with the two-year bond. Market forces would therefore put upward pressure on the rate on the two-year bond until $f_{1,2}$ again implied an equivalence between the two investments. In this example we end up with an even steeper spot curve; its slope has been driven higher by higher expected short-term rates.

Note that rising forward rates are not per se a reason to avoid longer-dated paper over shorter-dated paper. As we saw, an upward sloping forward curve can be consistent with the same expected return on different maturities. We therefore need to compare our own expectations with those expressed by the market. If our expectations imply higher forward rates than the implied forwards, we will have a motive to favor the shorter end of the curve, while the opposite will be true if our expectations point to lower rates than those predicted by the market.

The Yield Curve

Research has demonstrated that the pure expectations hypothesis does not suffice to explain observable yield curves. Additional explanations of the curve include:

- *Term Premium.* Historically, longer-dated bonds have offered higher yields than what is implied by forward rates. This is generally seen as a premium to compensate investors for the higher interest rate risk on longer-dated bonds[7] and for having their money tied up for longer ("liquidity preference"). This would explain the fact that yield curves tend to have a positive slope even in periods of relative stability of inflation (where central banks would be expected to hold rates relatively unchanged).
- *Segmentation.* Bonds with different maturities may not be perceived as perfect substitutes by investors. As an example, institutional investors such as pension funds and insurance companies have a natural preference for long-dated securities which can match their long-term liabilities, whereas investors such as banks are more active in the short-dated market due to their need for liquidity management. In the extreme, investors might have such a strong preference for a given segment ("*preferred habitat*") that only a significant premium would induce them to shift to a different maturity.

[7] This is also referred to as duration risk. The risk of a change in the price of a bond is approximately equal to the change in its YTM multiplied by its modified duration.

The ex ante term premium cannot be observed directly but can be inferred from the swap curve, from surveys on rate expectations and from statistical estimations. The ex post term premium, however, can be calculated directly by comparing the realized return on long-dated bonds over a given period with an investment in short-dated paper, which is rolled over. Dimson et al. (2002) report a ten-year term premium over the period from 1900 to 2000 of 0.7% for the US and an average of 0.5% for all the 16 countries covered in their study. Variations between countries are quite significant, however. As importantly, term premia are time-varying. Most studies suggest that higher uncertainty, especially over future inflation, tends to drive term premia higher while perceived stability in this respect will tend to drive them lower. The longer-term trend in term premia also appears to track the longer-term trend in bond yields, which is consistent with the inflation argument. This offers an explanation as to why estimates have suggested a negative term premium in recent years even if, as recognized by former Fed Chair, Ben Bernanke, in a recent post,[8] the current low level remains somewhat of a puzzle.

Ilmanen (2011) reviews the factors explaining the Bond Risk Premium (BRP), defined as the expected excess return of a default-free bond over a sequence of short-term bonds. He finds that the yield spread between ten-year bonds and three-month rates, that is, the slope of the yield curve, predicts excess returns on 7–10-year bonds over the next quarter and over the next year quite well. It shows little ability to forecast the BRP over the longer term, however. Figure 4.2 shows short-term rates represented by the rate on 90-day US T-bills, the yield on ten-year US Treasury bonds and the spread between the two, that is, the slope of the yield curve, since 1970. As can be seen, the slope of the curve has certainly varied over time, but rather than follow any longer-term trend it exhibits mean reversion. In contrast, ten-year yields saw a secular uptrend up until the early 1980s and a secular downtrend thereafter as did short-term rates. Ilmanen argues that the inability of the slope of the yield curve to capture such trends is due to its negative correlation with short-term rates. A very steep curve is consistent with relatively low short-term rates and expectations of higher future rates. A flat, or inverted, curve is consistent with relatively high short-term rates and expectations of lower future rates. These effects will often overshadow any risk premium built into the curve.

In a study of yield curve dynamics, Litterman and Scheinkman (1991) distinguish between *level, steepness* and *curvature*. In the short run, investors

[8] See also https://www.brookings.edu/blog/ben-bernanke/2015/04/13/why-are-interest-rates-so-low-part-4-term-premiums/

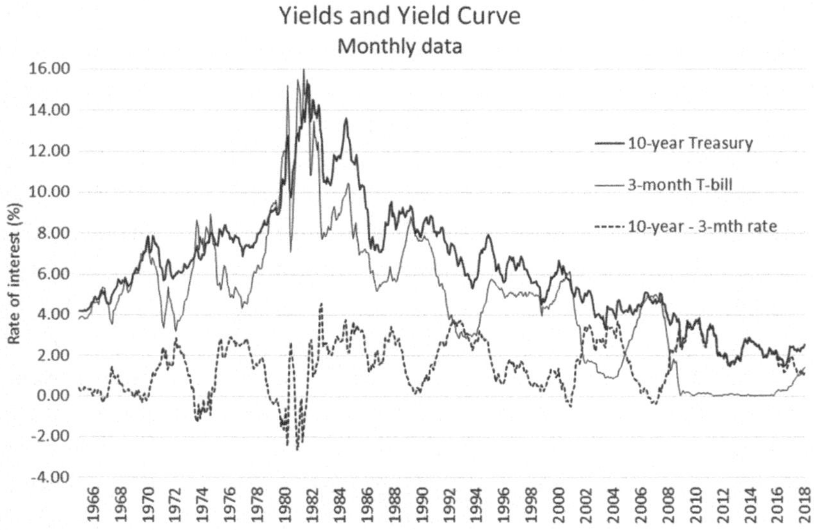

Fig. 4.2 Yield levels and the yield curve. (Source: Bloomberg)

are exposed to all three factors. In the long run, the *level* factor, which influences all maturities, is dominant. We noted the tendency to mean reversion of the slope of the yield curve. An implication of this is that even a maturity as distant as ten years will tend to track the longer-term *trend* of short-term rates. This brings us to the next subject: the influence of central bank policy.

Central Bank Policy

For countries or economic areas with a common currency, short-term interest rates are set by the central bank. At a given point in the cycle, central bank policy might be used counter-cyclically, to stimulate current growth or to reduce a particularly high level of inflation. Longer term, however, rates will be determined mainly by trend growth and inflation. One approach to gauging the monetary policy stance of the US Federal Reserve was suggested by Stanford professor John Taylor who gave name to the so-called Taylor rule.[9] In Taylor's original formulation, the Fed funds rate is determined as follows:

$$r_t = \pi_t + 0.5y_t + 0.5(\pi_t - \pi) + 2 \tag{4.3}$$

[9] Taylor (1993).

where

r_t= the Fed funds rate
π= inflation target, defined by Taylor as 2%
π_t= average rate of inflation over the previous four quarters
y_t= output gap; difference between actual GDP and targeted (potential) GDP
2= a proxy for the longer term equilibrium real growth in the economy

Following the Taylor rule, if, for example, inflation were 1% above the 2% target, with GDP at its target level, the Fed funds rate would be 1.5% above its neutral level. Conversely, if GDP were 1% below the target, with inflation at 2%, the Fed funds rate would be 0.5% below its neutral rate.

In the longer term, both types of deviations are assumed to be zero. In Taylor's framework the *neutral* nominal Fed funds rate is therefore equal to the sum of the longer-term growth rate and the inflation target, that is, 4%, whereas the neutral real rate is 2%. This understanding of central bank policy corresponds to seeing the long-term neutral Fed funds rate tending to converge with long-term nominal GDP growth.

Subsequent research has focused on the so-called real natural rate of interest or *R-star*, a longer-term equilibrium rate. John Williams of the Federal Reserve Bank of San Francisco[10] illustrates that in the US this rate of interest fluctuated between 2% and 2.5% in the 1990s until the mid-2000s, that is, around levels close to Taylor's neutral 2% real rate. But R-star then fell to around 0.5% around 2009 and has remained there throughout the recent years. Estimates for Canada, the UK, the euro area and Japan point to similar trends. The key explanation offered by the empirical research is the decline in trend GDP growth. In the US, the Fed updates its projections for the Fed funds rate regularly. As per June 2017, the median of its projection for the longer-run nominal Fed funds rate was 3%,[11] a full percentage point below the neutral rate implied by the Taylor rule. Given its projection of a 2% longer-term inflation, the longer-term real Fed funds rates are expected to be as low as 1%, a level closer to the R-star reported by John Williams.

Central banks set short-term rates at their discretion, while in normal circumstances the yield on long-dated bonds is set by the private market. This has led some commentators to argue that central banks have *no influence* over longer-dated yields. Indeed, some go as far as to suggest that the direction of causality might be the opposite: long-dated bond yields could be a driver of

[10] Williams (2017). See also Holston et al. (2016).

[11] See also https://www.federalreserve.gov/monetarypolicy/files/fomcminutes20170614.pdf

central bank rates rather than the other way around. This view, however, overlooks the influence of central bank policy on market expectations.

It is clear that recent years of unconventional monetary policies and direct interventions in the bond market constitute an exception to the rule that the long-dated bond yields are set exclusively by the private market. But even looking aside from such unconventional policies, central bank policy clearly influences market expectations. In previous times when central bank policy was more opaque than today, rate changes per se were often seen as precursors for future rate changes (markets would extrapolate). In more recent times main central banks such as the Fed have opted for greater transparency, communicating their own expectations about future rates, as discussed above. As an example, in the years after the Great Financial Crisis, the so-called *forward guidance* of the Fed contributed to holding long-dated bond yields at historically low levels, even when a recovery began to come into sight. It probably also worked to reduce the volatility of yields, thus reducing the term premium.

Bond Returns: The Historical Record

Long-dated bond yields have been driven by two secular trends in the post-WWII period:

- A period of gradually higher inflation, exacerbated by the oil price shocks of the 1970s, culminating in significantly tighter monetary policy in the US under Fed Chair Paul Volcker in the late 1970s to early 1980s.
- A period of gradually lower inflation since the early 1980s, referred to by economists as the Great Moderation.

This has given rise to a mediocre bond performance in the first period and a generally stellar performance in the second period. Looking forward, a repetition of the second period looks like a near impossibility unless one is willing to accept predictions of absurdly negative bond yields over a long period of time.[12] Eventually higher inflation and higher short-term rates than currently predicted, on the other hand, cannot be ruled out. This highlights that while the historical record of bond returns is not directly useful, the entry level of bond yields is clearly an important anchor for longer-term return expectations. To illustrate, the generally very low current yield levels create an asymmetric range

[12] Negative yields on bonds are not an impossibility. As an example, German ten-year Bunds briefly reached negative yield levels in the fall of 2016 under the influence of the Quantitative Easing (QE) program of the European Central Bank (ECB). There are no empirical examples of negative yields for extended periods, however.

of outcomes for longer-term bond returns: from slightly higher than the current YTM (assuming even lower yields over the time horizon) to negative or highly negative in the case of renewed inflationary pressures.

One weakness of the YTM measure is that institutional investors in the long-dated segment of the government bond yields are unlikely to hold bonds until they mature and will instead reinvest back into a certain maturity range as the average maturity of their bond portfolio shortens. If the yield curve is positively sloped this will give rise to a capital gain as, say, a ten-year bond eventually becomes nine-year bond with a lower yield. In bond parlance, this is referred to as "rolling down the yield curve". Depending on the steepness of the curve, this effect can more or less compensate the negative effect of generally rising yields. A forecast taking this into account would need to be explicit about the assumptions concerning the future shape of the yield curve.

How Do We Create Expectations About the Return on Government Bonds?

Our previous discussion has indicated that we can understand the observed bond yield as the sum of the chain of expected future short-term rates and a term premium. We could therefore rewrite Eq. (4.1) as follows:

$$(1+y_n)^n = (1+y_1)(1+f_{1,2})(1+f_{2,3})\ldots(1+f_{n-1,n}) + \text{term premium} \qquad (4.4)$$

In order to formulate expectations about future bond yields, we therefore need to contrast both observed expected futures short-term rates and the term premium with our own expectations.

An Example: Ten-Year Government Bonds Suppose that at present the YTM on ten-year government bonds is 2%, while three-month T-bills yield 1%. Observing the implied forward rates or using a statistical estimation on the basis of (4.4), we conclude that the term premium is currently 20 basis points against a historical average of, say, 50 basis points. We happen to disagree with the market in two respects. Firstly, our projection for future real GDP growth and inflation suggest higher future short-term rates than those implied by the market. When calculating the YTM that follows from the chain of our own expected short-term rates we get to a YTM of 2.7%. Secondly, we believe the current low term premium is unsustainable and expect a reversion to its long-term average of 50 basis points. Together these two elements of our expectations imply that the current YTM on ten-year bonds should be 3% rather than the current 2%.

Even if we are right, it is obviously not clear how quickly the market will get around to our way of thinking. To make our calculations easier, we might make the rough assumption that the market will reach the higher yield in a linear way over the coming ten years. This would imply that the yield on a ten-year bond should rise by 10 basis points per year. If our investment mandate dictates that we should reinvest back into the ten-year segment once a year (as described previously) we might then include a "roll-effect" of, say, −2 basis points per year, meaning that our projection would sum up to an increase in the YTM of 8 basis points per year over the coming ten years. Finally, we need to calculate the one-year horizon return for each of the ten years. Each year we would receive the coupon on the bond but would suffer a capital loss owing to the increase of 8 basis points in the YTM. The horizon return will therefore need to include both elements. Finally, we chain our projection of the horizon return for each of the ten years to get a total ten-year expected horizon return. In this example, it will clearly be lower than the current YTM on the ten-year bonds.[13]

Key questions are: does the outlook for growth and inflation look consistent with market expectation for monetary policy? If predicted future rates look too low, estimate an upward bias to future bond yields from this source (and vice versa). Compare the current term premium with its longer-term average. If it is significantly lower or higher, introduce a bias to future bond yields from this source based on the assumption of longer-term mean reversion.

4.4 The Credit Market

We have treated government bonds as being, in principle, free of default risk or *credit risk*. The market in bonds exposed to such risk is generally referred to as the credit market, where corporate bonds take up a prominent role. Credit rating agencies such as S&P, Fitch and Moody's assign ratings to bonds according to their credit risk. A general distinction is between *investment-grade* (IG) and *non-investment-grade* or *high yield* (HY) bonds (aka "junk bonds"). Investment grade corresponds to a rating of BBB or higher for S&P and Fitch or Baa or higher for Moody's; HY has a lower rating than this. This distinction is of particular importance to institutional investors many of which have policies which limit their fixed income investments to

[13] Horizon returns can be calculated directly on, for example, the Bloomberg system, inserting the relevant assumptions about future yields.

the investment-grade category. The difference in yield between bonds with a credit risk and ("risk-free") government bonds of the same maturity is referred to as the *credit premium* or *spread*. How good an indicator is this credit spread of the excess return over government bonds?

Ilmanen (2011) reports that the ex ante credit spread has generally overstated ex post excess returns significantly. In the US market, corporate bonds with investment-grade ratings have historically outperformed Treasuries by only 20 to 50 basis points against spreads well in excess of 100 basis points, with long-dated paper doing particularly poorly. A better performance has been seen for BB-rated bonds (HY, just below investment grade) and short-dated IG bonds. This pattern is seen despite the fact that average historical default rates have been considerably lower than credit spreads. What explains this? Ilmanen points to the following factors:

- **Embedded options.** Corporate bonds are often issued with a right to repay the bond at par before it matures which can account for 70–100 basis of the ex ante credit spread. Option-adjusted spread measures should correct for this, but reported spreads are not always explicit in this respect.
- **Downgrading.** Due to their policy constraints, index investors are forced to sell bonds which have left the index because they have fallen from an IG rating to a BB rating (or lower). This downgraded paper tends to perform better than bonds which were originally issued as HY, but index investors miss out on this performance.
- **Liquidity.** Corporate bonds are generally less liquid than government paper implying higher transaction costs for institutional investors needing to adjust portfolios for the reasons stated above.

These factors imply a significant difference between the situation facing most institutional investors and the pure Buy-and-Hold approach where the risk is in principle limited to the embedded options of some corporate bonds and the default risk. More generally, risk-free and highly liquid instruments such as US Treasuries and German Bunds tend to be the object of flight-to-quality flows during cyclical downturns and general increases in risk aversion which tend to affect both corporate bonds and equities negatively. This may or may not be an important argument for long-term investors, but it gives government paper an advantage over corporate paper in terms of diversification. It is clearly relevant from a more tactical point of view and we will return to this question in the TAA chapters of the book.

4.5 Equities

How Important Are Macro-Fundamentals?

Intuitively, the link between macro-fundamentals and equity returns seems straightforward. From an economic point of view, we would expect growth in an economy to translate into aggregate profits, earnings per share and ultimately returns on stocks. This understanding is reinforced by the observation that recessions are negative for corporate profits and invariably lead to market corrections, while recoveries do the opposite.

Intriguingly, however, empirical research has found no clear link over the very long term. In order to control for differences between countries in terms of population growth Dimson et al. (2002) focus on GDP per capita. Examining 16 developed economies over the period from 1900 to 2000, the authors find a correlation between the growth in real dividends and growth in real per capita GDP of −0.53. Focusing on the period from 1951 to 2000, when growth rates were higher than in the first half of the century, the correlation is no longer negative but still an insignificant 0.06. A similar result is found for total real returns on equities which show a correlation with growth in real per capita GDP of −0.32 over the period from 1900 to 2000 and of −0.03 from 1951 to 2000. Emerging markets show a similar pattern. Ritter (2005, 2012) confirms these findings for both developed and emerging markets.

What might explain these patterns? These are some of the suggested explanations:

- **International diversification.** Modern multinationals are more exposed to international economic trends than to their local economies. Dimson et al. (2002) make the point that this might explain recent trends, but would not apply to the same extent to the first half of the twentieth century. Klement (2015) argues that this explanation should imply a more direct correlation for small-cap firms which are on average more exposed to local economic trends. His studies, spanning the period of 1997 to 2013, however, find a negative correlation between stock market returns and growth in real GDP per capita for both small-, medium- and large-cap stocks, in both developed and emerging markets.
- **Competition between companies.** Progress in efficiency and technology ultimately translates into benefits for consumers, but a high degree of competition between companies can limit their ability to boost their profit margins on this basis.

- **New companies.** Bernstein and Arnott (2003) point out that growth in earnings per share will only match aggregate earnings for *existing investors* if no new shares are issued. Economic growth is in part due to the creation of new companies but this does not contribute to the growth in earnings and dividends of existing companies which will therefore be lower than the growth in aggregate earnings.
- **Stock markets expectations.** In the 1998 edition of his book *Stocks for the Long Run*, Siegel points out that because markets are forward-looking expectations of high future growth will tend to be built into prices at the outset. This will make the observable correlation between economic growth and stock market performance weaker. An extreme example of this was the Japanese stock market in the late 1980s which discounted several of decades of future growth.

These effects all illustrate why the fundamental analysis cannot stand alone. In the following we will look at different approaches to estimating future stock market returns and the importance of market valuations.

The Equity Risk Premium

In the spirit of the CAPM, we can decompose the return on equities into a risk-free component and a premium for risk, the equity risk premium (ERP). We can do this ex ante and understand the premium as an expected, or required, compensation for risk or we can do it ex post and understand it as a realized compensation for risk. The closest to a purely risk-free rate we can get is arguably short-maturity T-bills. But many analysts prefer to compare equities directly with the other main asset class and use the YTM on long-dated bonds. This way the ERP directly addresses the "Bonds vs. Stocks" question. The ERP is time-varying and arguably depends on the level of long-term bond yields. This makes it more workable to focus on the component parts of equity returns than on the ERP directly. In the following we will look at two of the best-known approaches.

The Dividend Discount Model

A natural starting point for modeling equity returns is the dividend discount model (DDM). While this model is often used for individual stocks, here we will think about the stock market as a whole. The price of stocks held for n years is equal to the discounted value of their future dividends plus their expected price at the end of the n years:

$$P_0 = \frac{D_1}{1+r} + \frac{D_2}{(1+r)^2} + \frac{D_3}{(1+r)^3} + \ldots + \frac{D_n}{(1+r)^n} + \frac{P_n}{(1+r)^n} \tag{4.5}$$

where

D_1= the expected dividend at the end of year 1
D_n= the expected dividend at the end of year n
P_n= the expected price at the end of year n
r = the discount rate (the required rate of return)

Unlike bonds, stocks of course have no maturity. As the time horizon extends into perpetuity, the discounted value of the end price, P_n, will approach zero. This allows us to write:

$$P_0 = \frac{D_1}{1+r} + \frac{D_2}{(1+r)^2} + \frac{D_3}{(1+r)^3} + \ldots \tag{4.6}$$

How do we estimate D_1, D_2 and so on? The well-known *Gordon Growth Model* makes the assumption that dividends will grow at a constant rate, g. This changes (4.6) to:

$$P_0 = \frac{D_1}{1+r} + \frac{D_1(1+g)^2}{(1+r)^2} + \frac{D_1(1+g)^3}{(1+r)^3} + \ldots \tag{4.7}$$

which can be reduced to[14]:

$$P_0 = \frac{D_1}{r-g} \tag{4.8}$$

[14] Equation (4.7) is a geometric series in which each term equals the previous term multiplied by $(1 + g) / 1 + r)$. Multiply (4.6) by $(1 + r) / 1 + g)$ to get $P_0 \frac{(1+r)}{(1+g)} = \frac{D_1}{1+g} + \frac{D_1}{(1+r)} + \frac{D_1(1+g)}{(1+r)^2} + \ldots$. Subtract (4.6) from this last expression to get $P_0 \frac{(1+r)}{(1+g)} - P_0 = \frac{D_1}{1+g}$ which implies that $P_0 = \frac{D_1}{r-g}$. Note that the model is rendered meaningless if $g > r$ which would imply an infinite value of stocks.

Decomposing the discount rate into a risk-free rate and the equity risk premium, we can write (4.8) as:

$$P_0 = \frac{D_1}{r_f + ERP - g} \tag{4.9}$$

The price of stocks will be high when the discount rate is low, that is, when either the risk-free rate, the ERP or both are low, or when dividend growth is high. Rearranging (4.8) we can express the expected return on the stocks as the sum of the dividend yield and the growth in dividends:

$$r = \frac{D_1}{P_0} + g \tag{4.10}$$

Note that if the dividend yield is constant, the price of stocks must grow by g. We can therefore think of the return on stocks as a composed of an income component (the dividend yield) and a capital gain component derived from the growth in dividends. Using this model to compute the expected return we need the dividend yield, $\frac{D_1}{P_0}$, and an estimate of the growth rate of future dividends, g.

What is the historical record of this input? Figure 4.3 shows the dividend yield of the S&P500 since 1950. As can be seen, this yield has been relatively stable the past 20 years after shifting significantly lower the prior 20 years. Dividends are not the full story, however. Companies both issue new stocks and buy back existing stocks and the net of the two can influence the effective equity *carry*. Ilmanen (2011) argues that the decline in dividend yield in the 1980s and 1990s was in part a reflection of an increase in net buybacks (buybacks minus issuance) driven by the fact that stock repurchases are more tax efficient than dividends. The dividend payout ratio (dividends/earnings) has therefore fallen. This can make net buybacks an important factor in the short term. Over the long run, however, buybacks show no persistent trend and their historical record therefore offers little guidance for the future.

Figure 4.4 illustrates the rolling 10- and 30-year annualized nominal growth in dividends for the S&P500. The latest figures for the two measures are relatively close, around 6%, but as can be seen the range of fluctuation over the 30-year window is around 2% against 6 percentage points for ten-year window. Is a 6% growth in dividends a realistic forecast for the next ten years? In the current scenario, most analysts believe it is too high.

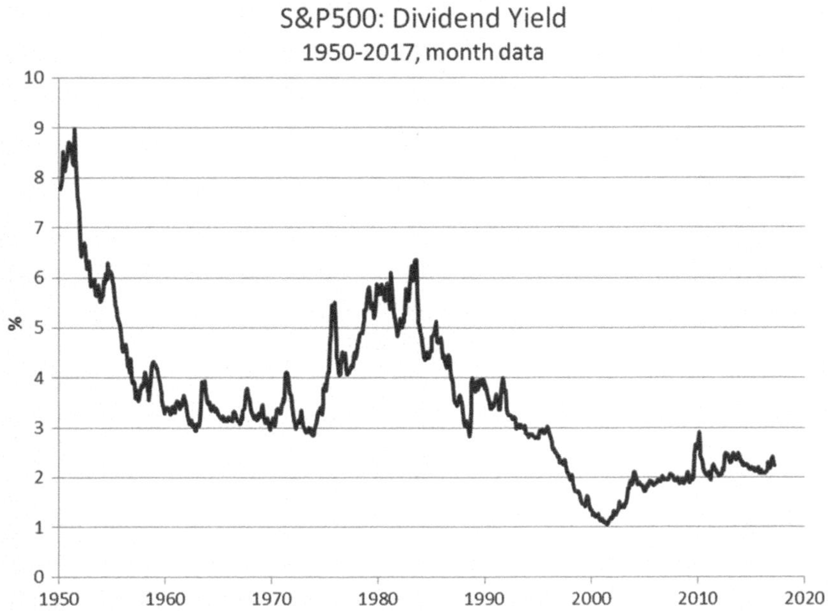

Fig. 4.3 S&P 500: dividend yield. (Source: Robert Shiller's data base)

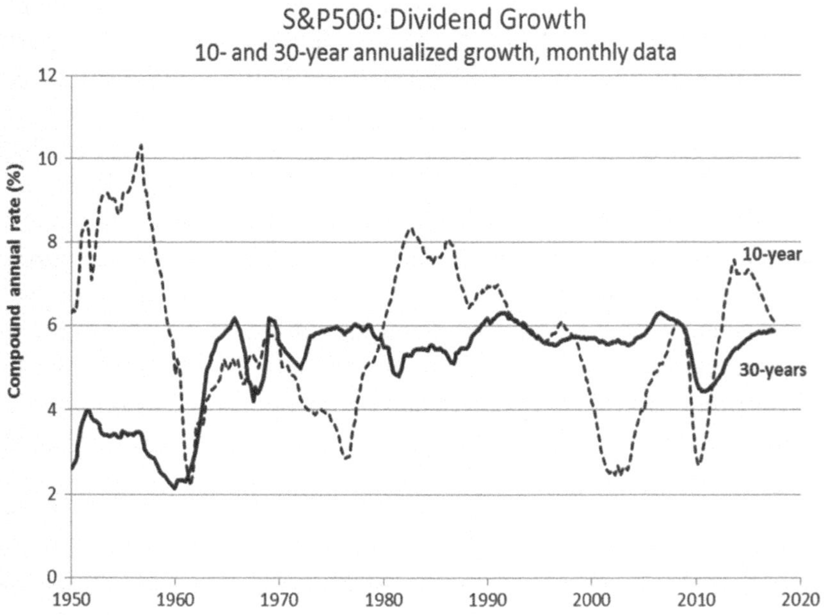

Fig. 4.4 S&P 500: dividend growth. (Source: Robert Shiller's data base)

So far we have not considered valuations. What price will the market be willing to pay for the future earnings which underlie future corporate dividends? We will look at this in the following two sub-sections.

The Bogle Approach to Decomposing the Equity Return

John Bogle (1991a, b) has suggested decomposing equity returns into an investment return and a speculative return. The investment return is represented by the dividend yield and the growth in earnings, while the speculative return is represented by the price which investors are willing to pay for those earnings, that is, the price-earnings (*P*/*E*) ratio. To see how these components combine, we start with a general expression of the return on a stock index from time t to time t+1:

$$1 + R_{t+1} = \frac{D_{t+1}}{P_t} + \frac{P_{t+1}}{P_t} \tag{4.11}$$

where $\frac{D_{t+1}}{P_t}$ and $\frac{P_{t+1}}{P_t}$ denote the dividend yield and the capital gain, respectively, over the period from time t to time t+1.

We can decompose the capital gain as follows:

$$\frac{P_{t+1}}{P_t} = \frac{E_{t+1}}{E_t} \frac{P_{t+1} / E_{t+1}}{P_t / E_t} \tag{4.12}$$

where $\frac{E_{t+1}}{E_t}$ represents the growth in earnings and $\frac{P_{t+1} / E_{t+1}}{P_t / E_t}$ represents the change in the *P*/*E* ratio.

Inserting (4.12) into (4.11) we get:

$$1 + R_{t+1} = \frac{D_{t+1}}{P_t} + \frac{E_{t+1}}{E_t} \frac{P_{t+1} / E_{t+1}}{P_t / E_t} \tag{4.13}$$

or

$$R_{t+1} = \frac{D_{t+1}}{P_t} + \frac{E_{t+1}}{E_t} \frac{P_{t+1} / E_{t+1}}{P_t / E_t} - 1 \tag{4.14}$$

which can be approximated by:

$$R_{t+1} = \frac{D_{t+1}}{P_t} + \frac{E_{t+1}}{E_t} + \frac{P_{t+1} / E_{t+1}}{P_t / E_t} \tag{4.15}$$

that is, the sum of the dividend yield, the growth in earnings per share and the change in the *P*/*E* ratio. Using this framework, Bogle and Nolan (2015) show that out of the compound annual return of 9.0% on the S&P500 over the period from 1871 to 2015, the investment return accounts for as much as 8.6% while the speculative return accounts for as little as 0.4%. The authors note that while the *P*/*E* has certainly exhibited significant swings, it tends to mean-revert over very long periods.

How well does this model predict future returns? Bogle and Nolan analyzed ten-year returns assuming reversion to a ten-year mean for earnings growth and to a 30-year mean for the *P*/*E* ratio.[15] For the period from 1915 to 2014, they find a correlation between the rolling ten-year returns using the model and actual returns of 0.65 and one as high as 0.81 for the more recent period from 1990 to 2015. The authors acknowledge that the main weakness of the model has been the sometimes significant swings in the *P*/*E* (ratio) over the investment period. We will return to this issue in the following sub-section.

Using a similar approach, but adding the annual rate of dividend growth as a fourth factor, Estrada (2007) examines the period from 1973 to 2005. He broadens the scope to include 11 non-US markets aside from the US considering different scenarios for the expected change in the *P*/*E* ratio. In a similar vein to the Bogle and Bogle and Nolan studies, he looks at a rolling ten-year window. In his base case, he assumes *reversion to the mean* of each of the compound annual growth in earnings, dividends and *P*/*E* ratios between 1973 and the point at which the forecast is made, using the dividend yield for the year before each prediction is made. In his first alternative scenario, he assumes that the *P*/*E* ratio remains unchanged, terming this the *random walk scenario.* In his second alternative scenario, he gives more weight to the recent past, using an equally weighted average of the mean *P*/*E* ratio over the prior five-year period and the mean over the period from 1973 to the date on which the forecast is made. This is termed the *adaptive expectations scenario.*

On this basis, he computes the correlation between the predicted and the observed return as well as the mean forecast error (MFE) and the absolute mean forecast error (MAFE) in each scenario.[16] Across the 12 markets, he

[15] Bogle's original formulation (1991a, b) assumed reversion to the 30-year mean for earnings.

[16] The MFE and the MAFE are calculated, respectively, as the average annual difference between the predicted and the observed annual compound returns and the absolute value of that difference.

finds a correlation of 0.64 and an MFE and MAFE of 2.0% and 4.9%, respectively, for the base-line mean reversion scenario. For the random walk scenario, the same readings are 0.49, −0.4% and 4.2%, respectively, whereas for the adaptive expectations scenario the readings are 0.62, 1.4% and 4.7%, respectively. Estrada notes that which expectations scenario is deemed to give the best result therefore depends on whether the correlation or the forecast errors are given the highest weight. Irrespective of this, however, he concludes that the model does significantly better than a "naïve" approach of simply basing expectations on the annual compound returns from 1973 to the date of the forecast. While the predictive power of the model varies across the countries, the study generally confirms the findings of Bogle and Bogle and Nolan.

Ferreira and Santa-Clara (2011) present a sum-of-the-parts (SOP) approach where each of the three components—dividend yield, earnings growth and *P/E*—are predicted separately. They use a 20-year moving average for earnings growth, but assume a zero growth in the *P/E*. Using *out-of-sample data* from 1927 to 2007 they report an R-squared of 1.3% using monthly data and 13.4% using yearly data, which implies a Sharpe ratio of 0.3 when used for market timing. This represents a significant improvement compared to using historical averages or traditional predictive regressions.

Using Historical Valuations

This leads us to the next question. We saw that *P/E* ratios tend to mean-revert in the very long run. Does this imply that we can ignore them for, say, a ten-year investment horizon? The historical record suggests otherwise. Figure 4.5 shows rolling ten-year total annualized returns on the S&P500 compared to rolling ten-year annualized changes in the *P/E* ratio. The difference between the two lines is the contribution of the dividend yield and the change in earnings. The spike in the *P/E* during the Great Financial Crisis in the late 2000s is the result of the collapse in earnings in this period and might be considered an outlier. Aside from this, however, we notice that at least in the post-WWII period mediocre stock market returns have tended to coincide with declines in the *P/E*, whereas periods of high returns have tended to coincide with expansions in the multiple. This begs the question of whether *P/E* ratios and valuation measures more broadly have predictive power for expected returns.

This was the question asked by Campbell and Shiller (1998) during the tech bubble years when the market *P/E* reached extreme highs and the dividend yield extreme lows. The authors first pose the question of whether the dividend yield forecasts future movements in dividends or stock prices. Using

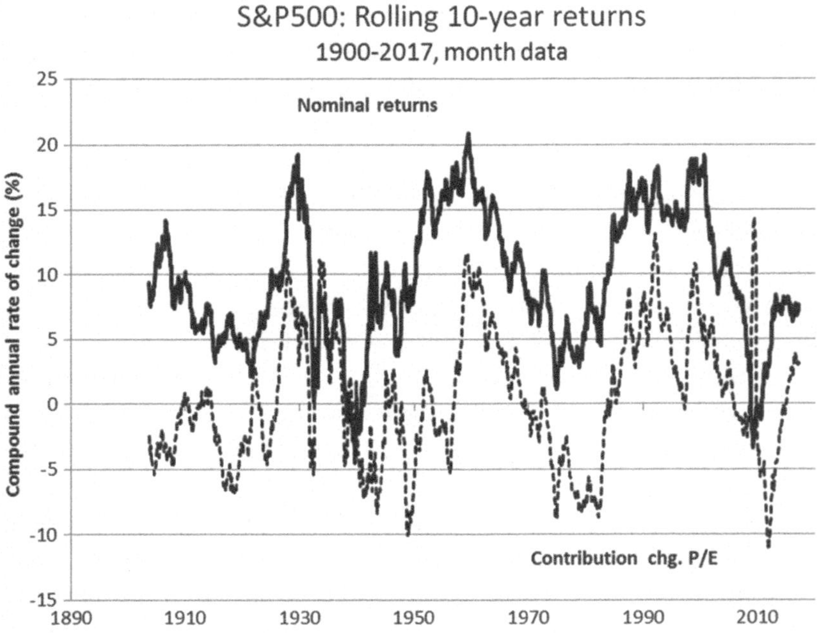

Fig. 4.5 Total annualized returns and the contribution from changes in the *P/E* ratio. (Source: Robert Shiller's data base)

data for the period since 1872, during which the dividend yield averaged 4.73%, they examine growth in real dividends from given years until the dividend yield crosses its long-term average. They find that movements in dividends explain practically no part of this reversion to the mean whereas the growth rate of real stock market prices explains as much as 64% of the adjustment. The authors acknowledge that this offers little guidance for forecasting since the historical range for the dividend yield crossing its average is as wide as 1–20 years. They therefore subsequently focus on fixed time horizons of one and ten years. For one-year periods they find that the dividend yield is able to explain about 15% of the annual variation in dividend growth but has practically no ability to explain variations in stock prices. Moving to a ten-year horizon, however, the dividend yield again explains practically none of the variation in dividend growth but some 15% of the variation in stock prices.

Campbell and Shiller note the weakness of the standard *P/E* ratio that recessions tend to temporarily depress earnings and create spikes in the ratio. They therefore calculate a ratio where the stock price in real terms is divided by an average of the real earnings for the past ten years. This smoothed measure, originally proposed by Graham and Dodd in their 1934 book,[17] has

[17] Benjamin Graham and David Dodd (1934), *Security Analysis*. Shiller proposed this measure in his book *Market Volatility*. See also Shiller (1990).

been termed the cyclically adjusted *P*/*E* (CAPE), the Shiller *P*/*E* or the *P*/*E*10. Regressing the CAPE against future ten-year real returns of the S&P500, the authors find a much more significant R-squared of 37%. Campbell and Shiller noted that the CAPE at the time of their writing was 28 which predicted a drop in the real value of the stock market of 40% over the subsequent ten years. The subsequent dramatic stock market correction in the early 2000s certainly appears to have vindicated their bearish call.

Figure 4.6 illustrates the CAPE and subsequent ten-year real stock returns. CAPE (the dashed line) is plotted against the left-hand scale which has been inverted, while subsequent compound annual real ten-year returns (the bold line) is plotted against the right-hand scale. The last reading of ten-year returns corresponds to the period from March 2007 to March 2017. As can be seen, the variation between the predicted and the realized return has at times been significant, but the CAPE does appear to capture the major swings in returns quite well.

A data analysis is offered by Asness (2012) who examines what different buckets of initial CAPE levels have implied for subsequent ten-year returns over the period from 1926 to 2012. The analysis reports both worst and best cases and the standard deviation of the realized returns in each bucket around its mean. His findings are summarized in Table 4.4.

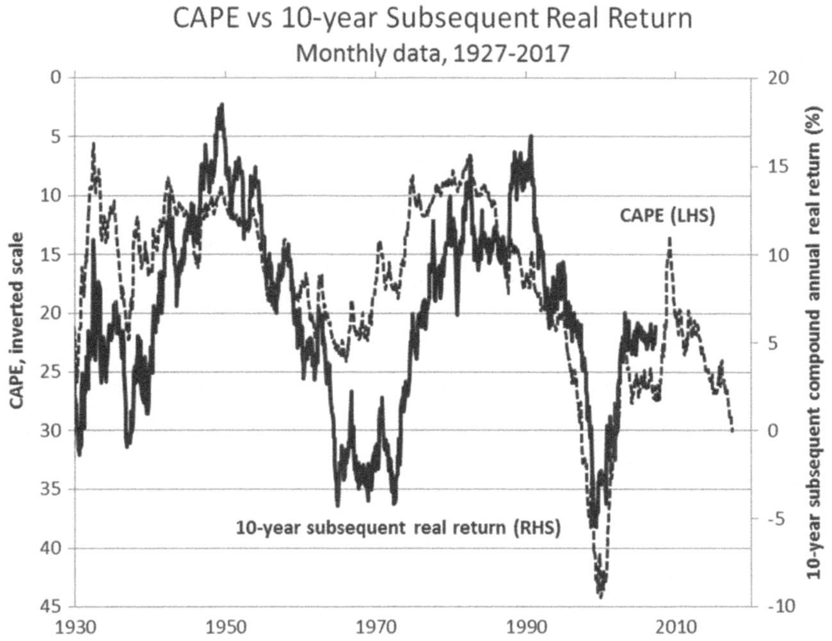

Fig. 4.6 CAPE and subsequent ten-year real returns. (Source: Robert Shiller's data base)

Table 4.4 CAPE and subsequent ten-year returns

Starting CAPE		Avg. real 10-yr return (%)	Worst real 10-yr return (%)	Best real 10-yr return (%)	Standard deviation (%)
Low	High				
5.2	9.6	10.3	4.8	17.5	2.5
9.6	10.8	10.4	3.8	17.0	3.5
10.8	11.9	10.4	2.8	15.1	3.3
11.9	13.8	9.1	1.2	14.3	3.8
13.8	15.7	8.0	−0.9	15.1	4.6
15.7	17.3	5.6	−2.3	15.1	5.0
17.3	18.9	5.3	−3.9	13.8	5.1
18.9	21.1	3.9	−3.2	9.9	3.9
21.1	25.1	0.9	−4.4	8.3	3.8
25.1	46.1	0.5	−6.1	6.3	3.6

Source: Asness (2012)

Asness notes that as the starting CAPE goes higher, the subsequent ten-year forward average returns invariably decreases, even if the range between worst and best cases is significant. He also observes that the standard deviation tends to be lower when the CAPE is at extremes, suggesting a higher reliability of the prediction in those cases. The level of the CAPE has risen to levels within the two lowest buckets in recent years, giving rise to new forecasts of low future returns from the adherents of using the CAPE for forecasting future returns.

Siegel (2014) offers a contrasting view. While generally lauding the value of the CAPE as a forecasting tool, he believes the current level of the CAPE is not directly comparable with average past levels. He suggests the following reasons for the elevated levels observed:

- **The Great Financial Crisis.** CAPE calculations for the past ten years still include the collapse in earnings which took place during the crisis years. This lowers the average earnings and increases the CAPE.
- **Changes in dividend policy.** As we saw previously, dividend payout ratios have fallen in recent decades as share buybacks have substituted cash dividends. This has increased the growth rate in earnings *per share* lowering the average of the ten-year average relative to current earning. This similarly pushes up the CAPE.
- **Changes in accounting standards.** Changes which were made in the 1990s required companies to mark to market any losses on assets held, whereas they were not allowed to report gains in asset values unless they were sold and a capital gain could be recorded. According to Siegel, the S&P500 treats its 500 components as if they belonged to a single company

which creates an "aggregation bias" when the losses of few companies offset the earnings of the rest, even though they are independent companies whose value can never go below zero. He advocates using corporate earnings from the national income and product accounts (NIPA) for the calculation of the CAPE.

The question is whether these factors suffice to justify the high readings of the CAPE and this controversy remains unsettled.[18] In his article, Siegel mentions another possible factor behind the high valuations without going into an explicit analysis of this: the low level of interest rates. We will examine this in the following sub-section.

The "Fed Model"

A common practice among investors has been to compare the earnings yield on stocks, E/P (the inverse of the P/E ratio), to the yield on ten-year government bonds. The decision rule that follows from this is that when the earnings yield exceeds the yield on bonds, equities are "cheap" relative to bonds, whereas the opposite applies when bond yields exceed the earnings yield. This is commonly referred to as the "Fed model" due to comments in a Humphrey-Hawkins Report from July 22, 1997, which made reference to the observed inverse relationship between changes on long-bond yields and the forward P/E ratio.[19] The Fed has never officially endorsed this model, however.

Figure 4.7 plots the relationship between the trailing P/E and the yield on ten-year US Treasury bonds from 1900 to 2017. As can be seen, the relationship is unclear in most of the period but seems to improve from the 1960s onwards.

Note that if the Fed Model holds true, this will provide a justification for maintenance of high P/E ratios under low inflation and low interest rates. This would effectively neutralize the reading from the CAPE analysis and is therefore of significant importance to expected long-term returns.

Asness (2003) rejects the Fed model as a decision rule on both conceptual and empirical grounds, even though he recognizes that it has a certain descriptive capacity. The conceptual problem with the model is that it compares what is essentially a measure in real terms (the earnings yield, E/P) with a measure

[18] See also the interesting recent exchange of views between Jeremy Siegel and Robert Shiller on this topic: https://www.advisorperspectives.com/articles/2017/05/23/jeremy-siegel-versus-robert-shiller-on-equity-valuations

[19] See also https://www.federalreserve.gov/boarddocs/hh/1997/july/reportsection2.htm

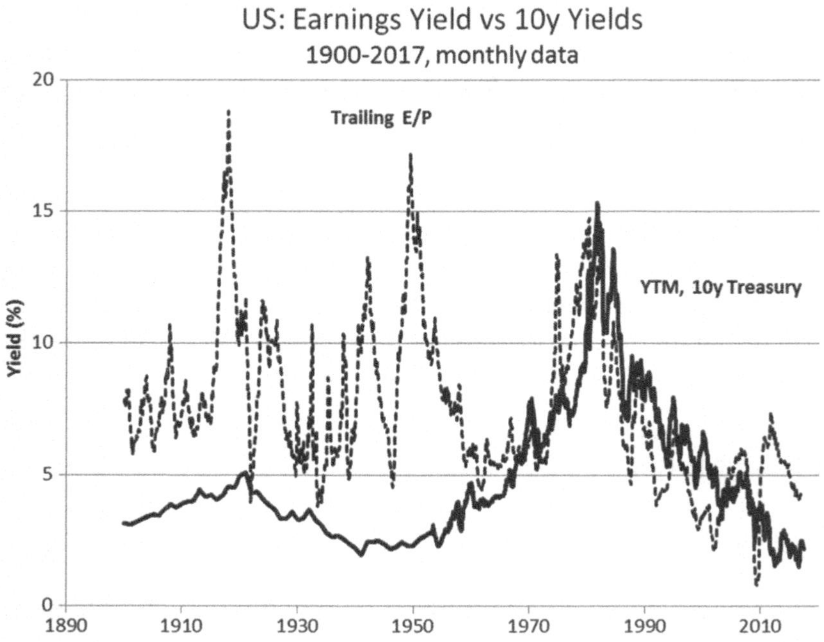

Fig. 4.7 Earnings yield versus ten-year treasury bond yield. (Source: Robert Shiller's data base)

in nominal terms (the bond yield). In principle, cost increases arising from inflation can be passed on to final prices by companies which leaves real earnings unchanged, whereas inflation will reduce the real value of a bond with fixed coupons. This is the key reason why stocks are generally considered a better hedge against inflation than stocks.

The author illustrates this key question by referring to the Gordon Growth Model which we looked at previously. As we saw, the model expresses the expected nominal return on stocks as the dividend yield plus the growth in dividends. This can be reformulated in terms of earnings by including the payout ratio, *D*/*E*. To simplify, Asness assumes *D*/*E* to be a fixed 0.5. Under this assumption, we can rewrite Eq. (4.10) as follows:

$$r = \frac{D_1}{P_0} + g = 0.5\frac{E_1}{P_0} + g \tag{4.16}$$

The growth in earnings will now be equal to the growth in dividends (*g*). The author then asks what is likely to happen to returns if expected long-term inflation falls. He argues that a one-to-one fall in nominal yields is likely, keeping the real expected return on both bonds and equities constant. In the case of bonds, this follows directly from the Fisher equation which states that the nominal rate of interest will equal the real rate of interest plus expected inflation. In the case of stocks, the fall in the nominal return can come about either from a fall in the earnings yield, $\frac{E_1}{P_0}$, corresponding to an increase in the *P*/*E* ratio, $\frac{P_0}{E_1}$, or from a fall in the nominal growth in earnings, *g*.

The Fed model implicitly assumes that the first case applies, so that a drop in inflation results in a higher *P*/*E* ratio. A much more likely outcome, according to Asness, is that a drop in inflation reduces the nominal growth in earnings, and keeps the real growth in earnings constant. This follows from the likely decline in corporate pricing power from the lower inflation. Researchers such as Feinman (2005) and Estrada (2007) reach conclusions similar to those of Asness while others—see, for example, Bekaert and Engstrom (2010)—have pointed to the importance of uncertainty over economic conditions and inflation. While investors may or may not suffer from "money illusion" using the Fed Model, they may be responding rationally to growing or falling uncertainty. This uncertainty will often rise in scenarios with sharply rising or falling inflation.

To put the Fed Model into perspective, note that higher or lower bond yields may follow either from higher or lower expected economic growth and from higher or lower expected inflation. Which situation applies matters significantly to the shorter-term correlation between the returns on bonds and equities. To illustrate, higher bond yields following from higher expected growth are much less likely to constitute a problem for equities than higher inflation on its own. The balance between growth and inflation varies over the cycle, giving rise to a different relative attractiveness between the two asset classes. We will examine this in depth in the chapters on TAA.

4.6 Asset Returns Over the Next Ten Years

To illustrate an application of the analysis discussed above we will briefly outline a view of returns over the coming ten years for the two main asset classes, long-dated government bonds and equities, concentrating on the US markets.

Starting with *secular trends*, there are so far no detectable changes in the pattern of low growth in the workforce and productivity in the developed economies, suggesting that *potential GDP growth* remains relatively low (slightly below 2%). At the same time, *actual GDP growth* has outstripped potential GDP in most developed countries in recent years, but especially in the US. This is illustrated in Fig. 4.8.

The difference between actual and potential GDP is referred to as the *output gap*. In the US case, the output gap was significantly negative at the height of the Great Financial Crisis, but most estimates suggest that the higher than potential growth seen in the period since then has now eliminated the gap (Fig. 4.9). By comparison, the output gap remains negative in, for example, the euro area.

If US growth remains above its potential rate, this will create a *positive* output gap which is associated with *eventual* inflationary pressures as capacity restraints in the economy set in. This could happen relatively slowly with inflationary pressures building up only very gradually which will allow the current expansion to last longer. Even on that assumption, however, the current situation must generally be characterized as *late cycle*.

Starting with *government bonds* we saw that the market has followed trends which are considerably more protracted than those seen in the stock market. Yields began to rise gradually from the 1960s, peaked in the early 1980s and trended lower thereafter. To see this as *mean reversion* would require a very long-term vision indeed. Even without assuming such mean reversion, however, current long-term bond yields look low on the following metrics:

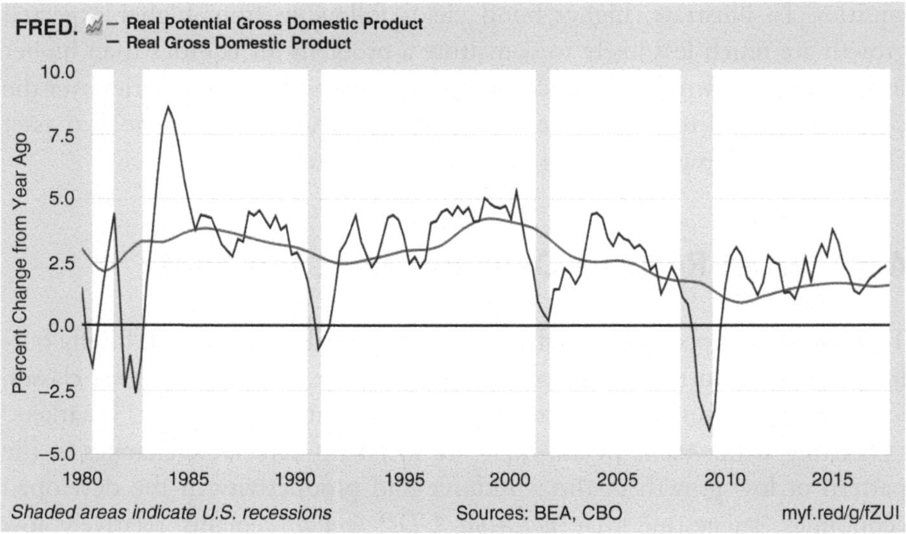

Fig. 4.8 US real potential versus actual GDP growth

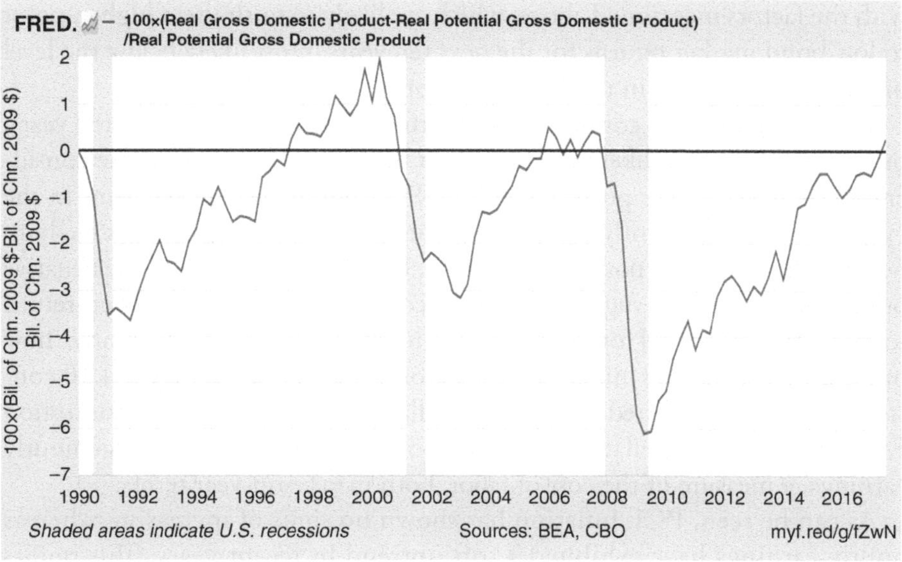

Fig. 4.9 US output gap

- *Real long-term yields* are unusually low in the US and negative in, for example, Germany. Real yields are low relative to real growth which suggests a long-term imbalance.
- The path for future *Fed funds* projected by the Fed itself sees rates stabilizing in a range of 2.5–3% by 2020 which contrasts with a level below 2% implied by futures on Fed funds. We see more upside than downside risk to the market view on future rates.
- The *yield curve*, which as we saw *has* exhibited mean reversion, is currently flat by historical standards.
- Estimates of the Fed of New York suggest that the *term premium* on long-dated bonds is currently negative.[20] Again, some long-term mean reversion looks plausible.

Some observers see the current low level of yields as explained predominantly by the unconventional policies of central banks in recent years, whereas others see them as consistent with the secular trend of low growth in potential GDP. We belong mostly to the second camp. But current bond yields look low even with this interpretation. The low entry level for yields combined

[20] See further *https://www.newyorkfed.org/research/data_indicators/term_premia.html*

with the factors mentioned above, which are likely to push them higher, point to low bond market returns for the next ten years, most likely below the level of current yields both in the US and Europe.[21]

Stocks look likely to continue to outperform bonds over the next ten years, but returns will most likely be lower than the historical average. One consideration is the *late-cycle* position of the US economy. The momentum in the cyclical recovery currently looks intact and the current expansion is likely to become the longest in post-WWII period. But the elimination of the negative output gap in the US suggests that the economy will, sooner or later, return to potential growth. How quickly this happens and, as importantly, how upward price pressures might develop beforehand, is crucial. Figure 4.10 contrasts the Fed's preferred measure of inflation, the Personal Consumption Expenditure (PCE) deflator excluding food and energy, with average hourly earnings, a measure of the cost of labor, both in year-on-year terms.

As can be seen, PCE inflation has shown no signs of increasing whereas hourly earnings have exhibited a soft uptrend in recent years. This points to two potential scenarios going forward. PCE inflation could eventually pick up prompting faster and more decisive tightening from the Fed. This would likely imply that the current economic expansion comes to an end sooner and that multiples would be more likely to contract than to expand. Alternatively, wage pressures could intensify widening the gap between the two measures to the benefit of household spending but to the detriment of corporate profit margins. We lean more toward the second scenario, but both would constitute a negative influence on long-term stock market returns.

Applying these considerations to the framework proposed by Bogle, we would look for a relatively unchanged level of dividend yields around 2% and growth in earnings per share in the region of 4% per annum on average over the ten-year period. At the time of writing the CAPE is at a level of 30.5. This is significantly below the level above 40 seen in early 2000 but significantly above the historical average around 17. For the coming ten-year, we would factor in a partial mean reversion corresponding to a negative valuation effect of around 1% per year. Summing up the components of the Bogle framework we would look for average stock market returns of around 5% per year.

[21] At the time of writing, ten-year government bond yields in the US and in Germany were 2.70% and 0.68%, respectively.

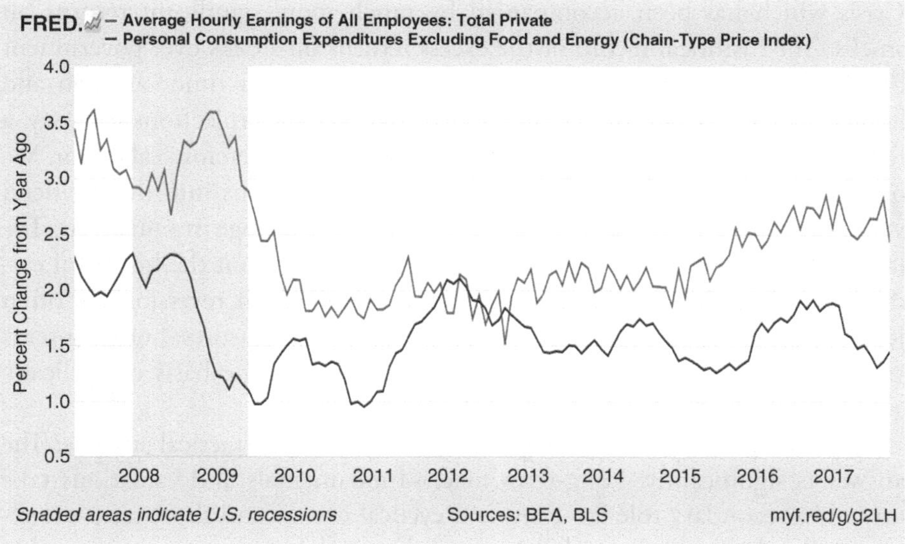

Fig. 4.10 Average hourly earnings versus PCE core deflator

4.7 Conclusion

Most projections for long-term asset returns use a ten-year time horizon. This will typically imply balancing secular trends and cyclical effects.

Long-term returns on government bonds are ultimately driven by trends in real economic growth and inflation. This link, however, is mediated through central bank policies which not only determine short-term rates but can exert a powerful influence on the yield curve as a whole. Projections of long-term returns on government bonds therefore involve both an analysis of macro-fundamentals and an assessment of future monetary policy. The result of this analysis must be contrasted with what is implied by the market in terms of forward rates and the term premium. This comparison provides the background for projected future levels of bond yields and, by implication, realized returns which take into account both incomes from coupons and expected capital gains or losses. The credit market trades off the government bond market. The credit spread expresses the risk of default, but as we saw this spread tends to overstate the ex post long-term excess returns over government bonds. Projections for future returns must therefore adjust for these effects.

The link between macro-fundamentals and long-term return is much less clear in the case of stocks. A good illustration of this is the recent period of relatively slow-paced economic recovery since the end of the Great Financial

Crisis which has been accompanied by much more significant returns on stocks. The historical record of the excess returns on stocks over government bonds or a short-term risk-free rate exhibits significant time variation and longer-term averages offer relatively little guidance for projections over, say, a ten-year period. A more forward-looking approach is therefore called for. We outlined one approach which decomposes equity returns into the dividend yield, expected growth in earnings per share and the change in valuations. The last of these components is clearly the most uncertain, but the historical evidence suggests that assumptions of partial or full mean reversion are often justified. Analysts use both trailing and forward *P*/*E* measures, but long-term valuations are arguably more objectively assessed on the basis of cyclically adjusted valuation measures such as the CAPE.

How much does such a strategic analysis differ from a tactical analysis? The answer is significantly. Long-term macro-fundamentals and valuations take up only a secondary role for TAA, and cyclical drivers and short-term monetary policy become essential drivers, understood in the context of market regimes. We will return to this in Part III of the book. Next we will take a closer look at the challenges of optimizing our strategic asset allocation, the subject of Chap. 5.

References

Asness, Clifford S. 2003. "Fight the Fed Model: The Relationship Between Future Returns and Stock and Bond Market Yields", *Journal of Portfolio Management*, Fall, 11–24.

Asness, Clifford S. 2012. "An Old Friend: The Stock Market's Shiller P/E". AQR Capital.

Bekaert, G., and E. Engstrom. 2010. "Inflation and the Stock Market: Understanding the 'FED Model", *Journal of Monetary Economics*, 57(3), 278–294.

Bernstein, William J., and Robert D. Arnott. 2003. "Earnings Growth: The Two Percent Dilution", *Financial Analysts Journal*, 59(5), 47–55.

Bogle, John C. 1991a. "Investing in the 1990s", *The Journal of Portfolio Management*, 17, 5–14.

Bogle, John C. 1991b. "Investing in the 1990s: Occam's Razor Revisited", *The Journal of Portfolio Management*, 18, 88–91.

Bogle, John C., and Michael W. Nolan. 2015. "Occam's Razor Redux: Establishing Reasonable Expectations for Financial Market Returns", *The Journal of Portfolio Management*, 42, 119–134.

Campbell J. Y., Shiller R. J. 1998. "Valuation Ratios and the Long-Run Stock Market Outlook", *Journal of Portfolio Management*, Winter, 11–26.

Dimson, Elroy, Paul Marsh, and Mike Staunton. 2002. "Triumph of the Optimists: 101 Years of Global Investment Returns". New Jersey: Princeton University Press.

Estrada, J. 2007. "Investing in the Twenty-First Century: With Occam's Razor and Bogle's Wit", *Corporate Finance Review*, May/June.

Feinman, J. 2005. "Inflation Illusion and the (Mis)pricing of Assets and Liabilities", *Journal of Investing*, Summer, 29–36.

Ferreira, M. A., and P. Santa-Clara. 2011. "Forecasting Stock Market Returns: The Sum of the Parts Is More than the Whole", *Journal of Financial Economics*, 100(3), 514–537.

Holston, Kathryn, Thomas Laubach, and John C. Williams. 2016. "Measuring the Natural Rate of Interest: International Trends and Determinants", FRB San Francisco Working Paper, December.

Ibbotson, Roger, Roger J. Harrington, and James P. Harrington. 2017. "Stocks, Bonds, Bills and Inflation (SBBI) Yearbook". Wiley.

Ilmanen, Antti. 2011. "Expected Returns: An Investor's Guide to Harvesting Market Rewards". Chichester, UK: John Wiley & Sons.

Klement, Joachim. 2015. "What's Growth Got to Do with It? Equity Returns and Economic Growth", *Journal of Investing*, 24(2), 74–78.

Litterman, R., and J. Scheinkman 1991. "Common Factors Affecting Bond Returns", *Journal of Fixed Income*, 1, 51–61.

Ritter, J. R. 2005. "Economic Growth and Equity Returns", *Pacific-Basin Finance Journal*, 13, 489–503.

Ritter, J. R. 2012. "Is Economic Growth Good for Investors?" *Journal of Applied Corporate Finance*, 24(3), 8–18.

Shiller, Robert. 1990. "Market Volatility". Cambridge, MA: MIT Press.

Siegel, Jeremy. 2014. "Stocks for the Long Run", 5th edition. New York: McGraw Hill.

Taylor, John B. 1993. "Discretion Versus Policy Rules in Practice", *Carnegie-Rochester Conference Series on Public Policy*, 39, 195–214.

Williams, John C. 2017. "Three Questions on R-star", FRBSF Economic Letter, February.

5

Optimizing the Strategic Asset Allocation

"It is better to be approximately right than precisely wrong."
—Warren Buffet

In the previous chapter, we discussed different approaches to forming expectations about future returns of the main asset classes but made only casual reference to the question of risk. In this chapter, we examine the issue of integrating risk and return, that is, optimizing the SAA. The mechanics of standard mean-variance optimization (MVO) are outlined in the Appendix to the book. Here we will focus on some of the challenges when applying MVO, possible remedies and alternative approaches.

5.1 Modern Portfolio Theory

The importance of the contribution to finance of modern portfolio theory (MPT) and its implementation in the form of MVO can hardly be overstated. Markowitz (1952, 1959) offered a framework for modeling risk on a portfolio level which marked a definitive departure from the focus on individual securities which had dominated practical finance beforehand. While the return on a portfolio is simply the weighted average of the return on each security in the portfolio, Markowitz showed that this does not apply to its risk, unless the returns on each of the securities are perfectly correlated. Assuming that investors are risk averse, he demonstrated how the expected return and variance (or standard deviation) of each asset and the correlation between their returns

H. Lumholdt, *Strategic and Tactical Asset Allocation*,
https://doi.org/10.1007/978-3-319-89554-3_5

could be combined to construct efficient portfolios which either maximize the return for a given level of risk or minimize the risk for a given level of return. Which exact portfolio investors would choose would depend on their degree of risk aversion as expressed by their utility function. But the rational choice would always be between the efficient portfolios. By implication, holding only a single asset was deemed in-optimal and the concept of diversification took on an exact meaning. Crucially, in the world of MPT, the risk of portfolios can be *measured* and *controlled.*

The contributions of Treynor (1962), Sharpe (1964), Lintner (1965a, b) and Mossin (1966) in developing the CAPM offered a simplified approach by assuming that all investors will hold the market portfolio. In this framework, only the systematic, or non-diversifiable, risk of individual assets, as represented by their beta, would be relevant to their expected, or required, return.

MVO is arguably even more relevant for asset allocation than for portfolios of individual securities with similar characteristics. As we noted in Chap. 1, the main source of diversification comes from investing across non-overlapping asset classes rather than from combining securities within each asset class. At the same time, using MVO in an asset allocation context reduces the number of computations considerably. These advantages notwithstanding, the practical application of MPT is plagued with complications which must be managed properly. We discuss this in the following.

5.2 Problems with MVO

The Normality Assumption

As the name implies, MVO works on the assumption that returns can be fully described by the two moments of mean and variance, consistent with a normal or Gaussian distribution. Empirical research has questioned this assumption and documented both *negative skewness* and *excess kurtosis* in return data.[1] Skewness is the third central moment of the probability distribution and is zero in the case of the symmetric normal distribution. A negative skewness implies that the distribution is tilted to the left so that its mean is smaller than its median which is smaller than its mode. Kurtosis is the fourth central moment of the distribution and refers to its peak and, more importantly in

[1] Early work in this field was done by Mandelbrot (1963a, b) and Fama (1965). For an overview of more recent studies, see, for example, Rachev et al. (2005).

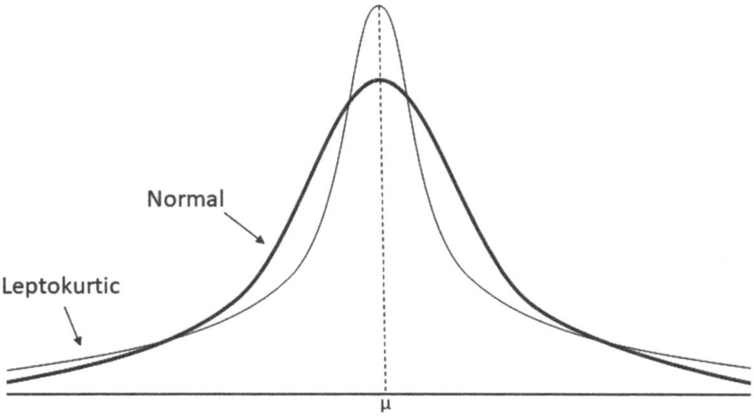

Fig. 5.1 Leptokurtic versus normal distribution

our context, the *fatness of its tails*. A normal distribution has a kurtosis of three. A distribution with a kurtosis in excess of three is referred to as leptokurtic or "fat-tailed".[2] Figure 5.1 gives an illustration.

Working on the assumption that returns are normally distributed in the presence of negative skewness and/or leptokurtosis in the actual return distributions will amount to underestimating risk. Specifically, the risk of extreme negative outliers which are not captured by the normal distribution will be overlooked. Kaplan (2009) gives a practical example. He notes that if the returns on the S&P500 had followed a normal distribution, the probability of returns of more than three standard deviations below the average would be as low as 0.135%.[3] Using 996 monthly stock market data since 1926, this would imply that such negative returns would occur between one and two times. The record, however, shows as many as ten occurrences over the period. Similarly, there have been as many as eight peak-to-trough declines of more than 20% since the mid-1920s. To this can be added the dramatic declines of

[2] Sample skewness is calculated as $\frac{n}{(n-1)(n-2)}\sum_{i=1}^{n}\left(\frac{x_i-\overline{x}}{\sigma_s}\right)^3$, where n is the number of observations, $\overline{x}$ is the mean of the sample and σ_s is the standard deviation of the sample. As n becomes large, this expression can be approximated by $\frac{1}{n}\sum_{i=1}^{n}\left(\frac{x-\overline{x}}{\sigma_s}\right)^3$. Excess kurtosis is calculated as $\frac{n(n+1)}{(n-1)(n-2)(n-3)}\sum_{i=1}^{n}\left(\frac{x_i-\overline{x}}{\sigma_s}\right)^4-3$ which can be approximated by $\frac{1}{n}\sum_{i=1}^{n}\left(\frac{x_i-\overline{x}}{\sigma_s}\right)^4-3$ for a large n.

[3] Corresponding to a one-sided 99.73% confidence interval.

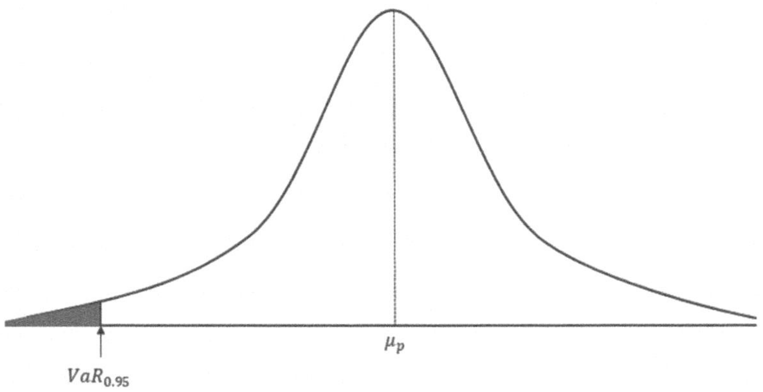

Fig. 5.2 Value at risk at 95% level

more than 40% in the two recent crises in the early 2000s and during the Great Financial Crisis 2007–2008, events of extreme unlikelihood under the assumption of normality of returns.

Correlations

Correlations between assets are time-varying and appear to be highest in periods of market stress or "bad times". Ang and Chen (2002) show that equity returns are more correlated during bear markets than during bull markets. The phenomenon applies to international markets as well where *contagion* can be pronounced in periods of stress. Longin and Solnik (2001) show that non-US markets, such as the UK, France, Germany and Japan, become more correlated with the US market when the US market is in a downturn. Bae et al. (2003) show similar patterns for emerging markets. The direct implication is that the benefits of diversification get reduced in exactly the periods when they are most needed. Static estimates of equity correlations may well overstate the benefits of diversification and bias the MVO toward asset weightings which are not subsequently justified. An equally important question is the correlation between risky assets, such as stocks, and risk-free assets, such as bonds, which is time-varying as well. We will look at the drivers of these correlations in Chap. 9.

The Data Input

MVO is based on historical estimates of risk, returns and correlations, but leaves open the question of how to choose a representative period. We discussed some of the intricacies of this for the estimation of expected returns in the previous chapter. Studies such as those of Best and Grauer (1991), and Broadie (1993) demonstrate that even small changes in the data input can cause significant changes in the optimized asset weights which tend to change frequently over time. Adjusting for this dynamically requires rebalancing which adds to transaction costs and reduces the return of the portfolio. Michaud (1989) notes that MVO will tend to overweight securities with large estimated returns, negative correlations and small variances, but that precisely such securities are likely to have the largest estimation errors. An additional complication is that MVO will tend to favor assets which have outperformed recently, ignoring any likelihood of mean reversion.

Britten-Jones (1999) lays out a procedure for testing the statistical reliability of estimates of efficient international equity portfolios. Using monthly data from MSCI for the period from January 1977 to December 1996 he derives the weights of 11 developed country markets from the point of view of a US investor, assuming no currency hedging and allowing for negative portfolio weights. He then divides the 20-year period into two 10-year periods to compare the results. The resulting weights are shown in Table 5.1. As can be seen, the estimated weights in several cases move from significantly positive to significantly negative between the two ten-year periods. The standard errors of the estimates are particularly high for the US (47%) but are generally so significant that the author is unable to reject the statistical hypothesis that the tangency portfolio of international equities for a US investor should be zero.

A related problem is the degree of *liquidity* of the assets in the portfolio. Investment strategies with relatively low liquidity, such as private equity and hedge funds, and illiquid assets will often exhibit generally lower volatility

Table 5.1 Estimated portfolio weights

	1977–1996	1977–1986	1987–1996
	Estimated weight (%)	Estimated weight (%)	Estimated weight (%)
Australia	12.8	6.8	21.6
Austria	3.0	−9.7	22.5
Belgium	29.0	7.1	66.0
Canada	−45.2	−32.7	−68.9
Denmark	14.2	−29.6	68.8
France	1.2	−0.7	−22.8
Germany	−18.2	9.4	−58.6
Italy	5.9	22.2	−15.3
Japan	5.6	57.7	−24.5
UK	32.5	42.5	3.5
US	59.3	27.0	107.9

Source: Based on Britten-Jones (1999)

than stocks in general, and lower correlations with liquid assets. These features may or may not hold up in a crisis situation. Since MVO makes no adjustment for liquidity this can result in a disproportionally high allocation to such assets.

5.3 Suggested Solutions

Risk Management

While MVO uses dispersion-based risk measures such as variance and standard deviation, risk management has focused on downside risk measures. One of the most widely used is *value at risk* (VaR). VaR is an estimate of the *maximum loss* over a given time horizon with a given level of confidence, such as 95% or 99%, stated either in money terms or in terms of a percentage. The time horizon can be as short as one day (relevant for trading) or as long as a month, quarter or year (relevant for asset allocation). By implication, the VaR also corresponds to the *minimum loss* with a probability of 1 minus the confidence level. We can therefore state VaR in two ways:

$$P\left(X \le \text{VaR}_{\alpha}(X)\right) = \alpha \tag{5.1}$$

or conversely

$$P\left(X \ge \text{VaR}_{\alpha}(X)\right) = 1 - \alpha \tag{5.2}$$

where X denotes the potential loss, α denotes the level of confidence and $\text{VaR}_{\alpha}(X)$ represents the value at risk at the α level of confidence. As an example, if a $\text{VaR}_{0.95}$=\$1,000,000 there is a 95% probability that our maximum loss will be \$1,000,000 over the chosen time horizon, and equally a 5% probability that it will be *greater* than this amount. This is illustrated in Fig. 5.1 where the shaded area corresponds to the loss outcomes in the distribution of returns.

To illustrate the calculation of the VaR for a portfolio when returns are normally distributed, suppose, for example, that the expected return of the portfolio, μ_p, is equal to 10%, that the standard deviation of the portfolio, σ_p, is equal to 20% and that we wish to compute the VaR at a 95% confidence level. To convert our return distribution to a standard normal distribution with an expected value of zero and a standard deviation of 1 we subtract the mean return, μ_p, from the VaR and divide the result by the standard deviation. This gives us the standard normal or z value:

$$z = \frac{\text{VaR} - \mu_p}{\sigma_p} \Rightarrow VaR = \mu_p + z\sigma_p \tag{5.3}$$

In the standard normal distribution, the one-tailed z value for a 95% confidence interval is 1.645 standard deviations below the mean.[4] In our example we therefore get:

$$\text{VaR} = 0.10 - 1.645 \times 0.20 = 0.229 \text{ or } 22.9\%$$

Given these assumptions, with a 95% probability, our maximum loss will be 22.9% of the value of our portfolio, while the loss will *exceed* this percentage with a probability of 5%.

It is clear that using the assumption of a normal distribution of returns when calculating VaR exposes the measure to the same problems of skewness and kurtosis as in the case of MVO. This can be countered by creating a return distribution from historical data or by using a forward-looking approach such as Monte Carlo simulation, even if the reliability of the results as guidance for the future will always be an issue. As importantly, researchers have pointed out that traditional VaR suffers from intrinsic problems as a risk measure.[5] One critique is that the measure is not sub-additive, implying that the VaR of two portfolios combined into one can be greater than the sum of the VaR of each of them, a feature which clearly conflicts with the idea of diversification. Another is that VaR fails to measure how large losses can be when the percentage thresholds have been breached. To return to our previous example, we calculated that the loss on the portfolio would exceed 22.9% with a probability of 5%. VaR says nothing about how large a loss will be incurred beyond this point, corresponding to the shaded area in Fig. 5.1.

One alternative measure which has been proposed to remedy this is the so-called *conditional value at risk* (CVaR), which does meet the sub-additivity criterion.[6] CVaR is defined as the loss incurred conditional on that loss being greater than or equal to VaR. It is calculated as a weighted average of the possible losses when this condition is met. Note that since CVaR includes the area beyond the VaR point, this measure will always be a higher figure than the VaR. We will look at one study which applies this measure in the following sub-section.

---

[4] This value can be calculated in Excel by using the NORMSINV function.

[5] See also Artzner et al. (1999).

[6] See further Rockafellar and Uryasev (2002).

Alternative Return Distributions

Researchers have suggested a host of non-normal distributions to better capture the skewness and kurtosis observed in the empirical data. Some of the earliest contributors were Mandelbrot (1963a, b) and Fama (1965) who proposed so-called stable Paretian or Lévy-stable distributions. The weakness of this type of distribution is that they have an infinite variance which clearly does not conform to empirical return data. A solution to this problem is to truncate the tails of the distribution giving rise to the so-called Truncated Lévy Flight (TLF) distribution.

Xiong and Idzorek (2011) simulate the returns of four hypothetical assets based on the TLF. They then compare the asset allocation resulting from standard MVO to an optimization applying the CVaR as the expression of risk. This is termed mean-conditional value at risk optimization or M-CVaR. The four different hypothetical assets have different returns and standard deviations and the authors vary their degree of kurtosis and skewness over four different scenarios and under the assumption of expected returns of 7%, 9%, 11% and 13%, respectively. Given the two different optimization methods, this gives rise to eight different asset allocations for each scenario.

The study shows that kurtosis uniformly distributed between the assets is of little importance when returns are symmetric. However, both negative skewness and high kurtosis concentrated on individual assets give rise to meaningful differences under the MVO and the M-CVaR methodologies, with the latter responding by lowering the allocations to such assets significantly.

The authors subsequently construct portfolios with the same four levels of expected returns mentioned previously for 14 different real-world asset classes over the period from February 1990 to May 2010. Table 5.2 shows some of the most important under- and overweights resulting from using the M-CVaR compared to MVO. Note that since the authors allow for short sales some of the weights are negative. As can be seen from the table, the differences in weights using the M-CVaR actually result in a higher standard deviation for the portfolio as a whole. In return for this, however, negative skewness is eliminated and kurtosis is reduced, highlighting the different emphasis of the M-CVaR approach. The authors note that while the M-CVaR methodology tends to underweight individual assets with higher skewness and kurtosis than the rest of the assets, what ultimately matters is the effect on the overall portfolio, as in the MVO approach.

To round off, the authors apply the same framework to the financial crisis of 2008 in an out-of-sample analysis. They find that using the M-CVaR rather

Table 5.2 Portfolio weights using M-CVaR versus MVO

	Weights (%), Exp. Ret.=7%		Weights (%), Exp. Ret.=9%		Weights (%), Exp. Ret.=11%		Weights (%), Exp. Ret.=13%	
	MVO	M-CVaR	MVO	M-CVaR	MVO	M-CVaR	MVO	M-CVaR
Underweights								
Commodities	3.62	1.12	4.03	1.38	4.71	2.17	4.85	2.59
US REITs	−2.55	−4.36	−0.74	−3.42	1.75	−1.69	4.73	0.98
Global high yld.	5.01	3.29	5.22	2.26	5.01	1.53	4.86	0.72
Overweights								
Non-US REITs	−2.83	−2.55	0.01	2.33	3.49	6.19	7.75	10.70
US bonds	28.18	28.30	22.91	24.11	17.35	20.26	11.16	14.46
Non-US bonds	9.27	15.62	9.01	14.10	8.82	12.27	8.08	11.02
Portfolio stats.								
Standard dev.	4.0%	4.6%	6.0%	6.7%	8.5%	9.2%	10.8%	11.5%
Skewness	−0.4	0.3	−0.3	0.3	−0.3	0.1	−0.4	0.0
Kurtosis	5.0	3.7	4.9	3.9	5.0	4.2	5.1	4.3

Based on Xiong and Idzorek (2011)

than MVO would have produced an outperformance ranging from 0.84% to 1.44% depending on the level of expected return of the portfolio.

The study by Xiong and Idzorek addresses one of the key critiques of MVO that investors tend to be more concerned with downfall risk than with volatility as measured by the standard deviation. The M-CVaR approach offers a way of utilizing more realistic assumptions about the distribution of returns and explicitly incorporating skewness and kurtosis into the optimization process, even if this inevitably comes at the price of higher complexity.

Checking for Robustness

A useful supplement to the optimization procedure is to simulate the behavior of the portfolio under varying market conditions to *stress-test* the SAA. One approach is to use historical periods, such as the recent crises, while another is to focus on particular factors of risk such as a significant change in monetary policy, a recession or a marked increase in global uncertainty. A broader approach might build different scenarios or "market regimes" which are assigned a probability in order to map a range of outcomes for returns and portfolio volatility. Chow et al. (1999) suggest criteria to distinguish between "quiet" and "turbulent" regimes and demonstrate how the two might be blended in the optimization of the portfolio. This approach is further developed in Kritzman and Li (2010). We will focus on the idea of market regimes more generally in Chap. 9.

Imposing Portfolio Constraints

We noted the risk that the MVO procedure leads to portfolios heavily biased in favor of or against certain asset classes due to sample errors in the data input. This problem is particularly pronounced when the historical data are limited, leading to a sample covariance matrix which produces unstable portfolios. Ledoit and Wolf (2003, 2004) propose a procedure for diminishing this problem through so-called shrinkage of the covariance matrix toward a target matrix which will be more biased but, in return, will suffer from less estimation error. A weighted average of this matrix and the sample matrix should then produce an estimate which is closer to the "true" covariance matrix. More generally, the portfolio manager may introduce portfolio constraints based on the view that some assets are over- or undervalued. It is clear that forcing the optimization process in this way introduces an element of subjectivity, but this may be justified on the grounds that it avoids outcomes of the MVO process which conflict excessively with more general views held by the manager.

5.4 Alternative Approaches

Several alternative approaches to structuring the SAA have been proposed. The first of the three might be classified as a complete departure from the idea of optimization, while the second and third optimize the SAA along different lines.

Equal Weighting: 1/N Approach

DeMiguel et al. (2009) compare a naïve strategy of equal (1/N) weighting of equity classes which are rebalanced periodically with 14 alternative approaches to portfolio optimization. The 1/N approach requires no data input and is therefore a useful reference against which to gauge the importance of estimation errors in the data input when using optimization. The criteria used for the comparison are the Sharpe ratio, the certainty-equivalent return and the turnover of the portfolio (to account for transaction costs). For most of the asset classes, the authors use data for the period from 1963 to 2004 and then perform out-of-sample optimizations for rolling 60- and 120-month periods.

The striking result of this study is that none of the optimization procedures outperform the naïve approach on the chosen criteria. The authors argue that this result is due to the estimation errors in the weights of the portfolio (extreme under- and overweights) being so large that this overshadows the allocation mistakes from using the naïve approach as opposed to optimization. The size of this error is a function of the number of securities in the optimization and the length of the estimation window. The authors find that the critical length of the estimation window for portfolios of 25 assets is 3000 months and as long as 6000 months for portfolios of 50 assets, in stark contrast with the 60 to 120 months typically applied.

Kritzman et al. (2010) take issue with these conclusions. Their main objection to the study by DeMiguel, Garlappi and Uppal is that the length of the historical data periods applied (60 and 120 months) is too short. As an alternative, they use data dating back as far as to 1926 to optimize 50,000 beta and alpha portfolios on the criterion of maximizing the expected Sharpe ratio. This study comes to the opposite conclusion that optimized portfolios generate superior results to that of the naïve approach. The authors recognize that investors should avoid basing their estimations on simple extrapolation of historical data and take into account "quiet" and "turbulent" periods, as proposed in the study mentioned previously.

Risk Parity

The idea of *risk parity* (RP) has received a lot of attention in recent years. RP takes its cue from the fact that the typical 60:40 stock-bond allocation of many investors implies that the main contribution to portfolio risk, often upwards of 80%, comes from the stock component. To achieve better diversification, RP advocates weighting each component in the portfolio so that each accounts for an equal proportion of portfolio risk.[7] Note that this approach requires no estimate of expected returns, but will typically imply a smaller weighting of stocks and other risk assets. Asness et al. (2012) argue that what is missing in this argumentation is a motivation for holding safer assets. They refer to studies which have found that a number of safer assets have empirically offered better risk-adjusted returns, that is, better Sharpe ratios than riskier assets, which beg the question of why investors are not taking advantage of this imperfection. To do so, investors aiming for higher returns than what would be achieved with a relatively high allocation to safer, and lower yielding, assets would need to apply leverage to boost the return. Many, however, either cannot do so or have aversion to leverage. This aversion might derive from the fact

[7] We provide an illustration of how weights are calculated using RP in the note at the end of the chapter.

that they are mainly evaluated on returns and may have benchmarks with higher beta assets. As a result they concentrate their investments in stocks which become expensive as a result, and consequently yield less, while doing the opposite in the case of bonds and other more defensive assets.

In the Appendix to the book, we show how the inclusion into MPT of a risk-free asset with a rate of interest at which investors can either lend or borrow gives rise to the *capital allocation line* (CAL). Portfolios on this line, representing combinations of the tangency portfolio and either lending (meaning that some of the portfolios are in cash) or borrowing (implying leverage), dominate all other portfolios in terms of their Sharpe ratio. The CAL will therefore constitute the efficient frontier. Using data from 1926 to 2010, Asness et al. find that US stocks have had an average annual return of 10.8% and a volatility of 18.9% whereas US Treasuries have had an average annual return of 5.2% and a volatility of 3.4%. Using these data, they estimate that the ex post tangency portfolio would have had an allocation of 88% to bonds and only 12% to stocks. The authors show that neither the 60:40 stock-bond allocation nor an investment in the weighted market portfolio would lie on the efficient frontier. Using RP with leverage, however, would give investors a result close to the line, after taking transaction costs into account. These results are illustrated in a stylized manner in Fig. 5.3.

When the authors expand the scope to include global stocks, US bonds, credit and commodities for the period of 1973 to 2010 and stocks and bonds

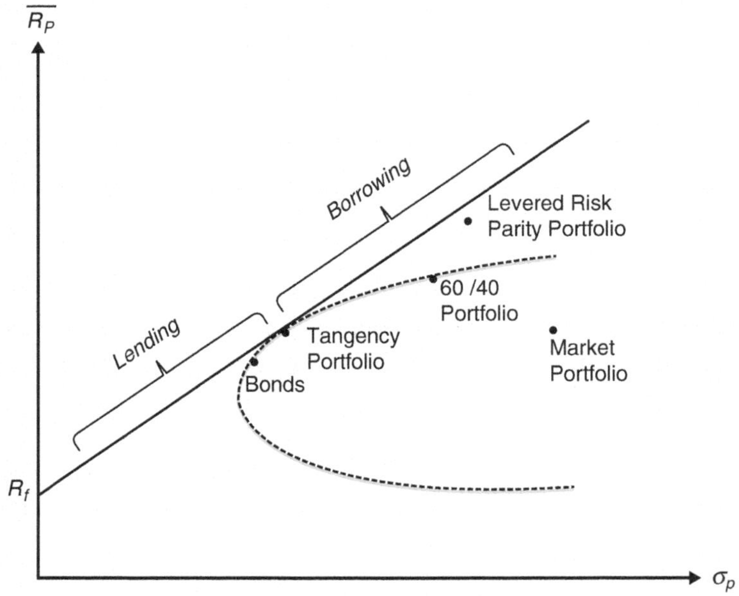

Fig. 5.3 Loosely based on Asness et al. (2012)

in 11 countries over the period from 1986 to 2010, they find similar results: the RP portfolio outperforms both the 60:40 portfolio and the weighted market portfolio.

Anderson et al. (2012) find a similar result for the long sample period from 1926 to 2010 but note that when taking into account transaction costs and costs of leveraging this conclusion no longer holds up. The authors note that these costs have varied considerably over sub-periods weakening the general conclusion that the RP strategy outperforms. Others have raised similar concerns, noting that periods of market stress might hinder access to funding for leverage while a general increase in interest rates could challenge portfolios with a high weighting of bonds. More generally, an explanation of why RP should represent a superior procedure to other optimization methods still appears to be missing, even if the empirical evidence might be seen to back up the RP approach.

Factor-Based Optimization

An investment strategy which has gained considerable importance is so-called factor investing. The idea is to redirect the focus from the asset class itself to style factors such as value, size and momentum and access the premia arising from these factors directly. Like assets, factors can be composed into portfolios which add a new dimension to the idea of optimization. This is the subject of the next two chapters of this book.

5.5 Conclusion

In this chapter we have reviewed some of the weaknesses of the standard MVO for SAA, suggested remedies and alternative approaches. No part of the critique presented suggests that investors should disregard the benefits of diversification deriving from the fact that different asset classes are less than perfectly correlated. But the MVO does assume a reliability of the data inputs which is clearly not met in practice. Remedies for this such as alternative return distributions and risk measures, stress-testing and the use of portfolio constraints can all improve the outcome but the thorny issues of estimating expected returns and changing correlations between the assets remain.

To benefit from the SAA as a long-term strategy, we should do our best to construct portfolios which are resilient to adverse conditions. But sticking strictly to SAA weights based on optimization *come hell or high water* represents an extreme proposition which is not supported by the uncertainties affecting the optimization process. Our view is that this makes a case for tolerance bands around the SAA which is where the TAA comes into the picture. The central tenet of this book is that to be efficient an asset allocation must assess the economic drivers of the markets as well as their statistical properties. Some of the problems facing MVO derive from changes in the economic scenario which can be identified and incorporated into the decision process. More on this later. Next we will look at Factor Investing, a relevant dimension of the SAA.

Technical Note: Finding Risk Parity Weights

We start with a simple two-asset portfolio and then generalize to n asset in the end. Most actual RP funds use the concept over a wider range of asset classes. In the Appendix to the book, we saw that the variance of a two-asset portfolio can be expressed as:

$$\sigma_p^2 = w_a^2\sigma_a^2 + w_b^2\sigma_b^2 + 2w_a w_b \sigma_a \sigma_b \rho_{ab} \tag{5.4}$$

For our purposes, we will assume that asset a is an index of stocks and asset b is an index of bonds and that w_a is the weight of stocks in portfolio while w_b ($= 1 - w_a$) is the weight of bonds. The contribution to the variance of the portfolio from each asset class can be written:

$$\text{Cont}_{\text{stocks}} = w_a^2\sigma_a^2 + w_a w_b \sigma_a \sigma_b \rho_{ab}$$

$$\text{Cont}_{\text{bonds}} = w_b^2\sigma_b^2 + w_a w_b \sigma_a \sigma_b \rho_{ab}$$

Setting $\text{Cont}_{\text{stocks}} = \text{Cont}_{\text{bonds}}$ and solving for w_a, we get:

$$w_a = \frac{\sigma_b}{\sigma_a + \sigma_b} \tag{5.5}$$

To illustrate, if stocks have a volatility of 15% whereas bonds have a volatility of 5%, our allocation to stocks will be (0.05)/(0.05+0.15) = 0.25 or 25% while our allocation to bonds will be 75%. If instead we want a 50% allocation to stocks, to maintain risk parity we would lever the bond component up to a weight of 150%. Note that the correlation sign ρ_{ab} cancels out in the two-asset case which will not apply to portfolios of more than two assets unless they have identical correlations. For such portfolios, we could apply the procedure set out in the Appendix to the book in order to calculate portfolio risk taking the diversification effect into account. Since portfolio risk will change as we change the weights, we could apply an iterative approach to find the risk parities. Alternatively, we could disregard this complication and apply a simple volatility weighting equivalent to (5.5). For the two-asset case, the calculation would be:

$$w_a = \frac{\frac{1}{\sigma_a}}{\frac{1}{\sigma_a} + \frac{1}{\sigma_b}} \tag{5.6}$$

which gives us the same result as (5.5). Generally, for n assets, each asset, $i = 1, \ldots, n$, would assume a weight of:

$$w_i = \frac{\sigma_i^{-1}}{\sum_{j=1}^{n} \sigma_j^{-1}} \tag{5.7}$$

References

Anderson, R., S. Bianchi, and L. Goldberg. 2012. "Will My Risk Parity Strategy Outperform?", *Financial Analysts Journal*, 75–93.

Ang, Andrew, and J. Chen. 2002. "Asymmetric Correlations of Equity Portfolios", *Journal of Financial Economics*, 63(3), 443–494.

Artzner, P., F. Delbaen, J.-M. Eber, and D. Heath. 1999. "Coherent Measures of Risk", *Mathematical Finance*, 9, 203–228.

Asness, Clifford S., Andrea Frazzini, and Lasse H. Pedersen. 2012. "Leverage Aversion and Risk Parity", *Financial Analysts Journal*, January/February, 68(1), 47–59.

Bae, K. H., G. A. Karolyi, and R. M. Stulz. 2003. "A New Approach to Measuring Financial Market Contagion", *Review of Financial Studies*, 16, 717–64.

Best, Michael J., and Robert G. Grauer. 1991. "On the Sensitivity of Mean-Variance-Efficient Portfolios to Changes in Asset Means: Some Analytical and Computational Results", *Review of Financial Studies*, 4(2), 315. 28p.

Britten-Jones, Mark. 1999. "The Sampling Error in Estimates of Mean-Variance Efficient Portfolio Weights", *The Journal of Finance*, 54(2), 655–671.

Broadie, M. 1993. "Computing Efficient Frontiers Using Estimated Parameters", *Annals of Operations Research*: Special Issue on Financial Engineering, 45, 21–58.

Chow, G., E. Jacquier, M. Kritzman, and K. Lowry. 1999. "Optimal Portfolios in Good Times and Bad", *Financial Analysts Journal*, 55(3), 65–73.

DeMiguel, Victor, Lorenzo Garlappi, and Raman Uppal. 2009. "Optimal Versus Naive Diversification: How Inefficient Is the 1/N Portfolio Strategy?", *Review of Financial Studies*, 22, 1915–1953.

Fama, E. F. 1965. "The Behaviour of Stock-Market Prices", *Journal of Business*, 38, 34–105.

Kaplan, Paul D. 2009. "Déjà Vu All Over Again", Morningstar Advisor, (February/March): 29–33.

Kritzman, M., and Y. Li. 2010. "Skulls, Financial Turbulence, and Risk Management", *Financial Analysts Journal*, 66, 30–41.

Kritzman, M., S. Page, and D. Turkington. 2010. "In Defense of Optimization: The Fallacy of 1/N", *Financial Analysts Journal*, 66(2), 31–39.

Ledoit, Olivier, and Michael Wolf. 2003. "Improved Estimation of the Covariance Matrix of Stock Returns with an Application to Portfolio Selection", *Journal of Empirical Finance*, 10, 603–621.

Ledoit, Olivier, and Michael Wolf. 2004. "Honey, I Shrunk the Sample Covariance Matrix – Problems in Mean-Variance Optimization", *Journal of Portfolio Management*, 30(4), 110–119.

Lintner, John. 1965a. "The Valuation of Risk Assets and the Selection of Risky Investments in Stock Portfolios and Capital Budgets", *Review of Economics and Statistics*, February, 47, 13–37.

Lintner, John. 1965b. "Security Prices, Risk and Maximal Gains from Diversification", *Journal of Finance*, December, 20, 587–615.

Longin, F. and Solnik, B. 2001. "Extreme correlation of international equity markets", Journal of Finance, 56(2), 649–676.

Mandelbrot, B. B. 1963a. "New Methods in Statistical Economics", *Journal of Political Economy*, 71, 421–40.

Mandelbrot, B. B. 1963b. "The Variation of Certain Speculative Prices", *Journal of Business*, 36, 394–419.

Markowitz, Harry. 1952. "Portfolio Selection", *Journal of Finance*, March, 7, 77–91.

Markowitz, Harry. 1959. Portfolio Selection: Efficient Diversifications of Investments. Cowles Foundation. Monograph No. 16. New York: John Wiley & Sons, Inc.

Michaud, R. 1989. "The Markowitz Optimization Enigma: Is Optimization Optimal?" *Financial Analysts Journal*, 45(1), 31–42.

Mossin, Jan. 1966. "Equilibrium in a Capital Asset Market", *Econometrica*, October, 35, 768–83.

Rachev, S. T., C. Menn, and F. J. Fabozzi. 2005. "Fat-Tailed and Skewed Asset Distributions". New York: Wiley.

Rockafellar, T. R., and S. Uryasev 2002. "Conditional Value-at-Risk for General Loss Distribution", *Journal of Banking and Finance*, 26(7), 1443–1471.

Sharpe, William F. 1964. "Capital Asset Prices: A Theory of Market Equilibrium Under Conditions of Risk", *Journal of Finance*, September, 19, 425–442.

Treynor, J. L. 1962. "Toward a Theory of Market Value of Risky Assets", Unpublished manuscript. Final version in Asset Pricing and Portfolio Performance, 1999, ed. Robert A. Korajczyk, 15–22. London: Risk Books.

Xiong, J. X., and T. M. Idzorek. 2011. "The Impact of Skewness and Fat Tails on the Asset Allocation Decision", *Financial Analysts Journal*, 67(2), 23–35.

6

Factor Investing I

"It's far better to buy a wonderful company at a fair price than a fair company at a wonderful price."
—Warren Buffett

So far, we have discussed investments from an asset class point of view. In this and the following chapter, we will zoom in on certain characteristics of segments of asset classes which have been shown to earn excess returns. This is the topic of *factor investing*. This type of analysis is not new. But the idea of making such factors directly investable through specialized vehicles is a relatively recent innovation which is causing a minor revolution in the asset management industry. The chapter is structured as follows:

We begin by classifying investment factors in Sect. 6.1. The theoretical framework underlying factors is outlined briefly in Sect. 6.2. This is followed by a review of empirical studies focusing on macro-factors in Sect. 6.3 and on style factors in Sects. 6.4 and 6.5.

In Chap. 7 we will review some of the key explanations behind factor rewards, their empirical record and the practical questions raised in the implementation of factor investing.

H. Lumholdt, *Strategic and Tactical Asset Allocation*,
https://doi.org/10.1007/978-3-319-89554-3_6

6.1 Classification of Factors

Overview

We can define investment factors as drivers of risk and return. Figure 6.1 offers a classification.

On the most general level, we can think of *macro-factors* such as real economic growth, inflation and interest rates. The next level can be referred to as *market* or *asset class factors*, that is, the drivers of risk for each asset class which explain their ability to generate returns in excess of the risk-free rate. Within given asset classes, we can refer to *style* or *fundamental factors* which are specific characteristics of asset classes such as size, value and growth for stocks and credit quality and maturity for bonds (which we touched upon in Chap. 1).

This classification warrants some comments. *Macro-factors* and *market factors* are clearly not *additive*. Systematic equity risk, which gives rise to the equity risk premium, is "macro" in nature as is the general risk on bonds as compared to cash or currency risk. Some therefore include them under the heading of macro-factors. We prefer to maintain the distinction. One reason is that the empirical research has taken different approaches. Some studies have linked macro-factors directly to returns, as we shall see later. Other research has focused on market and style factors directly, an approach where macro-factors are only implicit. Another reason is conceptual. Pervasive macro-factors affect all asset classes, although not equally and in the same direction, whereas, for example, "market risk" in the CAPM is specific to equities. Additionally, macro-factors are generally not *investable.*

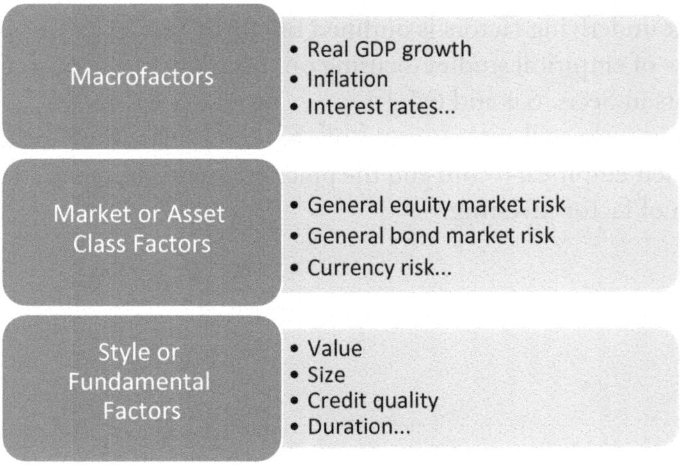

Fig. 6.1 Levels of factors

The distinction between *market factors* and *style factors* comes down to the degree of specification. The equity risk premium is general to this asset class, but the factor approach highlights that specific features of stocks, such as their book value versus their market valuation or their market capitalization size, can give rise to additional risk premia. Market and style factors therefore *can* be additive. Similarly, bonds in the broadest sense are generally riskier than cash or cash equivalents such as T-bills. But style features, such as their duration and credit risk, are even more important for their degree of excess return over the risk-free rate than in the case of stocks.[1]

Factor Analysis

A lot of the interest in factors focuses on returns. But the analysis can be applied *to risk management* as well where the identification of underlying portfolio factors can offer a more precise understanding of the drivers of risk. A prominent recent example of this approach is the study which was undertaken by professors Ang et al. (2009a) for the Norwegian Government Pension Fund Global (GPFG) which is one of the largest sovereign wealth funds in the world.[2]

The active management of the Fund generally produced an outperformance against its benchmark during the years prior to the Great Financial Crisis in 2007–2009, even though this was limited by the relatively tight tracking error allowed in its mandate. The crisis years gave rise to significant losses in the Fund, but public attention was centered on its *active management* which had seen a cumulative underperformance against the benchmark of around 3.5 percentage points over 2007 and 2008 prompting criticism. This underperformance was particularly pronounced in the area of fixed income.

The authors of the study did not vindicate the critics and found that the active management of the fund had actually played a minor role in its overall performance, accounting for less than 1% of the variation of its returns over

[1] Indeed, one might go as far as to state that style features are *all* that matter to bonds. Conceptually, as bonds become shorter and their credit risk is reduced, they converge on T-bills which are generally perceived as the closest thing to a risk-free asset available. The style features of bonds therefore arguably explain all of their risk premium, unlike in the case for stocks.

[2] The GPFG was established in 1990 to manage the wealth accruing from the country's petroleum exploration and production. The mandate of the Fund is to preserve the wealth for future generations and, apart from transfers to the Norwegian state, targeted at around 4% of its annualized real returns, it is managed independently of the government budget. The benchmark for the long-term management of the GPFG is decided by the Ministry of Finance and after reforms in 1998 generally implies a 60/40 percent allocation to stocks and bonds. Its active management is undertaken by Norges Bank Investment Management (NBIM), an arm of the central bank of the country.

the whole period from January 1998 to September 2009. But focusing on the crisis period, they concluded that despite the apparent diversification of the fund, approximately 70% of its active losses during the crisis period could be explained by its exposure to systematic risks. These risks include the type of factors which will discuss in this chapter, such as term, credit and liquidity risk for fixed income and value, size and momentum exposure for equities, as well as volatility risk which affected both asset classes. The authors argued that accessing such risk premia was rational for a fund with a long time horizon and a relatively low payout such as the GPFG. But rather than allowing the factor exposure to be a product of bottom-up decisions, a top-down approach of allocating explicitly to factors in its benchmark should be implemented. In sum, the study advocated a conscious approach to factors. This has inspired other comparable funds to adopt similar approaches to measuring and managing exposure risks in their portfolios.

6.2 The Theoretical Framework

From Single to Multifactor Models

The academic research underpinning factors dates back to the development of the CAPM[3] and the arbitrage pricing theory (APT). In the CAPM, the risk of an asset is measured exclusively by its contribution to the systematic risk of a portfolio, measured by its beta. This is the only risk which is rewarded. High-beta assets will command a high return and low-beta assets a low return. Idiosyncratic risk can be diversified away and commands *no risk premium*. The CAPM is, therefore, conceptually a *single factor model.* As is well known, the explanatory powers of the CAPM have generally found to be poor and researchers have looked for additional factors beyond general market risk to explain asset returns. This research in turn has created both the theoretical and empirical foundation for factor investing.

The APT developed by Ross (1976) represents the most important alternative to the CAPM. Whereas the CAPM sees the returns on individual assets and portfolios as relating exclusively to the single market factor, the APT expresses returns as linearly related to *multiple factors*, common to all assets and portfolios. The APT is not strictly speaking an equilibrium model and does not rely on the restrictive assumptions of the CAPM with respect to the distribution of returns and investor utility. Instead the model defines the

[3] See also the Appendix to the book.

return on individual assets and portfolios relative to that of other assets and portfolio from the point of view that any mispricing will be *arbitraged* away in an efficient market. Such arbitrage is assumed to be facilitated by perfect and frictionless capital markets, implying an absence of transaction costs.

The APT sees the return on an asset as the sum of an expected and unexpected component. Unexpected return is driven by the asset's exposure to common factors, the sensitivity of the asset to those factors and the specific risk component of the asset. This can be written as follows:

$$R_i = E(R_i) + b_{i1}F_1 + b_{i2}F_2 + \cdots + b_{ik}F_k + \varepsilon_i \tag{6.1}$$

where

R_i = the return on asset i.
$E(R_i)$ = the expected return on asset i.
b_{ik} = the sensitivity of the asset's return to factor k ("factor loading").
F_k = the unexpected change in the value of the kth factor, k = 1, …k.
ε_i = a random error term with a mean of zero and a variance of $\sigma^2_{\varepsilon i}$.

Investors are assumed to have homogeneous beliefs that such a k-factor model generates returns. Generalizing (6.3) to a portfolio of n securities, each with a weight of ω_i, we get:

$$R_p = \sum_{i=1}^{n} \omega_i E(R_i) + \sum_{i=1}^{n} \omega_i b_{i1} F_1 + \ldots + \sum_{i=1}^{n} \omega_i b_{ik} F_k + \sum_{i=1}^{n} \omega_i \varepsilon_i \tag{6.2}$$

The error terms represent *idiosyncratic risks* which are assumed to be mutually uncorrelated and uncorrelated with the factors. If the portfolio holds a sufficiently large number of securities, these risks will be diversified away and will therefore add up to zero:

$$\sum_{i=1}^{n} \omega_i \varepsilon_i = 0 \tag{6.3}$$

We can now create an *arbitrage portfolio* which consumes no wealth and has no risk. The first condition is met by using the proceeds from short sales to finance long positions. The second condition is met by having short and long positions with the same weighted sum of factor sensitivities which eliminates the *systematic risk*. These conditions can be expressed as follows:

$$\sum_{i=1}^{n} \omega_i = 0 \qquad \left(\text{total portfolio weights add up to zero}\right) \tag{6.4}$$

and

$$\sum_{i=1}^{n} b_{ik} = 0 \qquad \left(\text{systematic risks add up to zero}\right) \tag{6.5}$$

Under the assumption of efficient markets, in the APT such a portfolio cannot offer a positive return because arbitrage by investors would immediately eliminate such mispricing, increasing the price of the long position and/or lowering the price of the short position. Consistent with the *no arbitrage* condition of the APT, the expected return on such a portfolio must therefore be zero:

$$\sum_{i=1}^{n} \omega_i E\left(R_i\right) = 0 \tag{6.6}$$

Ross shows that under these assumptions, the expected return on any asset i can be expressed as[4]:

$$E\left(R_i\right) = \lambda_0 + \lambda_1 b_{i1} + \lambda_2 b_{i2} + \ldots + \lambda_k b_{ik} \tag{6.7}$$

The first term, λ_0, can be interpreted as the return on an asset with no factor sensitivity, corresponding to the return on a risk-free asset, R_f. λ_k can be understood as the risk premium on the kth systematic factor, that is

$$\lambda_k = \delta_k - R_f \tag{6.8}$$

where δ_k is the expected return on a portfolio with a *unit sensitivity* to the kth factor and zero sensitivity to all other factors. We can therefore write (6.7) as:

$$E\left(R_i\right) - R_f = \left(\delta_1 - R_f\right)b_{i1} + \left(\delta_2 - R_f\right)b_{i2} + \ldots + \left(\delta_k - R_f\right)b_{ik} \tag{6.9}$$

If we reduce the number of systematic factors to 1 and define b_{ik} as $\beta_i = \text{cov}\,(r_i, r_m)/\,\text{var}\,(r_m)$ (6.1), we effectively have the CAPM. The CAPM can therefore be seen as a special case of the APT with only one factor.

[4] This result follows from linear algebra. Two vectors are orthogonal, or perpendicular, if their scalar product is zero. If the vector of weights is orthogonal to a vector of 1's (6.6), to the vector of sensitivities (6.7) and to the vector of expected returns (6.8), then the vector of expected returns will be a linear combination of the vector of 1's and the vector of sensitivities. See further Ross (1976).

6.3 Empirical Research: Macro-Factors

In its pure theoretical form, the APT does not specify the factors, but later research has attempted to do this. The pioneering study is this field is that of Chen et al. (1986), who proposed a number of macro-factors of relevance for stock returns as proxies for the unidentified underlying factors in the APT:

$$R_i = \alpha_i + b_{i\mathrm{MP}}\mathrm{MP}_t + b_{i\mathrm{DEI}}\mathrm{DEI}_t + b_{i\mathrm{UI}}\mathrm{UI}_t + b_{i\mathrm{UPR}}\mathrm{UPR}_t + b_{i\mathrm{UTS}}\mathrm{UTS}_t + \varepsilon_i \quad (6.10)$$

where

- MP: The monthly growth rate of industrial production
- DEI: Change in expected inflation (measured by the CPI)
- UI: Difference between actual and expected inflation
- URP: The credit risk premium measured as the difference between the yield on low-grade (Baa) bonds and long-term government bonds with similar maturity
- UTS: Term structure of interest rates, expressed as the difference between the rate of interest on long-term and short-term government bonds (i.e. the slope of the yield curve)
- α_i: A constant regression term
- ε_i: An idiosyncratic error term

Consistent with the APT, the analysis focuses on *unanticipate*d changes in these variables, since current expectations about these variables are presumed to be already incorporated into market prices. The authors used as the economic criterion for choosing a factor that it should exert an influence on the expected discounted future dividends, that is, it should change:

$$P_o = \sum_{t=1}^{\infty} \frac{E(D_t)}{(1+r)^t} \quad (6.11)$$

where P_o is the price of the security, $E(D_t)$ is the expected future dividend at the end of period t and r is the discount factor. The authors offered an economic rationale for each of the macro-factors selected. Changes in the expected level of *industrial production* affect the current real value of future cash flows. Changes in expected *inflation* affect nominal cash flows and, to the extent it changes relative prices, may also change company valuation.

Insofar as the financial variables, the *credit risk premium* can be interpreted as a measure of changes in risk aversion, whereas the slope of the yield curve affects the value of distant versus near-term payments and can be seen as an expression of changes in time preferences.

The authors estimated this multifactor model for US stock returns over the period of 1953–1983 and for three sub-periods and found a strong relationship between the macro-factors and stock market returns. The most statistically significant factors were industrial production, changes in the credit risk premium and changes in the slope of the yield curve. The first two commanded a positive risk premium, which might be explained as the reward for the exposure to systematic production risks and unanticipated increases in the aggregate risk premium. The negative premium on the slope of the yield curve, on the other hand, could be due to a depressing effect of lower long-term rates on capital returns more generally. The inflation variable equally commanded a negative premium, which the authors suggested could be explained by the perception that equities are less exposed to inflation than other assets, and therefore tend to be bid up in price on this basis, resulting in lower future returns. However, the analysis found the inflation factor to be significant only in the stagflationary period from 1968 to 1977. More generally, the significance of the factors varied quite substantially between the three sub-periods.

Burmeister et al. (1994) proposed a different set of factors:

- *Confidence risk.* Unanticipated changes in investors' willingness to undertake risky investments, measured as the difference between the return on corporate and government bonds both with a maturity of 20 years.
- *Time horizon risk.* Unanticipated changes in investors' desired time to payouts, measured as the difference between the return on 20-year government bonds and 30-day Treasury bills.
- *Inflation risk.* Unanticipated changes in long- and short-term inflation rates, measured as the difference between expected and actual values.
- *Business cycle risk.* Unanticipated changes in the level of real business activity, measured as the difference in a business activity index between the end and the beginning of the period.
- *Market-timing risk.* Part of the return on the S&P500 which is not explained by the four macroeconomic factors.

The authors noted that different types of stocks should be expected to have different exposures to these factors than the market in general. Small caps, for example, are especially exposed to confidence risk, whereas growth stocks (which pay low or no dividends) are more exposed to time horizon risk than the market average. Exposure to inflation risk is more pronounced in industries that sell luxury goods than in industries that sell necessities, and real sectors are more exposed to business cycle risk than utility companies.

Macro-factors have the advantage of being economically intuitive. But different researchers have proposed different sets of factors[5] and it is safe to say that no single set of factors has been agreed upon. Unlike the macro-factors, the style or fundamental factors analyzed in the following are specific to the asset class and have the appeal of being directly investable.

Much of the research into style factors was originally undertaken with a view to testing the CAPM and capital markets theory more generally. But with good reason, practitioners have paid attention to the investment implications of the findings. We will begin with a brief review of the empirical research in the next section.

6.4 Empirical Research: Equity Style Factors

Value

Value is arguably the most prominent style factor and the one which has been subject to most empirical research. Its roots go back to the classic work by Graham and Dodd[6] and the foremost proponent of value investing is, of course, none other than Warren Buffett. Some of the key studies documenting *a value premium* include:

- Basu (1977) analyzed over 1400 industrial firms quoted on the NYSE over the period from 1957 to 1971. Ranking the stocks according to their P/E ratio and dividing them into quintiles of portfolios, he found that portfolios with low P/E ratios had an average annualized return of 16.3% against average annualized returns of 9.34% of high P/E stocks. The low P/E stocks also had better Sharpe ratios.
- Reinganum (1981) examined 566 stocks listed on the NYSE and AMEX over the period from 1975–1977 and reported similar results to those of

[5] See further, for example, Cutler et al. (1989), Chen (1991), Cheung and Ng (1998) and Flannery and Protopapadakis (2002).

[6] Graham and Dodd: *Security Analysis*, McGraw-Hill. The first edition is from 1934, but there are many later editions.

Basu (1977). However, the author showed a positive correlation between returns explained by P/E ratios and firm size (see below). Controlling for this, the P/E became much less significant and the author argued that size effectively subsumed it. This has subsequently been refuted in other research.

- Rosenberg et al. (1985) created long-short portfolios of US stocks with a high and low book-to-market value and found an average monthly return of 0.36% on this hedge portfolio over the period from 1973 to 1984.
- Fama and French (1992) studied stocks listed on NYSE, AMEX and NASDAQ over the period from 1963 to 1990 and documented an outperformance in average monthly returns of 0.58% between the decile of stocks with the higher book-to-market value and the decile of stocks with the lowest book-to-market value.
- Lakonishok et al. (1994) examined stocks on the NYSE and AMEX from 1963 to 1990 and segmented them into value and "glamor stocks" based on their price-to-book, price-to-cash-flow, P/E ratios and sales growth. The authors found that value stocks outperformed glamor stocks significantly.
- Chan et al. (1991) studied Japanese stocks over the period from 1971 to 1988 and found a strong positive relationship between book-to-market ratios and stock returns.
- Capaul et al. (1993) studied stock markets in France, Germany, Switzerland, the UK, Japan and the US over the period from 1981 to 1992 and found a similar strong evidence of superior returns on stocks with high book-to-market values.
- Bauman et al. (1998) examined stocks in 21 countries over the period from 1985 to 1996 and found that stocks with low P/E, price-to-book, price-to-cash flow and price-to-dividend ratios outperformed stocks with high readings on these metrics.
- Fama and French (1998) researched 13 international exchanges over the period from 1975 to 1995 and found that portfolios of value stocks outperformed in 12 of the 13 markets.

Size

The size effect or the size premium refers to the observation that small capitalization stocks tend to outperform large capitalization stocks. As we shall see, this factor appeared to vanish after being discovered in the original research. In spite of this, research in this field has continued and a recent study (see below) has suggested reasons to give it a new lease on life.

Key studies in this field include:

- Banz (1981) examined stocks listed on the NYSE over the period from 1926 to 1975 and divided them into five portfolios according to their size. Each portfolio was subsequently sub-divided into five portfolios according to their beta. The author examined the performance of these portfolios and reported a risk-adjusted average monthly return that was 0.40% higher for small-cap firms than for all other firms. The inverse relationship between size and returns was not linear, however; whereas small-cap stocks tended to outperform the market as a whole he found no significant difference in returns on averaged sized firms and large caps. More generally, Banz found that size had greater explanatory power than beta.
- Reinganum (1981)—study mentioned previously—reported that the smallest 10% of the stocks, which had a beta close to one, outperformed an equally weighted market index by approximately 1% per month.
- Keim (1983) studied stocks listed on the NYSE and AMEX over the period from 1963 and 1979 and reported that more than 50% of the excess returns on small-cap stocks were concentrated in January. The January effect could reflect that the market becomes very active at the beginning of each year and this effect appears to benefit small caps the most.
- Stoll and Whaley (1983) argued that transaction costs on trading small caps may, at least partially, offset the size effect. Analyzing stocks listed on the NYSE, they created ten portfolios ranked according to market value. They found that with a three monthly turnover the bid-ask spread for small-cap stocks would effectively offset the size effect.
- Later research[7] reported that the size effect had all but disappeared after the studies from the early 1980s. This was seen to be the case both in the US and internationally.
- In a recent paper, however, Asness et al. (2015) reported that the size effect is preserved after adjusting for *quality* (see further on the quality factor below). Small-cap stocks tend to be low quality measured on such metrics as profitability, growth in profits, level of payout, leverage and credit risk. This tends to work counter to the small-cap premium. The authors report a general risk-adjusted annual return of being long small caps and short large caps of 1.7%. This size premium, however, grows to 5.9% per year if the long position is limited to quality stocks. The authors find this premium to be stable through time, not concentrated on a particular month (as seen with the January effect), consistent internationally and not dependent on a low degree of liquidity of the stocks.

[7] See, for example, Dichev (1998), Horowitz et al. (2000), Chan et al. (2000), Amihud (2002), Schwert (2003), Van Dijk (2011) and Dimson et al. (2011).

A Three-Factor Model

Fama and French (1992) extended the formulation of the excess return in the CAPM, adding the value and size factors to the market factor. The additional factors were expressed as:

- *SMB* = Small Minus Big: the difference in returns between small and big stocks, mimicking the size factor.
- *HML* = High Minus Lower: the difference in return between high and low book-to-value stocks, mimicking the value factor.

Using monthly data for non-financial firms listed on the NYSE, AMEX and NASDAQ over the period from 1963 to 1990, the authors ranked stocks according to their size and book-to-market ratio in June of each year. They used a 50% breakpoint for size, such that stocks below this point were categorized as small (S) and stocks above this point as big (B). The breakpoints for the book-to-market ratio were 30% and 70%, implying that stocks below the 30% point were categorized as low (L), the next 40% as medium (M) and the highest 30% as high (H).

Combining these two dimensions they created six portfolios (S/L, S/M, S/H, B/L, B/M and B/H) from the intersection of the two size groups and the three book-to-value groups with their corresponding returns, R_{SL}, R_{SM}, R_{SH}, R_{BL}, R_{BM} and R_{BH}. Returns on the size factor portfolio and the book-to-market portfolio from July of each year to June of the following year were then calculated as follows:

$$R_{SMB} = \frac{1}{3}\left(R_{SL} + R_{SM} + R_{SH}\right) - \frac{1}{3}\left(R_{BL} + R_{BM} + R_{BH}\right) \tag{6.12}$$

$$R_{HML} = \frac{1}{2}\left(R_{SH} + R_{BH}\right) - \frac{1}{2}\left(R_{SL} + R_{BL}\right) \tag{6.13}$$

The authors formed 25 portfolios from 5 size quintiles and 5 book-to-market quintiles and regressed their excess return on the three-factor returns and a constant:

$$R_i - R_f = \alpha_i + b_i\left(R_m - R_f\right) + s_i\left(SMB\right) + h_i\left(HML\right) + \varepsilon_i \tag{6.14}$$

Where

- R_i: the return on portfolio i
- R_f: the return on the risk-free asset
- R_m: the return on the market portfolio
- α_i: the intercept of the regression
- b_i, s_i, h_i: the factor coefficients corresponding to factor sensitivities or loadings
- ε_i: statistical error term

Fama and French found that the two additional factors add significant explanatory power. They also found that the market betas of the portfolios were close to one implying that the contribution of the market factor in explaining returns, when the two style factors were included, was close to zero. The study therefore weakened the credibility of the CAPM considerably while it endorsed the existence of the two factor returns. The Fama-French model has become a standard reference in subsequent studies.

Momentum

Momentum refers to persistence in stock prices such that stocks which have performed well in the past continue to do so, and stocks which have underperformed continue to do so. Put differently, winners continue to be winners and losers continue to be losers.

Key studies include:

- De Bondt and Thaler (1985) studied stocks listed on the NYSE over the period from 1926 to 1982 and composed deciles of portfolios of securities with extreme high returns ("winners") versus the market portfolio or extreme low returns ("losers"). The authors found that losers over the past three years outperformed the market over the subsequent three years by a cumulative 19.6% whereas winners underperformed the market by 5%.
- Jegadeesh and Titman (1993) examined the performance of stocks listed on the NYSE and AMEX over the period from 1965 to 1989. On a monthly basis, they ranked stocks in ascending order based on their performance over the past 3–12 months (the formation period) and divided them into decile portfolios. They then measured the performance of a strategy of buying outperforming stocks (winners) and selling underperforming stock (losers) over subsequent periods of 3 to 12 months (the holding period). To allow for short-term reversals, they also measured this

performance, skipping a week between the formation and holding periods. The authors found that the return on this momentum strategy ranged from 0.32% per month, when both the formation and holding periods were three months and skipping a week, to 1.49% for a 12-month formation and a three-month holding period skipping a week. The return on an in-between strategy with a 6 × 6 formation and holding period was 1.10% or 0.92%, depending on whether a week was skipped or not. Jegadeesh and Titman (2001) documented that the momentum strategy had continued to produce positive results in the 1990s.
- Rouwenhorst (1998) examines 12 European markets over the period from 1980 to 1995 and reported results very similar to those in the US across each of these markets. Other studies of international markets have generally confirmed these findings as well.[8]
- Carhart (1997) extended the Fama and French model to include momentum. Using data for equity funds which had been in existence from 1962 to 1963 (to avoid survivorship bias), he formed decile portfolios of these funds and found that the best performers had positive exposure to momentum whereas the worst performers had negative exposure to this factor. The author found that the addition of the momentum factor to the Fama and French model added considerably to its explanatory power.

Low Volatility

A considerable amount of empirical work has documented that low volatility stocks have tended to outperform high volatility stocks. Some of the key studies include:

- Haugen and James Heins 1972, 1975) sampled 114 portfolios of 25 stocks listed on the NYSE over the period from 1926 to 1971 and calculated their mean return and standard deviation over the whole period as well as for nine periods of five years each. When regressing returns on standard deviations, they found that the portfolios of stocks with the lower variance had greater average returns than stocks with a high variance. This was one of the first studies documenting a negative relationship between risk and return, in apparent contradiction of standard finance theory.

[8] See, for example, Chan and Tong (2000), Hameed and Kusnadi (2002), Forner and Marhuenda (2003), Glaser and Weber (2003), Hon and Tonks (2003) and Muga and Santamaria (2007).

- Haugen and Baker (1991) reported similar results comparing the 1000 largest US stocks with the Wilshire 5000 index over the period from 1972 to 1989.
- Ang et al. (2006) examined US stocks listed on the NYSE, AMEX and NASDAQ over the period from 1963 to 2000 and documented a negative correlation between a stock's return and its idiosyncratic risk (proxied by its exposure to the VIX index) lagged by one month. Specifically, they found a difference in average returns between quintile portfolios with the highest and lowest idiosyncratic risk of −1.04% per month. The results were found to be robust when controlling for size, value, liquidity and volume and to hold up in both bull and bear markets. In a subsequent study, Ang et al. (2009b) reported similar results for 23 developed markets over the period from 1980 to 2003.
- Blitz and Van Vliet (2007) used all constituents of the FTSE World Developed index in a study for 1985 to 2006. Creating decile portfolios based on their historical volatility in this period, they reported a premium of 12% per annum from buying low volatility portfolios and selling high volatility portfolios. The results were confirmed specifically for both the US, European and Japanese markets, and were robust when controlling for size, value and momentum effects. In a later study, Blitz et al. (2013) examined stocks included in the S&P/IFC Investable Emerging Markets Index over the period from 1988 to 2010 and found similar results.
- Baker and Haugen (2012) studied 21 developed and 12 emerging markets over the period from 1990 to 2011. Computing the volatility of the total return for each company over the past 24 months and forming decile portfolios, the authors found that low volatility stocks outperformed high volatility stocks both across a sample of countries as a whole and in each individual country examined.
- Frazzini and Pedersen (2014) studied data for US stocks from the Center for Research in Security Prices (CRSP) over the period from 1926 to 2012 and data for 19 international stock markets from the MSCI developed universe over the period from 1989 to 2012. They constructed a "betting against beta" (BAB) factor which is long a portfolio of low-beta stocks and short a portfolio of high-beta stocks. The long and short positions were leveraged and de-leveraged, respectively, so that they both had a beta of one, making the BAB factor market neutral. The authors controlled for exposure to market, value, size, momentum and liquidity factors and found the BAB factor to deliver highly significant risk-adjusted returns both in the US and in the international markets.

Quality

The idea of *equity quality* is as old as the idea of value and indeed could be considered a dimension of the value factor. Most empirical research in this field, however, is of relatively recent date. One reason for this may be that there is no generally agreed on definition of quality, even though it is generally seen to be related to such features as the growth and stability of the earnings of a company and its degree of financial leverage of relevance to how safe a company is to economic downturns.

One of the broadest definitions is that of Piotroski (2000), who defined an F-score to measure the financial strength of firms within the universe of value stocks. The score is based on nine indicators for three areas of a firm's financial condition, each giving rise to individual scores of either 1 or 0. The F-score is calculated as the sum of the individual scores, which therefore ranges from 0 to 9. A score of 0 or 1 is classified as *low* whereas one of 8 or 9 is classified as *high*.

Profitability

- *ROA (Return on assets)*: score if positive in the current year: 1, otherwise: 0
- *CFO (Operating cash flow)*: score if positive in the current year: 1, otherwise: 0
- *ΔROA (current year's ROA less prior year's ROA)*: Score if positive: 1, otherwise: 0
- *ACCRUAL (operating cash flow/total assets)*: Score if CFO>than ROA: 1, otherwise: 0

Financial leverage/liquidity

- *ΔLEVER (Change in the ratio of total long-term debt to average total asset)*: score if lower in current year than prior year: 1, otherwise: 0
- *ΔLIQUID (change in ratio of current assets to current liabilities)*: score if higher in current year than prior year: 1, otherwise: 0
- *EQ_OFFER (change in number of shares)*: score if the firm did not issue common equity during the last year: 1, otherwise: 0

Operating Efficiency

- *ΔMARGIN (change in gross margin to total sales)*: score if higher in current year than prior year: 1, otherwise: 0
- *ΔTURN (change in turnover ratio (net sales to total assets))*: score if higher in current year than prior year: 1, otherwise: 0

Using data from the Compustat data base from 1976 to 1996, Piotroski divided stocks into quintiles based on their book-to-market ratio. Firms in the highest quintile, the value stocks, were then used to calculate performance. Within this group, small and medium caps were found to outperform large caps, whereas value stocks in general were found to outperform the market by 5.9%. Value stocks with a high F-score, however, did so by 13.4% per year, suggesting an additional quality premium of 7.5% per year.

Novy-Marx (2013) analyzed non-financial firms over the period from 1963 to 2010 using data from Compustat as well as accounting data. The author used a simple metric for quality: the ratio of a firm's gross profitability (revenues minus cost of goods sold) to assets. He argued that a firm must be considered more profitable than its competitors if its production costs are lower and its sales are higher, yet this may not show up in current earnings due to such costs as, for example, advertising or R&D. However, such costs will improve longer term earnings. Profitability measures therefore get "polluted" the farther down the income statement you go.

Sorting the data into quintiles, he found a difference in monthly returns between high and low profitability stocks of 0.31%. Sorting according to the book-to-market criterion, he found a difference in returns between high and low value stocks of 0.41%. The profitability and the value strategies did not overlap, however. Running the two strategies together in a 50:50 blend returned 0.71% per month and had a lower standard deviation than any of the two strategies. Novy-Marx pointed out that the high profitability stocks generally differ from the value stocks in the sense that they have higher book-to-market ratios and are generally larger. This gives rise to a negative correlation (−0.57) between the two strategies, offering an attractive diversification effect. To illustrate, the author showed that the profitability strategy performed poorly from the mid-1970s to the early 1980s and again over the middle of the 2000s. In contrast, the value strategy performed poorly over the 1990s. A combination of the two strategies, however, never saw a five-year period of losses over the period from 1963 to 2010.

The author also tested whether value strategies can be improved by controlling for quality and vice versa, which was done by double-sorting the data. This turned out to be the case. Selecting the highest value and profitability stocks was found to yield a monthly return which was 1.16% higher than that of the lowest value and profitability stocks. Generally, the study demonstrated the clear benefits of using the two criteria in conjunction.

Liquidity

The importance of liquidity is well known to finance practitioners. The ability to buy or sell significant quantities of securities quickly is often limited both by direct transaction costs and by the volume of trading in the market at any given time. On the other hand, empirical studies have demonstrated that precisely for those reasons illiquidity can command a premium for investors less in need of short-term liquidity.

In a seminal paper, Amihud and Mendelson (1986) focused on the implications of the bid-ask spread when transacting in the stock market. They noted that since this spread effectively reduces the *net return*, investors should require compensation in the form of a price discount, giving rise to a higher subsequent *gross return*. The bid-ask effect on the net return is greatest for short-term investors, who therefore have a preference for more liquid stocks, but gets smaller for investors who can spread it over a longer holding period and therefore focus less on liquid assets. They therefore hypothesized that the required return compensation should increase with the spread but at a decreasing rate, implying a concave relationship.

Their findings confirmed these ideas. Using stock data from the NYSE over the period from 1960 to 1979, they calculated bid-ask prices on the basis of the last trading day of each year and used an average of beginning and year-end spreads for the year as a whole. Ranking securities according to their bid-ask spread for each year and subsequently according to their systematic risk (β), they formed 49 portfolios. The authors then regressed expected returns in each subsequent year on the systematic risk, the spread and a year-effect variable. They found that the monthly excess return on a stock with a 1.5% spread was 0.45% higher than that of a stock with a 0.5% spread, but that the monthly return on a stock with a 5% spread was only 0.09% higher than that of a stock with a 4% spread. In sum, high-spread stocks have higher returns but their returns vary less with the spread than is the case for low-spread stocks.

Subsequent studies have expanded the measure of liquidity beyond the bid-ask spread used by Amihud and Mendelson. This has shifted the emphasis, but the negative relationship between liquidity and stock returns has generally been confirmed. Key studies include:

- Brennan and Subrahmanyam (1996) distinguished between the *fixed* and *variable costs* of trading in the market, both serving as proxies for the illiquidity of stocks. The fixed costs were represented by the bid-ask spread whereas the variable costs were represented by *the price impact* of trading (the effect on the price of orders to buy or sell) which is related to trading volume. Using intra-day data for stocks traded on the NYSE over the period from 1984 to 1991, they found that both fixed and variable costs contribute to creating a premium on illiquidity.

- Daniel et al. (1998) used *turnover*, defined as the ratio of stock volume to the number of shares outstanding, as a proxy for liquidity. Using data for non-financial companies listed on the NYSE over the period from 1962 to 1991, they estimated the return of a cross-section of stocks controlling for size, book to market and beta and found a strong negative relation to stock turnover.
- Pástor and Stambaugh (2003) analyzed temporary price fluctuations induced by *order flow* as a *market-wide* measure of liquidity. Using data from the NYSE and AMEX over the period from 1966 to 1999, they constructed this measure of market liquidity for each month using daily data within the month. The exposure of individual stocks to market liquidity, a non-diversifiable risk, was represented by their "liquidity beta". The authors argued that stocks which have a greater exposure to market liquidity, that is, stocks with a higher liquidity beta, should command a greater premium because they are more exposed to unexpected declines in overall market liquidity. Their findings confirmed this. Adjusting for market, size, value and momentum, they reported that stocks with high liquidity betas outperformed stocks with low liquidity betas by 7.5% per annum. This sensitivity was found to be higher for small-cap stocks, suggesting that it may explain part of the size premium discussed previously. The relevance of the systematic risk identified in this study was highlighted in the 2008–2009 financial crisis when extreme risk aversion caused general market liquidity to collapse.
- Amihud (2002) developed a proxy of price impact termed ILLIQ. This was defined as the absolute value of the daily stock return divided by its daily dollar volume averaged over some period. It is a measure of illiquidity because a large absolute return happening on a small volume is a reflection of low liquidity (what traders would refer to as a "thin market") while a small return with a large volume signals the opposite. The appeal of this measure is the easy access to the relevant data even for long periods of time. Amihud used a monthly measure of ILLIQ for stocks traded on the NYSE over the period from 1963 to 1997 and found a strong positive relationship between expected returns and this measure of illiquidity even when controlling for size, beta and momentum (the author did not control for value).
- Acharya and Pedersen (2005) proposed an asset pricing model which incorporates liquidity risk into the "frictionless" CAPM. In this liquidity-

adjusted model (LCAPM), the expected return on a security increases with the security's *expected illiquidity* and its "net beta". The net beta consists of the market beta of the standard CAPM and three betas representing different types of *liquidity risk*:

1. $\mathrm{cov}(c^i, c^M)$: the covariance of a security's liquidity with the liquidity of the market
2. $\mathrm{cov}(r^i, c^M)$: the covariance of a security's return with the liquidity of the market
3. $\mathrm{cov}(c^i, r^M)$: the covariance of a security's liquidity with the market return

The first risk reflects a *commonality in liquidity*. Investors demand a premium for holding securities that become illiquid when the market in general becomes illiquid. The second risk reflects that investors have a preference for securities with high returns during declines in market liquidity. The third risk implies that investors have a preference for securities which maintain their liquidity in a down market or "flight to quality" situation.

Using data for stocks listed on the NYSE and AMEX stocks for the period from 1963 to 1999, the authors found that differences in expected liquidity implied a difference in annual returns between liquid and illiquid stocks of 3.5% but that the three additional betas added an additional 1.1% risk premium. Among these, the first two had a relatively limited impact, commanding risk premia of 0.08% and 0.16% per year, respectively, while the third beta proved to be more important, showing a premium of 0.82% per year. The key insight of this study is that not only do differences in expected liquidity matter, unexpected *changes* in liquidity, or *liquidity risks*, need to be considered as well.

In a more recent study, Ibbotson et al. (2013) examined how liquidity compares to the best-known style factors, size, value and momentum. Using data from the NYSE, AMEX and NASDAQ over the period from 1972 to 201, the authors selected the top 3500 stocks with a market capitalization exceeding $5 million by the end of each year. From this selection of stocks, they recorded:

- Size: measured by *year-end capitalization*
- Liquidity: measured as *annual share turnover* (sum of 12 monthly volumes divided by each month's shares outstanding)
- Value: measured by the *trailing earnings-to-price ratio*
- Momentum: measured by the previous *12-month return*

They subsequently ranked the universe of stocks into quartiles of equally weighted portfolios assigning a quartile number for turnover, size, value and momentum. These portfolios were rebalanced annually. For each quartile they reported annual returns (geometric and arithmetic mean) and standard deviation. The results are shown in Table 6.1.

Several observations stand out. Firstly, the difference in returns between the low and the high liquidity portfolios is as great as the differences in the high and low quartiles of the other factors; liquidity ranks alongside the other styles as a differentiating factor. Secondly, there is no clear relationship between risk (as measured by standard deviation) and liquidity. Lower liquidity has empirically implied higher risk in the case of the size portfolios, but the opposite appears to be the case for both the value and momentum portfolios, where risk is actually inversely related to liquidity. This suggests that liquidity is very much a factor in its own right.

Ibbotson, Chen, Kim and Hu subsequently examined whether liquidity might be a proxy for the other factors. This was done by constructing equally weighted portfolios double-sorted in quartiles of size, value and momentum. The results are summarized in Table 6.2, which shows compound returns for the three styles across different levels of liquidity. As the table illustrates, the difference in annual returns between low and high liquidity portfolios of microcaps has been particularly pronounced. But it is significant for the other cap sizes as well and is more than 300 basis points even in the case of large caps, which are generally perceived to be liquid. Size, in other words, does not

Table 6.1 Liquidity compared to size, value and momentum

Cross-section	Result (%)	Q1	Q2	Q3	Q4
Size	Geometric mean	13.04	11.93	11.95	10.98
Q1=micro	Arithmetic mean	16.42	14.69	14.14	12.61
Q4=large	Standard deviation	27.29	24.60	21.82	18.35
Value	Geometric mean	16.13	13.60	10.10	7.62
Q1=value	Arithmetic mean	18.59	15.42	12.29	11.56
Q4=growth	Standard deviation	23.31	20.17	21.46	29.42
Momentum	Geometric mean	12.85	14.25	13.26	7.18
Q1=winners	Arithmetic mean	15.37	16.03	15.29	11.16
Q4=losers	Standard deviation	23.46	19.79	21.21	29.49
Liquidity	Geometric mean	14.50	13.97	11.91	7.24
Q1=low	Arithmetic mean	16.38	16.05	14.39	11.04
Q4=high	Standard deviation	20.41	21.50	23.20	28.48
Universe	Geometric mean	12.15			
Aggregate	Arithmetic mean	14.46			
	Standard deviation	22.39			

Source: Ibbotson et al. (2013)

Table 6.2 Based on Ibbotson et al. (2013)

	Compound annual returns			
Quartile	Low liquidity	Mid-low liquidity	Mid-high liquidity	High liquidity
Size				
Microcap	15.36	16.21	9.94	1.32
Small-cap	15.30	14.09	11.80	5.48
Mid-cap	13.61	13.57	12.24	7.85
Large-cap	11.53	11.66	11.19	8.37
Value				
High value (high E/P)	18.43	16.69	15.97	9.98
Mid-value	14.75	14.44	12.67	11.76
Mid-growth	12.53	12.09	9.96	6.58
High growth (low E/P)	9.99	12.32	8.39	2.24
Momentum				
High momentum (winners)	16.03	15.18	12.97	8.53
Mid-high momentum	16.02	15.31	13.43	9.05
Mid-low momentum	14.61	14.65	12.85	7.97
Low momentum (losers)	10.30	9.62	7.52	3.03

capture the liquidity premium. On the other hand, the size factor is not consistent for all levels of liquidity. For portfolios with low and mid-low liquidity, a smaller size does indeed imply a higher return, but the opposite applies to portfolios with high liquidity.

Similar results were found across the value and momentum factors. The difference between low and high liquidity portfolios was particularly large within the high value segment. But it even held up in the case of high growth (i.e. low value) where portfolios with low liquidity were seen to outperform those with high liquidity by more than 700 basis points per year. Again, liquidity is seen to constitute a distinct factor, separate from value. The same is seen to apply to momentum portfolios. As the table shows, the highest compound return is achieved by combining high momentum with low liquidity (16.03%) whereas the lowest return follows from combining low momentum with high liquidity (3.03%).

Finally, the authors constructed long-short and long-only portfolios to isolate the risk premium. The long-short portfolios were created by subtracting the returns of the less liquid quartile from those of the most liquid quartile to construct a dollar-neutral liquidity factor. These two series were then regressed on the three factors of the Fama-French model and the four factors of the Carhart model. In all cases the authors found a positive and significant alpha component, implying that liquidity is not fully captured by those factors. Liquidity, in other words, constitutes an important addition to the other factors.

The Ibbotson, Chen, Kim and Hu study is particularly relevant from an investment point of view because it documents that liquidity is an economically significant driver of returns across, and separate from, other style factors such as size, value and momentum.

6.5 Empirical Research: Corporate Bond Style Factors

Do style factor similar to those found in the equity space apply to fixed income? Recent studies suggest that this might indeed be the case. Before reviewing the studies, it is useful to recapitulate the standard understanding of bond risk.

We noted in Chap. 4 that an investment in a bond over n periods (years, quarters, months, etc.) can always be substituted with an investment in a one-period bond which is rolled-over when the short-term bond matures. Similarly, an investment over one period can be made in a one-period bond or in an n-period bond which is sold after one period. The *expectations hypothesis* states that investors should be indifferent between any such two alternatives and that bonds of all maturities are effectively perfect substitutes. The critique of this theory is that unless a bond is held to maturity the return on this investment will not necessarily coincide with its "promised yield" (i.e. its yield-to-maturity). This risk will grow the longer is the maturity (or, more precisely, the duration) of the bond and is variously referred to as interest rate risk, duration risk or term risk. The market compensation for this risk is called the *term premium.*

Secondly, an investment in bonds can imply a risk of default. A bond with such a risk should command a premium over a bond with a similar maturity and payment profile but free of such risk. On a practical level, corporate bonds are normally seen to offer a *default risk premium* over government bonds, the size of which is related to their credit ratings. Finally, as in the case of stocks, bond issues can be more or less liquid. Of particular relevance to the bond market is the fact that the most recent, "on the run", issues tend to be the more liquid than "off the run" bonds, which are less actively traded. Less liquid bonds will command a premium over more liquid bonds.

As discussed in Chap. 4, the data supplied by Ibbotson et al. confirm the existence of a *term premium* over the very long term. But the data also demonstrated that the term premium is time-varying[9] and appears to depend significantly on both the economic cycle and monetary policy. Figure 6.2 shows the

[9] This is consistent with the findings in such studies as, for example, Fama and Bliss (1987) and Campbell and Shiller (1991) which also rejected the expectations hypothesis.

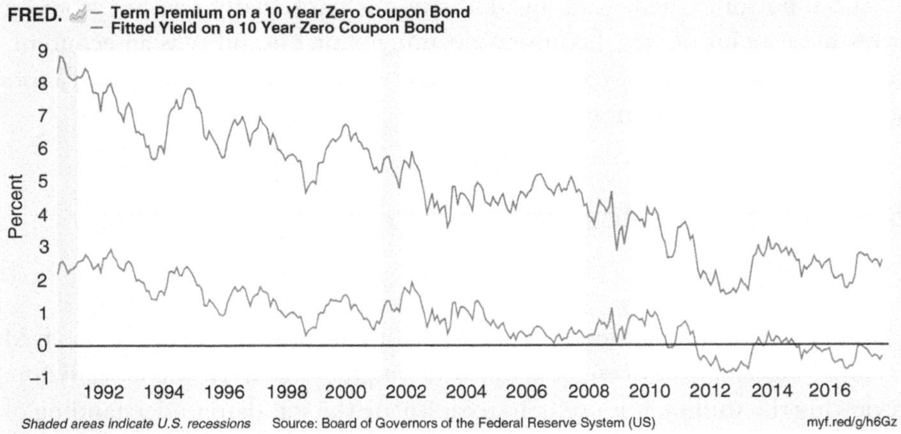

Fig. 6.2 Ten-year term premium

term premium and the yield on a ten-year zero-coupon bond since 1990. As can be seen, the term premium has tracked the trend of long-term interest rates and in crisis periods, such as the early 2000s and 2008–2009 with "flight to quality" into government bonds, the term premium has fallen as well. As can be seen in the figure, the term premium turned negative for the first time around 2012 and, at the time of writing, is back in slightly negative territory.

There is no consensus on what is behind this. Former Fed chair, Ben Bernanke, has suggested that international bond demand might be the reason. Others see the negative term premium as the outcome of unconventional monetary policies. Ultimately, the two explanations need not be contradictory. The Fed terminated the Quantitative Easing (QE) program in 2014, but both the ECB and the Bank of Japan have continued theirs. The extreme low levels of yields in those markets have likely prompted a search for yield in the US Treasury market. This also suggests that the negative term premium will eventually disappear as those programs get terminated.

In Chap. 4 we also noted the long-term excess return of corporate bonds over government bonds with similar maturities. Figure 6.3 illustrates the yield spread of Baa-rated (investment-grade) and of high-yield (option-adjusted) corporate bonds over ten-year US Treasury bonds. Naturally, the lower is the credit quality of the bond the higher is the yield spread, but does this spread only reflect the default risk of the bond? Both recorded data on default rates (adjusting for partial recoveries) and empirical studies suggest otherwise and have documented that credit spreads exceed default risks considerably.[10] We

[10] See, for example, Vazza and Kraemer (2017), Fons (1987) and Altman (1989).

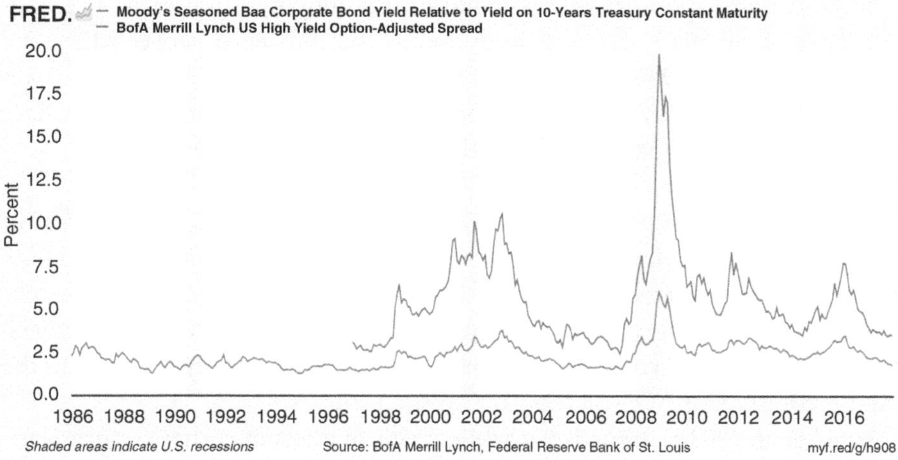

Fig. 6.3 Ten-year spread between baa-rated corporate bonds and US treasuries

will review a few of these studies first and subsequently turn to studies examining a range of factors similar to those in the equity space:

- Elton et al. (2001) examined the yield difference between corporate bonds with AA-, A- and BBB-rating(s) and US government bonds over the period from 1987 to and 1996. They decomposed corporate yields spread into (1) expected default, (2) tax differences between corporate bonds and Treasury bonds and (3) a systematic risk premium. They found that default risk alone explained no more than 25% of the variation in corporate spreads. Since corporate bonds are subject to state and local tax in the US, whereas government bonds are not, the authors adjusted for this factor as well but still found that a large part of the spreads remained unexplained. Finally, they regressed this unexplained part of the spread on the three Fama-French factors and found that betas on these equity factors explained between 65% and 85%. The authors concluded that investors in corporate bonds require a risk premium for the same systematic risks which affects stocks.
- Collin-Dufresne et al. (2001) studied data on 688 different investment-grade corporate bonds over the period from 1988 to 1997, applying a structural model of default risk. They found that the model explained only around 25% of the variation in the spread while the remaining 75% was explained by a factor common to all bonds and therefore not related to default risk. Huang and Huang (2012) using a similar methodology verified these findings in an updated study.
- Longstaff et al. (2005) used the Credit Default Swap (CDS) spread as the measure of default risk. They found that this accounts for a more significant part of

the total yield spread than was found in the study by Elton et al. The non-default component was then measured as the difference between the total spread and the CDS spread. The authors found that this part of the spread was mostly explained by measures of bond liquidity. Several other studies have emphasized the importance of liquidity in corporate bond spreads.[11]

More recently, studies have applied factors similar to the ones identified in the equity space to fixed income. It is generally understood that corporate bonds share characteristics with equities, which has prompted some researchers to apply factor exposures in equities directly to fixed income. Others, however, have taken a different approach, "re-thinking" equity factors into the fixed income space. We will look at two such studies:

Israel et al. (2016) argued that while credit markets may share return characteristics with equities, their underlying risks are not identical. As an example, corporate events such as leveraged buyouts tend to benefit shareholders but at the expense of bondholders. Moreover, bonds and stocks are traded in different markets and are typically held by different investors with different risk aversion, liquidity demands and so on. The same factors identified in the equity space must therefore be interpreted in the credit context. Using monthly data from the Bank of America Merrill Lynch investment-grade, high-yield and corporate bond indices over the period from 1997 to 2015, the authors selected large, liquid corporate bonds from the sample to avoid the high transaction costs typical for smaller issues. In the average month, the sample consisted of 59% investment-grade paper and 41% high yield.

The authors then examined four determinants of the excess returns on corporate bonds, defined according to the following metrics:

- *Carry*: the option-adjusted spread (OAS).
- *Defensive* (or *quality)*: based on market-leverage, gross profitability and duration.
- *Momentum*: trailing six-month excess return and equity momentum of bond issuer.
- *Value*: spread relative to default risk.

Running monthly cross-sectional regressions of bond returns on the four factors, the authors ranked issues by their characteristic values. Table 6.3 shows annualized performance statistics for quintile portfolios (Q1 to Q5) formed on the four factors and long-short portfolios which subtract the bottom from

[11] See, for example, Houweling et al. (2005), Driessen (2005), Chen et al. (2007), Lin et al. (2011), Dick-Nielsen et al. (2012) and Acharya et al. (2013).

Table 6.3 Annualized performance statistics

		Q1	Q2	Q3	Q4	Q5	Q5 – Q1
Carry	Return	−0.4%	1.1%	1.5%	3.7%	3.7%	4.1%
	Volatility	2.9%	4.4%	6.6%	8.7%	13.9%	11.7%
	Sharpe ratio	−0.12	0.26	0.22	0.43	0.27	0.35
Defensive	Return	0.0%	1.4%	2.0%	1.9%	2.7%	2.7%
	Volatility	6.0%	5.8%	6.4%	6.2%	5.6%	2.4%
	Sharpe ratio	0.00	0.24	0.31	0.32	0.49	1.11
Momentum	Return	−0.2%	1.3%	1.5%	1.4%	2.7%	2.9%
	Volatility	7.2%	6.1%	5.2%	5.3%	6.5%	3.4%
	Sharpe ratio	−0.03	0.21	0.28	0.27	0.41	0.85
Value	Return	−0.4%	0.7%	1.6%	2.4%	3.5%	3.9%
	Volatility	5.5%	5.8%	6.3%	6.8%	5.6%	2.2%
	Sharpe ratio	−0.07	0.13	0.25	0.35	0.62	1.75
Combined	Return	−0.5%	1.0%	1.5%	2.3%	4.9%	5.4%
	Volatility	5.6%	5.6%	6.3%	6.8%	6.0%	2.5%
	Sharpe ratio	−0.09	0.18	0.24	0.34	0.81	2.19

Source: Israel et al.

the top quintile (Q5 – Q1). The authors also created portfolios exposed to all four factors at the same time ("combined") by using equal-risk weighted scores from the four styles.[12]

The risk premia were found to be highly statistically significant except for the carry factor. As can be seen from the table, both returns and Sharpe ratios are generally higher in the top quintiles (high score on the style measure) than in the low (low score on the style measure), but carry scores below the other styles in terms of Sharpe ratio due to its high volatility. Equally important, the equal-risk weight combined portfolio shows a significantly higher Sharpe ratio than any one style alone, suggesting a clear diversification effect.

Table 6.4 shows the pairwise correlations between excess returns on each long-short quintile portfolio for the carry, defensive, momentum and value styles. As can be seen, carry shows a negative correlation with the other styles which creates a justification for including it in a portfolio despite its inferior performance as a stand-alone investment. Finally, the authors created an optimized long-only portfolio combining the four styles and found an equally clear outperformance after taking into account estimated transaction costs.

Houweling and van Zundert (2017) performed an analysis similar to that of Israel et al., focusing on four style factors, including size but excluding carry. In a similar vein to the previous study, they applied bond-specific measures, although with somewhat different definitions:

[12] This was done using linear programming where the objective is to maximize the multifactor portfolios exposures to the four factors subject to a series of constraints. The resulting portfolios are therefore different from a simple weighted average of the individual factor portfolios. See further Israel and Ross (2017).

Table 6.4 Pairwise correlations

	Carry	Defensive	Momentum	Value
Carry	1.00			
Defensive	−0.18	1.00		
Momentum	−0.30	0.40	1.00	
Value	−0.09	0.28	−0.16	1.00

Source: Israel et al.

- *Size*: based on total company debt (as opposed to size of individual bonds).
- *Low Risk*: based on maturity, and credit rating.
- *Value*: differential between actual and "fair" credit spread which is estimated on the basis of maturity, rating and the three-month change in the bond's credit spread.
- *Momentum*: based on previous six-month return with one-month implementation lag.

The authors used monthly data from the Barclays US Corporate Investment Grade Index and the Barclays US Corporate High Yield Index over the period from 1994 to 2015. For each month, they constructed an equally weighted decile portfolio with the highest and lowest exposure to each of the four factors. On this basis, they formed portfolios long in the top decile portfolio and short in the bottom decile portfolio. To control for systematic equity risk, the authors estimated alphas of these factor portfolios regressing returns on both the CAPM and the equity factors of the Fama-French-Carhart model.

For *investment-grade* bonds, the two approaches gave relatively similar results with annualized alphas ranging from around 1.2% for size and low risk to 2.5%–3.0% for value, all which were highly statistically significant. The analysis, however, showed no momentum effect. For *high-yield* bonds, both the CAPM and Fama-French-Carhart factors were highly significant for both value and momentum, with alphas of 5% and 8%, respectively. For low-risk, however, only the CAPM alpha was statistically significant. Pairwise correlations between the CAPM alphas were generally below 20%, except between value and size (41%). In sum, the corporate bond factors analyzed showed an outperformance which was not explained by systematic equity factors. Moreover, combining factors showed a clear diversification effect.

Houweling and van Zundert, however, argued that the long-short approach may overstate the outperformance due to the transaction costs from shorting bonds, especially when relatively illiquid issues are involved and holding periods are assumed to be as short as one month. They therefore performed the same analysis using a *long-only* approach with holdings of overlapping periods of 12 months. The key results of this analysis are showed in Table 6.5 which

Table 6.5 Annualized performance statistics, long-only portfolios

		Size	Low-Risk	Value	Momen-tum	Multi-factor
Investment grade	Outperformance	1.12%	0.41%	1.30%	0.30%	0.78%
	Tracking error	2.29%	2.85%	3.07%	1.84%	1.18%
	Information ratio	0.49	0.14	0.42	0.16	0.66
	t-value	2.15	0.60	1.35	0.72	2.79
High yield	Outperformance	5.50%	1.45%	4.26%	2.04%	3.31%
	Tracking error	7.95%	5.02%	5.66%	3.86%	3.38%
	Information ratio	0.69	0.29	0.75	0.53	0.85
	t-value	2.24	1.16	2.28	2.20	3.04

Source: Houweling and van Zundert (2017)

shows performance statistics for both single factor portfolios and a multifactor portfolio which combines the four-factor portfolio with an equal weighting of 25% in each.

As can be seen, for investment-grade bonds all four factors show a meaningful outperformance, although this is especially the case for size and value, which also exhibit the highest t-values. These results are even more pronounced for high-yield bonds where the outperformance is considerable across all the four factors. As importantly, the multifactor portfolios show a statistically significant outperformance for both investment-grade and high-yield bonds and a relatively low tracking error. The authors concluded that the multifactor approach is generally more robust and preferable to trying to "cherry-pick" any particular factor.

References

Acharya, V. V., and L. H. Pedersen 2005. "Asset Pricing with Liquidity Risk", *Journal of Financial Economics*, 77, 375–410.

Acharya, V. V., Y. Amihud, and S. Bharath. 2013. "Liquidity Risk of Corporate Bond Returns: A Conditional Approach", *Journal of Financial Economics*, 110, 358–386.

Altman, E. I. 1989. "Measuring Corporate Bond Mortality and Performance", *Journal of Finance*, 44(4), 909–922.

Amihud, Yakov, and Haim Mendelson. 1986. "Asset Pricing and the Bid–Ask Spread", *Journal of Financial Economics*, December, 17(2), 223–249.

Amihud, Yakov. 2002. "Illiquidity and Stock Returns: Cross-Section and Time-Series Effects", *Journal of Financial Markets*, January, 5(1), 31–56.

Ang, Andrew, Robert J. Hodrick, Yuhang Xing, and Xiaoyan Zhang. 2006. "The Cross-Section of Volatility and Expected Returns", *Journal of Finance*, 61, 259–299.

Ang, Andrew., W. Goetzmann, and S. Schaefer. 2009a. "Evaluation of Active Management of the Norwegian Government Pension Fund–Global", Norwegian Government Pension Fund.

Ang, Andrew, Robert J. Hodrick, Yuhang Xing, and Xiaoyan Zhang. 2009b. "High Idiosyncratic Volatility and Low Returns: International and Further U.S. Evidence", *Journal of Financial Economics* 91, 1–23.

Asness, Clifford S., Andrea Frazzini, Ronen Israel, Tobias J. Moskowitz, and Lasse Heje Pedersen. 2015. "Size Matters, If You Control Your Junk", Fama-Miller Working Paper, January 22.

Baker, N. L., and R. A. Haugen. 2012. "Low Risk Stocks Outperform Within All Observable Markets of the World". Available at SSRN 2055431.

Banz, R. 1981. "The Relationship Between Return and Market Value of Common Stock", *Journal of Financial Economics*, 9, 3–18.

Basu, S. 1977. "Investment Performance of Common Stocks in Relation to Their Price-Earnings Ratios: A Test of the Efficient Market Hypothesis", *The Journal of Finance*, 663–682.

Bauman, S. W., M. C. Conover, and R. E. Miller. 1998. "Growth Versus Value and Large-Cap Versus Small-Cap Stocks in International Markets", *Financial Analysts Journal*, 75–89.

Blitz, David, and Pim Van Vliet. 2007. "The Volatility Effect: Lower Risk Without Lower Return", *Journal of Portfolio Management*, 102–113.

Blitz, D., J. Pang, and P. van Vliet. 2013. "The Volatility Effect in Emerging Markets", *Emerging Markets Review*, 16, 31–45.

Brennan, Michael J., and Avanidhar Subrahmanyam. 1996. "Market Microstructure and Asset Pricing: On the Compensation for Illiquidity in Stock Returns", *Journal of Financial Economics*, July, 41(3), 441–464.

Burmeister, Edwin, Richard Roll, and Stephen A. Ross. 1994. "A Practitioner's Guide to Arbitrage Pricing Theory", in A Practitioner's Guide to Factor Models, ed. John W. Peavy III, 1–30. Charlottesville: The Research Foundation of The Institute of Chartered Financial Analysts.

Campbell, J. Y., and R. J. Shiller. 1991. "Yield Spreads and Interest Rate Movements: A Bird's Eye View", *Review of Economic Studies*, 58(3), 495–514.

Capaul, C., I. Rowley, and W. F. Sharpe. 1993. "International Value and Growth Stock Returns", *Financial Analysts Journal*, 27–36.

Carhart, Mark M. 1997. "On Persistence in Mutual Fund Performance", *The Journal of Finance*, March, 52(1), 57–82.

Chan, Kalok., A. Hameed, and W. Tong. 2000. "Profitability of Momentum Strategies in International Equity Markets", *Journal of Financial and Quantitative Analysis*, 35, 153–172.

Chan, Louis K. C., Y. Hamao, and J. Lakonishok. 1991. "Fundamentals and Stock Returns in Japan", *The Journal of Finance*, 1739–1764.

Chan, Louis K. C., J. Karceski, and J. Lakonishok. 2000. "New Paradigm or Same Old Hype in Equity Investing?", *Financial Analysts Journal*, 56(4), 23–36.

Chen, Nai-Fu, Richard Roll, and Stephen A. Ross. 1986. "Economic Forces and the Stock Market", *Journal of Business*, 59(3), 383–403

Chen, Nai-fu. 1991. "Financial Investment Opportunities and the Macroeconomy", *Journal of Finance*, June, 529–554.

Chen, L., D. Lesmond, and J. Wei. 2007. "Corporate Yield Spreads and Bond Liquidity", *Journal of Finance*, 62, 119–149.

Cheung, Y. Wong, and L. K. Ng. 1998. "International Evidence on the Stock Market and Aggregate Economic Activity", *Journal of Empirical Finance*, 5, 281–296.

Collin-Dufresne, P., R. S. Goldstein, and J. S. Martin. 2001. "The Determinants of Credit Spread Changes", *Journal of Finance*, 56, 2177–2207.

Cutler, D. M., J. M. Poterba, and L. H. Summers. 1989. "What Moves Stock Prices?", *Journal of Portfolio Management*, 15, 4–12.

Daniel, Kent, David Hirshleifer, and Avanidhar Subrahmanyam. 1998. "Investor Psychology and Security Market Under- and Overreactions", *Journal of Finance*, 53, 1839–1886.

De Bondt, W., and R. Thaler. 1985. "Does the Stock Market Overreact?", *Journal of Finance*, 40, 793–805.

Dichev, I. D. 1998. "Is the Risk of Bankruptcy a Systematic Risk?", *The Journal of Finance*, 53(3), 1131–1147.

Dick-Nielsen, J., P. Feldhütter, and D. Lando 2012. "Corporate Bond Liquidity Before and After the Onset of the Subprime Crisis", *Journal of Financial Economics*, 103, 471–492.

Dimson, E., P. Marsh, and M. Stuanton. 2011. "Investment Style: Size, Value and Momentum", in Credit Suisse Global Investment Returns Sourcebook 2011, Credit Suisse Research Institute, Zurich, 41–54.

Driessen, J. 2005. "Is Default Event Risk Priced in Corporate Bonds?", *Review of Financial Studies*, 18, 165–195.

Elton, E. J., M. J. Gruber, D. Agrawal, and C. Mann 2001. "Explaining the Rate Spread on Corporate Bonds", *Journal of Finance*, 56, 427–465.

Fama, E., and R. Bliss. 1987. "The Information in Long-Maturity Forward Rates", *American Economic Review*, 77, 680–692.

Fama, E. F., & French, K. R. 1992. "The Cross-Section of Expected Stock Returns", *Journal of Finance* 47 (2), 427–465.

Fama, E. F., and K. R. French. 1998. "Value Versus Growth: The International Evidence", *The Journal of Finance*, 1975–1999.

Flannery, M. J., and A. A. Protopapadakis 2002. "Macroeconomic Factors Do Influence Aggregate Stock Returns", *The Review of Financial Studies*, 15(3), 751–782.

Fons, J. S. 1987. "The Default Premium and Corporate Bond Experience", *Journal of Finance*, 42(1), 81–97.

Forner, C., and J. Marhuenda 2003. "Contrarian and Momentum Strategies in the Spanish Stock Market", *European Financial Management*, 9(1), 67–88.

Frazzini, A., and L. Pedersen. 2014. "Betting Against Beta", *Journal of Financial Economics*, 111, 1–25.

Glaser, M., and M. Weber. 2003. "Momentum and Turnover: Evidence from the German Stock Market", *Schmalenbach Business Review*, 55, 108–135.

Hameed, A., and Y. Kusnadi. 2002. "Momentum Strategies: Evidence from Pacific Basin Stock Markets", *Journal of Financial Research*, 25(3), 383–397.

Haugen, Robert A., and A. James Heins. 1972. "On the Evidence Supporting the Existence of Risk Premiums in the Capital Markets", Wisconsin Working Paper, December.

Haugen, Robert A., and A. James Heins. 1975. "Risk and the Rate of Return on Financial Assets: Some Old Wine in New Bottles", *Journal of Financial and Quantitative Analysis*, 10, 775–784.

Haugen, Robert A., and Nardin L. Baker. 1991. "The Efficient Market Inefficiency of Capitalization-Weighted Stock Portfolios", *The Journal of Portfolio Management*, 35–40.

Hon, M. T., and I. Tonks. 2003. "Momentum in the United Kingdom Stock Market", *Journal of Multinational Financial Management*, 13(1), 43–70.

Horowitz, J. L., Loughran Tim, N. E. Savin. 2000. "The Disappearing Size Effect", *Research in Economics*, 54.

Houweling, P., A. Mentink, and T. Vorst. 2005. "Comparing Possible Proxies of Corporate Bond Liquidity", *Journal of Banking & Finance*, 29(6), 1331–1358.

Houweling, Patrick, and Jeroen van Zundert. 2017. "Factor Investing in the Corporate Bond Market", *Financial Analyst Journal*, 73(2), 100–115.

Huang, J., and M. Huang. 2012. "How Much of the Corporate-Treasury Yield Spread Is Due to Credit Risk?", *Review of Asset Pricing Studies*, 2(2), 153–202.

Ibbotson, R., Z. Chen, D. Kim, and W. Hu. 2013. "Liquidity as an Investment Style", *Financial Analysts Journal*, 69(3), 30–44.

Israel, R., D. Palhares, and S. A. Richardson. 2016. "Common Factors in Corporate Bond and Bond Fund Returns", AQR Working Paper.

Israel, Ronen, and Adrienne Ross. 2017. "Measuring Factor Exposures: Uses and Abuses", *The Journal of Alternative Investments*, 20(1), 10–25.

Jegadeesh, N., and S. Titman. 1993. "Returns to Buying Winners and Selling Losers: Implications for Stock Market Efficiency", *Journal of Finance*, 48(1), 65–91.

Jegadeesh, N., and S. Titman. 2001. "Profitability of Momentum Strategies: An Evaluation of Alternative Explanations", *Journal of Finance*, 56(2), 699–720.

Keim, D. B. 1983. "Size-Related Anomalies and Stock Return Seasonality: Further Empirical Evidence", *Journal of Financial Economics*, 12, 13–32.

Lakonishok, J., A. Shleifer, and R. W. Vishny. 1994. "Contrarian Investment, Extrapolation, and Risk", *Journal of Finance*, 49, 1541–1578.

Lin, H., J. Wang, and C. Wu. 2011. "Liquidity Risk and Expected Corporate Bond Returns", *Journal of Financial Economics*, 99, 628–650.

Longstaff, F., S. Mithal, and E. Neis. 2005. "Corporate Yield Spreads: Default Risk or Liquidity? New Evidence from the Credit-Default-Swap Market", *Journal of Finance*, 60, 2213–2253.

Muga, L., and R. Santamaria. 2007. "The Momentum Effect in Latin American Emerging Markets", *Emerging Markets Finance and Trade*, 43(4), 24–45.

Novy-Marx, R. 2013. "The Other Side of Value: The Gross Profitability Premium", *Journal of Financial Economics*, 108, 1–28.

Pástor, Ĺuboš, and Robert Stambaugh. 2003. "Liquidity Risk and Expected Stock Returns", *Journal of Political Economy*, June, 111(3), 642–685.

Piotroski, Joseph D. 2000. "Value Investing: The Use of Historical Financial Statement Information to Separate Winners from Losers", *Journal of Accounting Research*, 38. Supplement.

Reinganum, M. R. 1981. "Misspecification of Capital Asset Pricing: Empirical Anomalies Based on Earnings' Yields and Market Values", *Journal of Financial Economics*, 9, 19–46.

Rosenberg, B., K. Reid, and R. Lanstein. 1985. Persuasive Evidence of Market Inefficiency, *The Journal of Portfolio Management*, Institutional Investor Journals, 11, 9–16.

Ross, Stephen. 1976. "The Arbitrage Theory of Capital Asset Pricing", *Journal of Economic Theory*, 13(3), 341–360.

Rouwenhorst, K. G. 1998. "International Momentum Strategies", *Journal of Finance*, 53(1), 267–284.

Schwert, G. W. 2003. "Anomalies and Market Efficiency", in Handbook of the Economics of Finance, ed. G. M. Constantinides, M. Harris, and R. M. Stulz, 939–974. Boston: Elsevier.

Stoll, H. R., and R. E.Whaley. 1983. "Transaction Costs and the Small Firm Effect", *Journal of Financial Economics*, 12, 57–79.

Van Dijk, M. A. 2011. "Is Size Dead? A Review of the Size Effect in Equity Returns", *Journal of Banking & Finance*, 35(12), 3263–327.

Vazza, D., and N. Kraemer. 2017. "2016 Annual Global Corporate Default Study and Rating Transition", Standard & Poor's Rating Services, April 13.

7

Factor Investing II

This chapter continues the analysis of factor investing, focusing on two main questions. Firstly, what gives rise to factor returns and are these returns likely to be persistent? Secondly, which are the key issues to be considered in the practical implementation of factor investing?

The chapter is structured as follows: Sect. 7.1 gives an overview of the many explanations offered for why factors command a premium and assesses their relevance. Section 7.2 discusses what is new in the factor approach and how many factors are likely to be relevant from an investment point of view. Section 7.3 reviews the long- and short-term performance record of factors while Sect. 7.4 discusses questions of implementation. We round off with a conclusion putting factor investing into the context of asset allocation. An appendix to this chapter, written by the CIO of Kirk Kapital, Teis Knuthsen, examines the topic of factor cyclicality.

7.1 What Explains Factor Rewards?

We will first review some of the most important explanations which have been offered and subsequently discuss their investment implications.

This chapter draws on charts and tables from MSCI Inc. with their kind permission. Please note that: *The MSCI data contained herein is the property of MSCI Inc. (MSCI). MSCI, its affiliates and its information providers make no warranties with respect to any such data. The MSCI data contained herein is used under license and may not be further used, distributed or disseminated without the express written consent of MSCI.*

H. Lumholdt, *Strategic and Tactical Asset Allocation*,
https://doi.org/10.1007/978-3-319-89554-3_7

Explanations for the observed factor premia can be broadly classified into three groups:

1) *Reward for risk-taking*: exposure to factors represents systematic risk which is rewarded accordingly in the markets. Factor rewards are consistent with efficient markets and rational investors.
2) *Behavioral patterns*: factor rewards are driven by collective biases which are not captured by the standard models of rational investor behavior.
3) *Structural/institutional limitations:* particular investor circumstances might impede their access to factor premia and may explain their persistence.

Risk Explanations

The general idea behind these explanations is that factors are proxies for underlying systematic risks which cannot be diversified away and therefore command a premium. Suggestions and findings from empirical research include:

Value

- *Leverage and risk of distress:* value firms tend to have a high degree of financial leverage and are more susceptible to financial distress (Fama and French 1998; Chen and Zhang 1998).
- *Irreversibility of investments*: in contrast with growth firms, the stock price of value firms consists primarily of tangible assets, which are harder to downscale in periods of economic weakness. This makes value firms riskier (Zhang 2005).
- *Macro-sensitivity:* value stocks tend to outperform growth stocks in periods of economic expansion, reducing the book-to-market spread between the two. The opposite happens in downturns. Value stocks are also more sensitive to restrictive monetary policy than growth stocks (Jensen and Mercer 2002; Black et al. 2009).

Size

- *Insufficient information*: the scarcity of information about small caps could lead some investors to exclude this market segment in their portfolio diversification. This in turn gives rise to an excess market return (Banz 1981).
- *Efficiency and leverage*: small firm portfolios generally contain more marginal firms with lower efficiency and higher degrees of leverage. These firms

are more exposed to periods of tight credit (Chan and Chen 1991) and are more likely to be distressed (Dichev 1998).

- *Profitability:* small caps have lower returns on equity, and there is greater uncertainty over their earnings. This makes them more sensitive to economic downturns (Fama and French 1995).
- *Liquidity:* small-cap issues are less liquid than the average stock issue (Amihud and Mendelson 1986; Liu 2006).

Momentum

- *Macro-sensitivity*: returns to momentum strategies are positive only in periods of expansion and become negative in recessions (Chordia and Shivakumar 2002). Winners have higher loadings to the growth rate in industrial production and are more exposed to growth shocks (Liu and Zhang 2008).

Behavioral Explanations

These explanations depart from the assumption of efficient markets and rational investors and point instead to cognitive biases and systematic errors among investors.

Value

- *Extrapolation:* investors tend to base expectations of earnings on the recent past and consistently overestimate the future growth rates of growth (or "glamor") stocks relative to value stocks; investors are effectively overpaying for growth stocks. This systematic error is what gives rise to the superior performance of value stocks as actual growth rates subsequently become known (Lakonishok et al. 1994). Consistent with this, La Porta et al. (1997) found that earnings announcements tended to produce disappointments as far as growth stocks were concerned, while the opposite applied to value stocks.
- *Mental accounting and loss aversion:* some investors regard stocks individually rather than as a portfolio, a result of narrow framing in their mental accounting. Their degree of "loss aversion" tends to depend on previous performance; a loss coming after a recent gain is less painful because the previous gain creates a cushion. Conversely, a loss following a prior loss is particularly painful. Put differently, investors get more sensitive to additional losses after having suffered initial losses. In this framework, value stocks, which have typically had a very negative prior performance, will be

considered riskier and investors will therefore apply a higher discount rate to their future earnings, which equates to a value premium (Barberis and Huang 2001).

Momentum

- *Overreaction:* investors tend to overreact to the most recent information while giving less weight to past information. This leads to excessive optimism from good news and excessive pessimism from bad news and causes stocks to deviate from their intrinsic value (De Bondt and Thaler 1985).
- *Conservatism* and *representativeness*: investors believe the profitability of companies follows one of two regimes: mean reversion or trending. When the idea of mean reversion dominates, investors will exhibit a conservative bias and react only partially to good or bad news. But as evidence of a trend gets sufficiently convincing, they will see this as representative of the future and extrapolate recent performance. Initial underreaction is therefore followed by a delayed overreaction which gives rise to a momentum effect (Barberis et al. 1998).
- *Overconfidence* and *biased self-attribution:* overconfident investors will overestimate the value of their private information. They will attribute a positive reaction to new information of given stocks to their own skills and a negative reaction to bad luck. As they get more confident in their ability to pick winners, they will push up the price of outperforming stocks which eventually depart from their fundamental value. These traits are consistent with an overreaction over the short- to medium-term and eventual reversals (Daniel et al. 1998).
- *Investor heterogeneity:* investors can be divided into "newswatchers" and "momentum traders", both with bounded rationality. Investors in the first group base their trades on fundamental information but ignore the information in price history. Conversely, investors in the second group trade only on price movements and ignore fundamental information. Information therefore diffuses with a delay across all investors and is at first only partly incorporated into prices, consistent with underreaction and momentum. This incentivizes momentum traders, who subsequently drive prices beyond their fundamental value, consistent with a longer-term overreaction. Eventually, stock prices revert to their fundamental value (Hong and Stein 1999).
- *Adjustment and anchoring bias:* investors could use the 52-week high of individual stocks as a reference point and rank stocks according to the ratio of their current price to this reference point. When stocks reach a level

close to the 52-week high, investors are initially reluctant to push the price higher, even if this is warranted by positive information. Eventually, however, the information prevails and the price continues higher. A similar pattern, in reverse, applies to stocks far below their 52-week high. George and Hwang (2004) noted that such behavior is consistent with an "adjustment and anchoring bias" and demonstrated that stocks with the highest ratio to the 52-week high outperformed stocks with the lowest ratio significantly over the subsequent 6–12 months.

Low Volatility

- *Lottery effect*: some investors use stocks with a high volatility as lotteries, that is, they are willing to accept a lower expected return for getting access to the chance of a big win even if its probability is low. As a consequence, they overpay for high volatility stocks and underpay for low volatility stocks, which create a low volatility premium (Kumar 2009; Baker et al. 2011).
- *Analyst optimism*: sell-side analysts have a tendency to inflate earnings forecasts, which is particularly pronounced when it comes to volatile stocks where such a practice is harder to detect. This tends to push up the prices of such stocks, leading to overvaluation, as seen, for example, in forward E/P estimates, and subsequent inferior returns (Hsu et al. 2013).

Structural/Institutional Explanations

These explanations are based on the practical observation that investor circumstances do not always allow their access to factor rewards or may discourage it. This in turn could explain factor persistence.

Value

- *Time horizon* and *institutional herding:* not all investors have a sufficiently long time horizon to take advantage of the value premium. Institutional investors, in particular, may be concerned that a temporary underperformance compared to their peers could lead to withdrawal of investor funds (De Long et al. 1990; Shleifer and Vishny 1990). Related to this, studies have demonstrated a herding tendency among institutional investors (see, e.g. Lakonishok et al. 1992a; Dasgupta et al. 2011).

- *Agency problems:* institutional investors may favor glamor stocks because they appear to be more prudent to sponsors even if they are not truly safer (Lakonishok et al. 1992b).

Low Volatility

- *Institutional benchmarks* and *tracking error*: the benchmarks of institutional investors may discourage overweighting low volatility stocks because this could lead to excessive tracking errors (Baker et al. 2011).
- *Leverage constraints*: institutional investors are often barred from using leverage while others have aversion to it or face excessive borrowing costs. To boost returns they therefore favor high beta stocks rather than exploiting the low volatility premium through the use of leverage (Frazzini and Pedersen 2014).

Which "School of Thought" Is Right?

The risk explanations may seem to make factor investing less attractive as they imply efficient markets and no "free lunch". Arguably, however, factor rewards stemming from systematic risks are more likely to be persistent. To illustrate, the equity risk premium clearly varies over time and harvesting it presupposes a long time horizon and the ability to withstand short-term volatility. But an absence of a risk premium would be inconsistent with any long-term equilibrium in capital markets. A similar reasoning can be applied to factor risk. By comparison, behavioral patterns might, by their very nature, be more changeable, while constraints from structural and institutional circumstances could eventually be reduced.

So which "school of thought" is right? Our view is that the rational explanations present a convincing case when it comes to macro-sensitivities of such factors as *value* and *size*. The common theme of the sensitivity of factors to *bad economic times* where *leverage* takes its toll and *market liquidity* drops significantly rings particularly true after the experience during the 2008–2009 financial crisis and emphasizes that such risks cannot somehow be arbitraged away.

But something is still missing. Both the *momentum effect* and the *low volatility premium* are hard to justify on purely rational grounds and both behavioral and institutional explanations have filled some of the gap. The common theme of initial underreaction to news, possibly driven by anchoring, followed by overreaction, driven perhaps by overconfidence and herd behavior, makes a better case than the rational school in explaining the *momentum effect*. In a similar vein, the preference for volatile stocks of some investors (suggesting short-termism) and the tendency of sell-side analysts to overrate such stocks provide plausible explanations for the *low volatility premium* observed. The structural/institutional explanations are conceptually somewhere between the rational and the behavioral school. The particular value of these contributions is that they rely less on conjectures and refer instead to well-known investor circumstances, such as adherence to a cap-weighted benchmark and leverage constraints. These explanations seem relevant across most of the factor premiums observed.

So the realistic answer to the question is that returns across factors likely encompass an element of all three explanations, even if their relative weights will vary. Our starting point must therefore be the empirical record to which we turn in Sect. 7.3.

7.2 Pertinent Questions

What Is New in the Factor Approach?

Harvesting factor rewards through targeted investments is neither new nor particularly rare. Research has found that mutual funds often have tilts toward certain factors, such as value or size. Moreover, long-short strategies have long been standard practice among investment bank traders and hedge funds who seek to reduce or eliminate the market effect. So what is new?

Firstly, factor analysis is now used more explicitly in risk management of institutional investors, as discussed in the first part of the previous chapter. This is based on the idea that uncovering factor exposures across asset classes can provide relevant information which is not captured in the traditional portfolio optimization approach.

Secondly, access to single factors has been increasingly *commoditized* in recent years through funds offering *smart beta* (aka strategic or alternative beta) products, which are an outgrowth of the trend toward passive investment through ETFs and similar vehicles. Estimates suggest that smart beta funds have now surpassed the $1 trillion threshold.[1] Single-factor funds still dominate, but multifactor vehicles have been gaining ground more recently, in a second round of commoditization. This is clearly happening at the expense of traditional actively managed funds.

[1] See also https://www.ft.com/content/16d47d2c-6324-11e7-8814-0ac7eb84e5f1

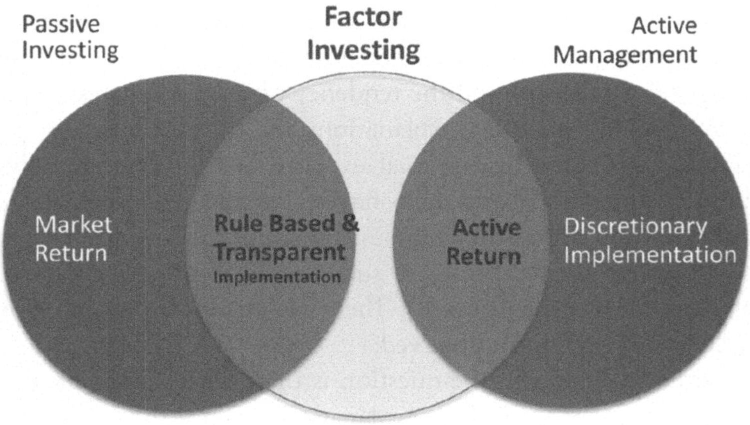

Fig. 7.1 Factor investing between passive and active management. (Source: © MSCI Inc. Used with permission)

The features of these investment products which are most commonly cited are the following:

- *Low cost* as compared to both traditional active management and hedge funds
- *Rules-based* as opposed to discretionary investment
- *Transparency* in the investment approach

Factor investing can reasonably be classified as somewhere between traditional active management and passive investment, as illustrated in Fig. 7.1. It is active in the strict sense that it involves a deviation from capitalization-weighted indices. But it is not active in a discretionary sense: both the composition and subsequent rebalancing of factor exposures are based on algorithms rather than on manager decisions.

How Many Factors?

Some researchers have questioned the validity of the numerous empirical tests on financial data in search of a pattern. Yee (2010) noted that a "phantom pattern" will exhibit statistical significance at the 1% level approximately 1% of the time. If researchers test 100 of such patterns one of them will have a 63.4% chance ($1 - 0.99^{100}$) of exhibiting significance at the 1% level; the probability grows to 99.3% if 500 tests are carried out. This problem derives from so-called *data-snooping* or *data mining*, which refers to the practice of using data for a given period to first detect a pattern and then subsequently to test for that pattern on the same data. Lo and MacKinlay (1990) illustrated the pitfalls of data-snooping in tests of the CAPM and demonstrated how using firm characteristics from data rather than from an economic theory can lead to significant biases.

Two recent studies stand out. Harvey et al. (2016) documented as many as 316 factors identified in empirical research and concluded on statistical grounds that most of them are likely false. The authors argue that the traditional cutoff level of two for the *t*-value should be raised to three when new factors are being considered. Hou et al. (2017) performed a comprehensive study reviewing 447 anomalies identified in the empirical literature. The authors pointed out that many of the anomalies were concentrated among small-cap stocks, which make up 60% of all listings but account for only 3% of market capitalization. Many studies have given these stocks equal weightings with other stocks despite their higher transaction costs and the fact that there are more statistical outliers among them. Correcting for this, the authors found that 286 of the 447 anomalies were *not* significant at the 5% level, while increasing the threshold for the *t*-value to 3%, as proposed by Harvey, Liu and Zhu, raised this number to 380. The factors which fared the best were generally the best-known ones but even here the authors found less significant outperformance than reported in previous studies. Hou, Xue and Zhang concluded that many of the studies on market anomalies were infected by "p-hacking", defined by the authors as "selecting sample criteria and test procedures until insignificant results become significant".

The immediate conclusion of these studies is that factors should meet at least two criteria:

- They should have proved persistent in out-of-sample tests, across different geographic markets and over time. This generally speaks against including newly discovered factors.
- They should have a strong rationale, be it risk-based, behavioral or structural/institutional. Factors classified as anomalies do not meet this criterion.

7.3 Factor Performance

Long-term Risk and Return

Figure 7.2 shows 40 years of gross equity factor returns and their annualized risk represented by MSCI factor indices using the MSCI World as the parent index. All data are in USD terms. The size factor (small caps) is represented by

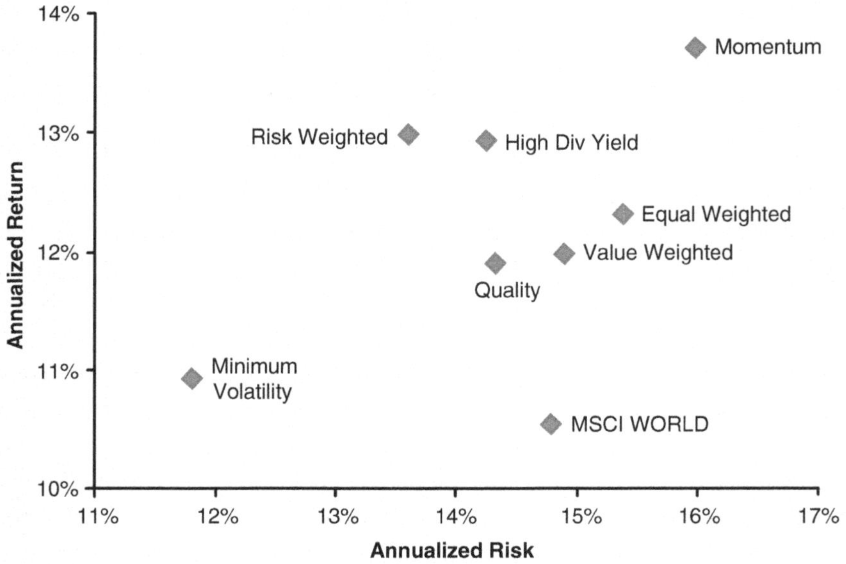

Fig. 7.2 Factor risks and returns 1975–2014. (Source: © MSCI Inc. Used with permission)

the Equal-Weighted index while low volatility is captured both by the Minimum Volatility index and the Risk-Weighted index. The latter, however, has a bias toward stocks with lower size and therefore captures two factors.[2]

As can be seen, all the factors exhibit a long-term excess return over the MSCI World index, four of them with a lower recorded volatility than the parent index and three with a higher volatility. Tables 7.1 and 7.2 put this into perspective by showing the frequency of outperformance of the factors and the frequency of factors having a lower volatility than the MSCI World index, respectively, as a function of the time invested. These tables include a Quality Mix index, which combines the quality, value-weighted and minimum volatility indices and a Balanced Mix, which combines the equal-weighted, high dividend yield, momentum, quality, value-weighted and minimum volatility indices.

Table 7.1 indicates that the likelihood of the factors outperforming the parent index clearly grows the longer is the investment horizon, akin to the picture seen with equities versus government bonds. This relationship gets even stronger when it comes to the two mixed indices. With respect to volatility, however, the picture is less clear. The likelihood of a lower volatility than the MSCI World index clearly grows with a longer time horizon for the high dividend, risk-weighted and minimum volatility indices. But this relationship is weaker in the case of quality and value, and appears to be the opposite for the equally weighted and momentum factors. Note, however, that the mixed

[2] For more on methodology, see https://www.msci.com/msci-factor-indexes

Table 7.1 Frequency of outperformance versus the MSCI World index, based on monthly prices on a rolling basis from 1975–2014

Rolling Window	Equal Weighted	High Div Yield	Momentum	Quality	Risk Weighted	Value Weighted	Minimum Volatility	Quality Mix	Balanced Mix
1 Y	62%	61%	66%	53%	61%	69%	46%	57%	72%
3 Y	73%	73%	77%	59%	76%	70%	52%	68%	88%
5 Y	83%	82%	91%	62%	83%	77%	55%	77%	92%
10 Y	76%	98%	99%	75%	88%	99%	65%	87%	100%
15 Y	85%	99%	100%	88%	95%	100%	66%	100%	100%
20 Y	89%	100%	100%	99%	98%	100%	72%	100%	100%
25 Y	100%	100%	100%	100%	100%	100%	91%	100%	100%

Source: © MSCI Inc. Used with permission

Table 7.2 Frequency of lower volatility versus the MSCI World index, based on monthly prices on a rolling basis from 1975–2014

Rolling Window	Equal Weighted	High Div Yield	Momentum	Quality	Risk Weighted	Value Weighted	Minimum Volatility	Quality Mix	Balanced Mix
1 Y	41%	61%	32%	54%	76%	49%	93%	88%	79%
3 Y	29%	68%	32%	60%	80%	56%	99%	93%	84%
5 Y	26%	67%	26%	61%	89%	67%	100%	100%	94%
10 Y	15%	80%	11%	70%	97%	80%	100%	100%	100%
15 Y	7%	100%	0%	64%	100%	78%	100%	100%	100%
20 Y	1%	100%	0%	67%	100%	74%	100%	100%	100%
25 Y	27%	100%	0%	77%	100%	66%	100%	100%	100%

Source: © MSCI Inc. Used with permission

Table 7.3 Long-term correlations between factor indices based on monthly returns from 1975–2014

	Equal Weighted	High Div Yield	Momentum	Quality	Risk Weighted	Value Weighted	Minimum Volatility
Equal Weighted	1.00						
High Div Yield	0.26	1.00					
Momentum	-0.11	-0.03	1.00				
Quality	-0.17	0.41	0.22	1.00			
Risk Weighted	0.81	0.49	0.01	0.01	1.00		
Value Weighted	0.56	0.73	-0.32	0.14	0.52	1.00	
Minimum Volatility	0.13	0.45	0.08	0.19	0.58	0.16	1.00

Source: © MSCI Inc. Used with permission

indices again present a more favorable picture than the individual factors, suggesting a clear long-term diversification effect.

This long-term diversification effect is equally visible in factor correlations, as illustrated in Table 7.3. As the table illustrates, pairwise correlations between factors are generally low and, in the case of value and momentum, expressly negative. Ilmanen and Kizer (2012) found the diversification effect, and the potential improvement in Sharpe ratios, to be higher between factors than between asset classes, but especially so when a long-short approach is used.

Time Dependence

Figure 7.3 shows factor performance relative to the MSCI World over time. Factor returns are clearly time-dependent and given factors have exhibited periods of significant underperformance. Some prominent examples of this include:

- *Quality*: protracted underperformance from around 1975 to around 1988.
- *Value*: underperformance during the tech bubble years of the late 1990s and from around 2006 to the present.
- *Small size:* underperformance during the tech bubble of the late 1990s and during the financial crisis, 2007–2008.
- *Momentum:* sharp underperformance twice in the early 2000s and especially during the early months of 2009.
- *Low volatility:* underperformance in the late 1990s and following the market recovery from 2009.

This pattern partly reflects the particular traits of each factor. Factors such as quality and low volatility are generally more defensive and tend to do well in periods of low or declining growth, whereas small caps and value stocks are

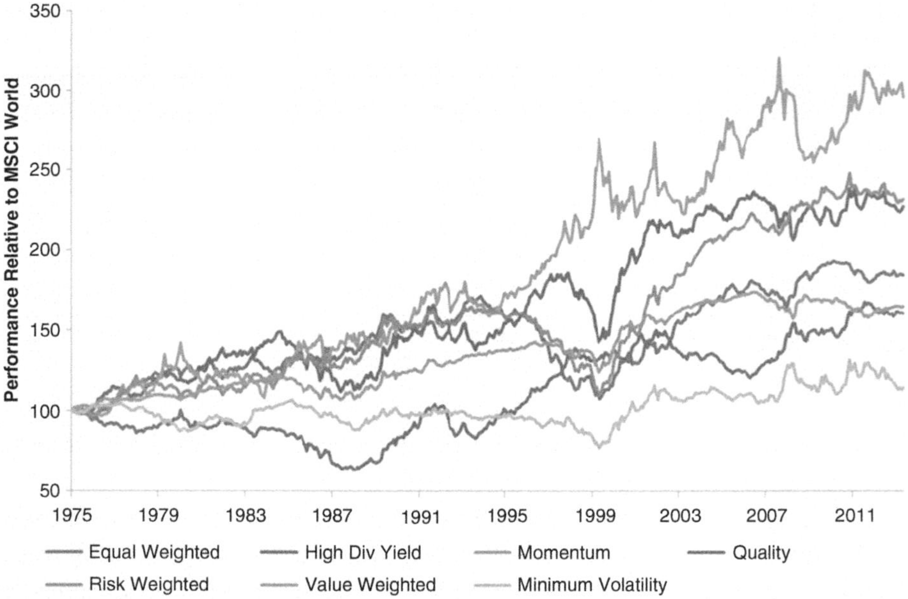

Fig. 7.3 Cumulative excess factor returns versus the MSCI World index, 1975–2014. (Source: © MSCI Inc. Used with permission)

more pro-cyclical. Momentum is somewhere in between and tends to perform the best during periods when growth is stable and both upticks and setbacks are limited. This factor, on the other hand, tends to suffer during periods of sudden changes in market sentiment. A case in point was early 2009, which saw a sharp market recovery after the significant losses seen from 2007 to 2008. In such periods, the "winners" over the past 6 or 12 months of previous market decline will tend to be low-beta stocks which subsequently become the least favored segment of the market during market rallies.

On a more general level, both value and low volatility tend to be more interest rate sensitive than the other factors. A low interest environment, as typically seen in periods of low growth, tends to coincide with underperformance of the value factor but tends to work to the benefit of the low volatility factor.

These performance characteristics translate into different patterns of performance during different phases of the business cycle. We examine this in more detail in the Appendix to the chapter written by Teis Knuthsen.

7.4 Implementation

Implementing a factor approach can encompass the three decision-levels outlined in Fig. 7.4. The first level involves determining the existing portfolio exposures. As discussed in the previous chapter, an analysis such as the one undertaken by professors Ang, Goetzmann and Schaefer for the Norwegian Sovereign Wealth Fund might conclude that the fund in question has an undue exposure to unrewarded macro-risks, such as the level of interest rates

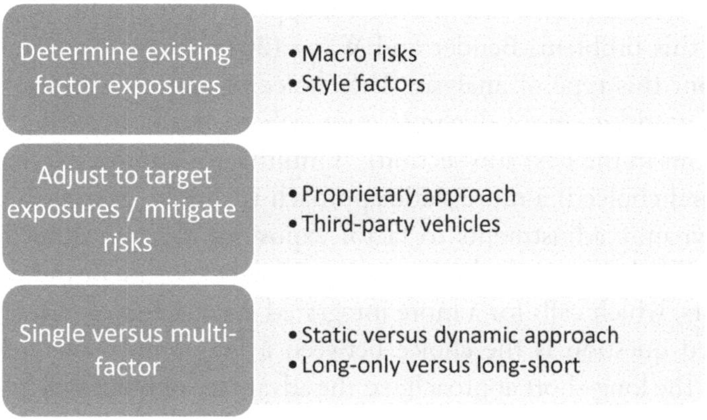

Fig. 7.4 Implementation

or oil prices, which might be mitigated through a different portfolio composition. Or the fund may have a larger than wanted exposure to given style factors and a smaller than wanted exposure to others. The analysis should include both the proprietary part of the portfolio management and any third-party management involved. With respect to the latter, uncovering factor exposures will allow a better segregation of performance into "true alpha" and more or less hidden beta exposures, as discussed in Chap. 2. Israel and Ross (2017) offer a practical framework for measuring factor exposures.

To the extent the first level of analysis uncovers a higher, lower or different factor exposure than that desired, the adjustment can be undertaken either through a proprietary approach or through the use of third-party vehicles. In the former case, the adjustment will involve a bottom-up process in which securities are screened for their exposure to more than one factor. The advantage of this approach is that a more precise overall exposure can be achieved.

Alternatively, third-party vehicles may be used. The advantage of this approach is the greater ease of adjustment and potentially lower administrative and transaction costs. As an example, the managers may conclude that the portfolio's exposure to the value or size factor should be increased or that overall volatility should be reduced and decide to supplement the existing securities portfolio with value, size or low volatility ETFs.

Finally, a general decision regards the choice between a single and a multifactor approach. A single-factor approach clearly offers greater flexibility when third-party vehicles are involved. Exposure to more than one style factor can still be targeted, but this is then done through the use of several single-factor ETFs. The potential disadvantage of the single-factor approach is that interactions between factors may remain undetected. Single-factor vehicles may have a primary exposure to, say, value, but a secondary exposure to, say, size. The bottom-up selection used in a multifactor approach can double-sort factors to minimize this problem. Bender and Wang (2016) suggest a framework for carrying out this type of analysis. The choice of approach is also related to whether a static or more dynamic approach to factor investing is applied (more on this in the next sub-section). A multifactor approach is arguably the most natural choice if a more static approach is chosen, even if this does not exclude dynamic adjustments to factor exposures through other means. Its relevance will also grow the higher is the general exposure of the portfolio to style factors, which calls for a more integrated approach.

A related question is the choice between a long-only versus a long-short approach. The long-short approach has the advantage of offering a full exposure to the factor reward. The empirical research on, for example, the value factor suggests both an outperformance of value stocks and an underperformance of growth stocks. A long-only approach can only buy the supposedly cheap factor but is excluded from selling the supposedly expensive one. Portfolios of long-short factors will also by their very nature have lower internal correlations and be more or less market-neutral.

The potential disadvantages of the long-short approach, on the other hand, is that it implies a greater short-term risk if the long and the short "legs" of the position, for whatever reason, happen to respectively underperform and outperform simultaneously, a problem well-known to traders. Another challenge is that not all stocks lend themselves to shorting at low cost at all times. Finally, the market-neutrality implies that the reward from general market exposure is left out, which can be an issue for institutions which are generally restricted from using leverage.

More generally, investors are well advised to conduct the necessary due diligence when it comes to third-party vehicles. Weighting procedures can vary considerably between funds, giving rise to different factor exposures, and differences in rebalancing routines can imply higher or lower transaction costs.

Should Factor Investing Be Timed?

Factor investing is not *macro-consistent*, as we defined it in Chap. 2: if all investors targeted factor premia at the same time, those premia would by definition disappear. Put differently, someone in the market has to take the opposite view or be unable or unwilling to target factor premia, as argued in the structural/institutional explanations. The growth in factor funds has given rise to concerns for at least two reasons:

- *Commoditization* of factors through smart beta funds and higher general awareness of factor premia in the investing public have led to large inflows and greater positioning than previously. The rules-based nature of factor funds implies that they cannot adjust to potentially crowded trades.
- The *transparency* of a rules-based system has the disadvantage that factor premia might be arbitraged away with greater ease. Related to this, some observers worry that traders might attempt to front-run rules-based rebalancing by factor funds.

Cahan and Luo (2013) discuss metrics to detect crowded trades. Arnott et al. (2016a, b) take a longer-term view and highlight the importance of valuations. The authors argue that both investors and empirical studies have focused excessively on the past performance of factors and ignored relative valuations. If past performance is based in great part, or, exclusively, on rising valuations, the value added is more likely to prove "situational" than structural. As an example, in 1977, at the time when the value premium was first documented in the academic literature, a value portfolio consisting of the 30% of stocks with the highest book-to-price ratio was priced richer to a growth portfolio consisting of 30% of stocks with the lowest book-to-price ratio than at any time since 1926. It never subsequently reached a higher level. Similarly, when the size factor was first documented in 1981, it was close to the end of a powerful run starting in 1975. It subsequently underperformed significantly all the way up to 1999. The authors suggest using relative valuations, comparing the spread between the long and short leg of a factor to its historical record, and find this measure to be a good predictor of subsequent five-year returns. This can be used in a contrarian approach, favoring factors with low valuations with respect to their historical record, and vice versa.

Asness (2016a, b) takes the opposite view.[3] His key objection is that valuations are meaningful only if factor portfolios remain constant over time. The case where this applies the least is the momentum strategy which, with its high turnover, will see the long-short portfolio change significantly over time. But even for a factor like value, its historical record will give significantly different answers depending on whether, for example, a book-to-price or sales-to-price criterion is used. Finally, factor timing involves a cost in terms of a lower diversification. Asness does concede, however, that valuations can become relevant in extreme cases.

Our view is that factor valuations are relevant from a strategic point of view, in the same vein that the CAPE provides useful information for longer-term stock market returns. Even though the caveats stressed by Asness are clearly relevant, factor valuations are likely to offer relevant information in deciding the level of individual and general factor exposures from a strategic point of view. From a more tactical point of view, however, we believe the cyclicality of factors makes a more compelling case for timing the exposure. As already mentioned, we explore this in the Appendix to the chapter.

Is factor investing SAA or TAA? We believe it can be both. It is a natural strategic overlay to the general exposure to asset classes in the SAA, and many portfolios created from a bottom-up approach may, more or less inadvertently, imply exposures to style factors. But factor dynamics also suggest that some variation in factor tilts over time can make sense. We still believe, however, that the lion's share of the TAA should be done through the asset classes themselves. This is the subject of the remaining chapters of the book.

---

[3] See also Asness et al. (2017).

7.5 Conclusion

Factors come in different forms. Macro-factors are general to all asset classes and are generally not investable or rewarded. They are particularly relevant to our understanding of what drives risk and return across asset classes and, as we will see in the following chapters, take up a more prominent role in TAA than in SAA.

Market and style factors, on the other hand, do give rise to market rewards. The discovery in empirical studies of factor rewards beyond that of the general market factor has driven financial theory much closer to the observable realities of markets. It has also caused a general reorientation in our approach to investment management.

Which are the most relevant factors? We have reviewed some of the best documented factors in the empirical literature, but recent studies also emphasize that some of the published factors may in fact be more the result of "creative" research methods than of realistic, investable opportunities in the markets. Factors come with a health warning: focus on the ones that are truly well-documented and which make economic sense.

What gives rise to these factor rewards? In this field, theory has arguably lagged behind the empirical observations. But we are not completely clueless. Factor rewards are likely to reflect risks which come in different shapes and forms. They probably also reflect behavioral and institutional traits of investors which have received much more attention in recent research. Whether or not these explanations capture the whole picture is debatable, but they do serve as a useful starting point.

Ultimately, however, we need to look at market performance in its own right. Style factors have shown an impressive long-term outperformance but we can also see from the data that this comes at the price of periodic underperformance. Can this time dependency be managed? Our answer is that there is some scope in this area using a cyclical approach to factors. This drags factor investing somewhat into the tactical field, even if the objective of diversification in our SAA portfolio must remain key.

The factor approach forces us to answer a central question: unless we are 100% passive investors, what is our current exposure to factors? The most likely result of such an analysis is that we probably have some built-in factor tilts in our portfolio. So there is clear case for dealing with this explicitly. If style factors are important to risk and returns, are we correctly positioned for them in our asset allocation? Put differently, do we currently have the factor exposures we should, or would like to, have? There are no hard and fast rules on how much factor exposure we should seek, and this ultimately must depend on circumstances such as time horizon and maximum tracking error. For most investors, however, factor investing will constitute a relevant complement or overlay to their general exposure to asset classes.

The practical question is how to implement a factor approach. If we have determined our current factor exposure and decided to modify it, we have more than one way to do this. Should we target single factors and or should we adopt a more integrated approach, managing factor exposures as a whole? As we have seen, there are pros and cons to both approaches but the basic trade-off is between flexibility and consistency. Another question is whether we should manage all factor exposure in-house. Given the sufficient computational and management capacity, this might give the optimal result. For many investors, however, the use of third-party vehicles constitutes a convenient and possibly lower cost alternative. This does not, of course, free us from the duty of examining each such vehicle carefully to determine the best fit.

Appendix: Factor Cyclicality

By Teis Knuthsen, Chief Investment Officer, Kirk Kapital

We have seen that style factors offer potential long-term rewards but also that their main risks are macroeconomic in nature. We also noted, however, that each factor reflects these risks differently, giving rise to distinct patterns of performance under different scenarios. This begs the question of whether we can improve our factor strategy by varying our exposure to different factors according to the phase of the business cycle. This appendix takes a closer look at this question.

The Relevance of the Business Cycle

Investors are confronted with a plethora of economic data and an equal amount of takes on economic trends, which suggests a clear advantage of using a simplified and consistent approach to eliminate some of the "noise".

We will contrast factor returns with one broad indicator of the business cycle: the composite leading indicator (CLI) published monthly by the Organisation for Economic Co-operation and Development (OECD).[4] The CLI is an amplitude-adjusted leading indicator for the global economy, and

[4] See further https://data.oecd.org/leadind/composite-leading-indicator-cli.htm

by considering both the level and the change of the CLI, we may divide the economic business cycle into four distinct phases[5]:

- *Recovery*: level of activity below trend, change positive
- *Expansion*: level of activity above trend, change positive
- *Slowdown*: level of activity above trend, change negative
- *Downturn*: level of activity below trend, change negative

The four phases have an average length of approximately nine months and each occurs with a probability of close to 25%, providing a relatively robust data set going back to the 1960s. The CLI is published with a lag of 5–6 weeks but captures a great part of the systematic relationship between economic trends and the performance of financial markets.

We will focus on five MSCI World factor indices (size, value, quality, minimum volatility and momentum) that form the basis for the iShares risk factor ETFs. These series express total returns, measured in euros, and we have limited the investment horizon to 20 years. We match the performance of these factors with the phase of the cycle, using annualized returns and standard deviations.

Figure 7.5 shows the risk/return relationship over the past 20 years for the five risk factors plotted against the MSCI All Countries global benchmark. We see a pattern similar to that shown in Fig. 7.3. In particular, three of the factors exhibit higher returns than the benchmark, in the case of momentum and value with a higher risk. Two of the factors exhibit lower risk but with a level of risk similar to that of the benchmark.[6]

Once we account for the business cycle, however, a much more detailed picture emerges. Table 7.4 shows annualized returns and risk conditioned on the four specific stages of the business cycle.

One general observation is the substantial returns of both the general market and the style factors in the early recovery phase and the equally significant losses during the downturn phase.[7] More specifically, however, we see the significant variation between the different factors in each phase. Value and size outperform significantly in the early part of the business cycle

---

[5] This corresponds to defining the phase of the cycle according to the position of and change in the output gap, as outlined in the following chapter.

[6] We also found (not shown here) that an equally weighted portfolio of the five factors yields a higher risk-adjusted return than the benchmark, in line what we saw previously.

[7] Arguably, markets price both phases incorrectly which highlights the relevance of Warren Buffett's famous dictum: *"be fearful when others are greedy and greedy when others are fearful"*.

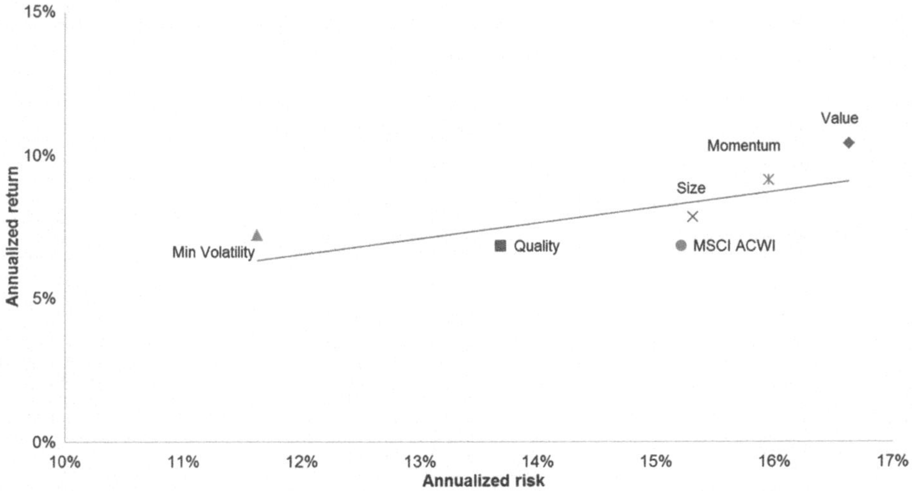

Fig. 7.5 MSCI World risk factors versus MSCI All Countries, 1998–2018, % p.a. (Source: Bloomberg, Macrobond)

Table 7.4 Risk factors and the economic cycle, 1998–2018, % p.a.

	Recovery		Expansion		Slowdown		Downturn		Total	
Factors	Return p.a.	Risk p.a.	Return p.a.	Risk p.a.	Return p.a.	Risk p.a.	Return p.a.	Risk p.a.	Return p.a.	Risk p.a.
MSCI ACWI	41.1%	11.4%	17.5%	10.4%	3.6%	13.5%	-24.5%	19.3%	6.8%	15.2%
Value	54.9%	13.1%	21.4%	10.4%	7.9%	14.0%	-26.7%	20.9%	10.4%	16.6%
Quality	30.9%	11.1%	15.1%	10.3%	6.1%	11.5%	-20.6%	17.7%	6.8%	13.7%
Min Volatility	21.7%	9.9%	11.7%	8.4%	10.5%	11.7%	-12.1%	14.5%	7.2%	11.6%
Size	46.4%	12.3%	19.8%	9.3%	2.7%	13.3%	-25.3%	19.3%	7.8%	15.3%
Momentum	28.4%	11.1%	24.7%	14.9%	8.4%	16.2%	-20.5%	17.1%	9.1%	15.9%

Source: Bloomberg, Macrobond

(the recovery phase), whereas momentum outperforms in the later upswings (the expansion phase) and minimum volatility survives the best in the downturn phase. The business cycle approach suggests a clear potential benefit from weighting the different factors accordingly. Figure 7.6 shows annualized returns across the four economic phases. A particular reading of this chart is that investors stand to benefit from reducing risk exposures during the slowdown phase in preparation for an eventual downturn.

The factor strategy outlined in this appendix is relatively easy to replicate. The composite leading indicator is published monthly, and since the four phases of the business cycle have an average length of nine months, the timing strategy can be implemented with a low frequency of trading in liquid ETFs.

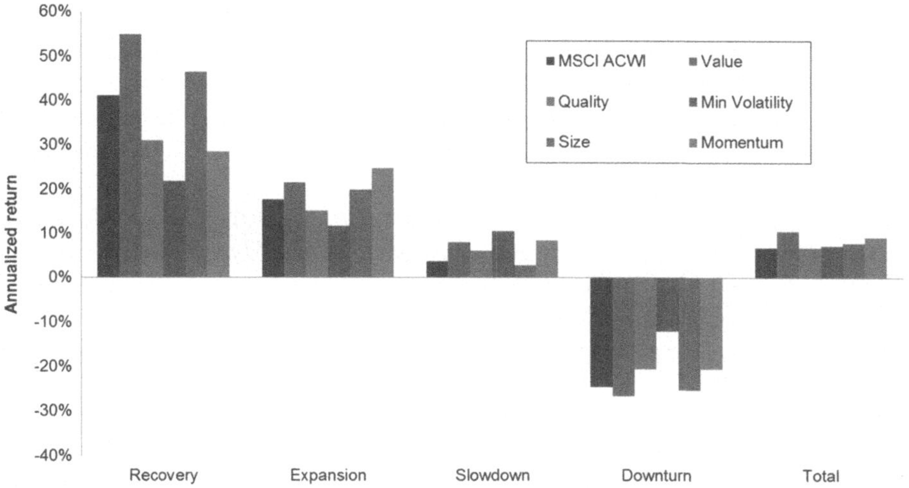

Fig. 7.6 Risk factors and the economic cycle, 1998–2018, % p.a.

References

Amihud, Yakov, and Haim Mendelson. 1986. "Asset Pricing and the Bid–Ask Spread", *Journal of Financial Economics*, December, 17(2), 223–249.

Arnott, Rob, Noah Beck, Vitali Kalesnik, and John West. 2016a. "How Can 'Smart Beta' Go Horribly Wrong?", Research Affiliates, February.

Arnott, Robert D., Noah Beck, and Vitali Kalesnik. 2016b. "To Win with 'Smart Beta' Ask If the Price Is Right", Research Affiliates, June.

Asness, Clifford S. 2016a. "The Siren Song of Factor Timing", *The Journal of Portfolio Management*, Special QES Issue, 42(5), 1–6.

Asness, Clifford S. 2016b. "My Factor Philippic", *AQR Capital Management*.

Asness, Clifford S., Swati Chandra, Antti Ilmanen, and Ronen Israel. 2017. "Contrarian Factor Timing is Deceptively Difficult", *The Journal of Portfolio Management*, 43, 72–87.

Baker, Malcolm, Brendan Bradley, and Jeffrey Wurgler. 2011. "Benchmarks as Limits to Arbitrage: Understanding the Low-Volatility Anomaly", *Financial Analysts Journal*, 67(1), 40–54.

Banz, R. 1981. "The Relationship Between Return and Market Value of Common Stock", *Journal of Financial Economics*, 9, 3–18.

Barberis, Nicholas, Andrei Shleifer, and Robert Vishny. 1998. "A Model of Investor Sentiment", *Journal of Financial Economics*, 49(3), 307–343.

Barberis N., and M. Huang. 2001. "Mental Accounting, Loss Aversion, and Individual Stock Returns", *Journal of Finance*, 56, 1247–1292.

Bender, Jennifer, and Taie Wang. 2016. "Can the Whole Be More than the Sum of the Parts? Bottom-Up Versus Top-Down Multifactor Portfolio Construction", *The Journal of Portfolio Management*, 42(5), 39–50

Black, Angela J., Bin Mao, and David G. McMillan. 2009. "The Value Premium and Economic Activity: Long-Run Evidence from the United States", *Journal of Asset Management*, 10(5), 305–317.

Cahan, Rochester, and Yin Luo. 2013. "Standing Out from the Crowd: Measuring Crowding in Quantitative Strategies", *Journal of Portfolio Management*, 39, 14–23.

Chan, K. C., and Nai-Fu Chen. 1991. "Structural and Return Characteristics of Small and Large Firms", *The Journal of Finance*, 46.

Chen, Nai-fu, and Feng Zhang. 1998. "Risk and Return of Value Stocks", *Journal of Business*, 71(4).

Chordia, T., and L. Shivakumar. 2002. "Momentum, Business Cycle and Time-Varying Expected Returns", *Journal of Finance*, 57, 985–1019.

Daniel, Kent, David Hirshleifer, and Avanidhar Subrahmanyam. 1998. "Investor Psychology and Security Market Under- and Overreactions", *Journal of Finance*, 53, 1839–1886.

Dasgupta, Amil, Andrea Prat, and Michela Verardo. 2011. "The Price Impact of Institutional Herding", *Review of Financial Studies*, 24(3), 892–925.

De Bondt, W., and R. Thaler. 1985. "Does the Stock Market Overreact?", *Journal of Finance*, 40, 793–805.

De Long, J. B., A. Shleifer, L. Summers, and R. Waldmann. 1990. "Noise Trader Risk in Financial Markets", *Journal of Political Economy*, 98, 703–738.

Dichev, I. D. 1998. "Is the Risk of Bankruptcy a Systematic Risk?", *The Journal of Finance*, 53(3), 1131–1147.

Fama, E. F., and K. R. French. 1995. "Size and Book-to-Market Factors in Earnings and Returns", *Journal of Finance*, 50(1), 131–155.

Fama, E. F., and K. R. French. 1998. "Value Versus Growth: The International Evidence", *The Journal of Finance*, 1975–1999.

Frazzini, A., and L. Pedersen. 2014. "Betting Against Beta", *Journal of Financial Economics*, 111, 1–25.

George, Thomas, and Chuan-Yang Hwang. 2004. "The 52-Week High and Momentum Investing", *Journal of Finance*, 59, 2145–2176.

Harvey, C. R., Y. Liu, and H. Zhu. 2016. "… and the Cross-Section of Expected Returns", *The Review of Financial Studies*, 29(1), 5–68.

Hong, Harrison, and Jeremy C. Stein. 1999. "A Unified Theory of Underreaction, Momentum Trading and Overreaction in Asset Markets", *Journal of Finance*, 54, 2143–2184.

Hou, Kewei, Chen Xue, and Lu Zhang. 2017. "Replicating Anomalies", NBER Working Paper No. 23394.

Hsu, J. C., H. Kudoh, T. Yamada. 2013. "When Sell-Side Analysts Meet High-Volatility Stocks: An Alternative Explanation for the Low-Volatility Puzzle", *Journal of Investment Management*, 11(2), 28–46.

Ilmanen, Antti, and Jared Kizer. 2012. "The Death of Diversification Has Been Greatly Exaggerated", *Journal of Portfolio Management*, Spring, 38(3), 15–27.
Israel, Ronen, and Adrienne Ross. 2017. "Measuring Factor Exposures: Uses and Abuses", *The Journal of Alternative Investments*, 20(1), 10–25.
Jensen, Gerald, and Jeffrey Mercer. 2002. "Monetary Policy and the Cross-Section of Expected Stock Returns", *Journal of Financial Research*, Spring, 55, 125–139.
Kumar, Alok. 2009. "Who Gambles in the Stock Market?", *Journal of Finance*, August, 64(4), 1889–1933.
Lakonishok, Josef, Andrei Shleifer, and Robert W. Vishny. 1992a. "The Impact of Institutional Trading on Stock Prices", *Journal of Financial Economics*, 32, 23–43.
Lakonishok, Josef, Andrei Shleifer, and Robert W. Vishny. 1992b. "The Structure and Performance of the Money Management Industry", *Brookings Papers on Economic Activity: Microeconomics.*
Lakonishok, J., A. Shleifer, and R. W. Vishny. 1994. "Contrarian Investment, Extrapolation, and Risk", *Journal of Finance*, 49, 1541–1578.
La Porta, Rafael, Josef Lakonishok, Andrei Shleifer, and Robert Vishny. 1997. "Good News for Value Stocks: Further Evidence on Market Efficiency", *Journal of Finance*, 52, 859–874.
Liu, W. 2006. "A Liquidity-Augmented Capital Asset Pricing Model", *Journal of Financial Economics*, 82(3), 631–671.
Liu, X., and L. Zhang. 2008. "Momentum Profits, Factor Pricing, and Macroeconomic Risk", *Review of Financial Studies*, 21, 2417–2448.
Lo, A., and A. MacKinlay. 1990. "Data-Snooping Biases in Tests of Financial Asset Pricing Models", *Review of Financial Studies*, 3, 431–467.
Shleifer, A., and R. Vishny. 1990. "Equilibrium Short Horizons of Investors and Firms", *American Economic Review Papers and Proceedings*, 80, 148–153.
Yee, Kenton K. 2010. "Combining Fundamental Measures for Stock Selection", in Handbook of Quantitative Finance and Risk Management, Springer.
Zhang, Lu. 2005. "The Value Premium", *The Journal of Finance*, 60(1), 67–102.

Part III

Tactical Asset Allocation

8

Tactical Macro-Drivers

"Successful investing is about having everyone agree with you ... later"
—Joseph C. Robillard

In this chapter, we lay the foundation for a business cycle approach to TAA which will be elaborated further in Chap. 9. Section 8.2 first outlines standard business cycle analysis and the dating of business cycles. We will then shift our attention to the concept of the output gap and its evolution over time, giving rise to four separate phases for the economy. Section 8.3 discusses the relevance of this to monetary policy and examines how changes in policy rates are reflected in the yield curve.

8.1 Why Not Ignore the Short Term?

Proponents of a pure long-term approach to asset allocation, that is, having no or very limited tolerance bands around the SAA, point to the evidence of persistent long-term risk premia, which are particularly evident in the equity space. This evidence is hard to refute and constitutes the main reason for placing the main emphasis on SAA. So why not stick 100% to the SAA with no short-term adjustments aside from rebalancing?

Throughout the previous chapters of the book, we have highlighted some of the challenges to the pure SAA approach. To recapitulate:

H. Lumholdt, *Strategic and Tactical Asset Allocation*,
https://doi.org/10.1007/978-3-319-89554-3_8

- *Long-term returns*: the historical record of asset returns offers only limited guidance for time horizons such as ten years where cyclical effects will need to be balanced with more structural factors. Forward-looking models can clearly help, but expectations of full or partial reversion to the mean is the best we can offer when it comes to valuations.
- *Time diversification:* a longer time horizon works to the benefit of investors, but the argument can only be pushed so far. Uncertainty over the terminal value of the investment grows as the time horizon gets longer and, more importantly, so does within-period uncertainty.
- *Portfolio optimization:* mean-variance optimization offers a rational approach to portfolio composition, which is more relevant to SAA than to TAA. But the robustness of this approach depends critically on the reliability of the data input and statistical assumptions which are often challenged in the practical application.

Is the short term not prone to even more uncertainty than the long term? In one respect it clearly is. Market sentiment can exert a very powerful influence in the short run and is in part driven by hard-to-model behavioral factors. In contrast, however, the relationship between asset returns and the performance of the economy, as represented by the *business cycle*, gets clearer in the shorter term. This is a key motivation for including this information in our investment decisions and allowing room for tactical adjustments to our portfolio.

8.2 The Business Cycle

The Standard Business Cycle

The traditional analysis of business cycles focuses on four moments:

- Expansion
- Peak
- Contraction
- Trough

A much-used definition of a *recession* is a contraction in GDP over two successive quarters. The National Bureau of Economic Research (NBER), which in the US is officially in charge of dating the business cycle, uses a broader, and more demanding, definition:[1]

[1] See also http://www.nber.org/cycles/jan08bcdc_memo.html

A recession is a significant decline in economic activity spread across the economy, lasting more than a few months, normally visible in real GDP, real income, employment, industrial production, and wholesale-retail sales. A recession begins just after the economy reaches a peak of activity and ends as the economy reaches its trough. Between trough and peak, the economy is in an expansion.

This broader definition is justified on several grounds. Firstly, a decline in GDP sometimes occurs because of a contraction in specific sectors of the economy, for example, due to shocks of one kind or another. This can technically lead to a drop in GDP, but if it does not affect other parts of the economy to the same degree it might be misleading. Secondly, while the NBER recognizes the GDP as the single best measure of aggregate economic activity, its mandate is to date the cycle on a monthly basis; the GDP is published quarterly. The NBER's dating of the cycle is the most reliable source for empirical studies. But it has the drawback that turning points in the cycle are published with a considerable delay, often upwards of a year. Other, timelier, indicators are therefore needed in shorter-term analyses.

The NBER has dated cycles back to the mid-nineteenth century. For the period since the end of WWII, it has identified 11 full cycles, as illustrated in Table 8.1.

The average cycle has lasted about six years, but as can be seen from the table, the range of variation is considerable. One pattern is clear, however. The average length of the cycles (trough to trough or peak to peak) has increased

Table 8.1 Dating the business cycle

Business cycle Reference dates		Duration in months			
Peak	Trough	Contraction	Expansion	Cycle	
		Peak to trough	Previous trough to this peak	Trough from previous trough	Peak from previous peak
Nov 1948	Oct 1949	11	37	48	45
July 1953	May 1954	10	45	55	56
Aug 1957	April 1958	8	39	47	49
April 1960	Feb 1961	10	24	34	32
Dec 1969	Nov 1970	11	106	117	116
Nov 1973	March 1975	16	36	52	47
Jan 1980	July 1980	6	58	64	74
July 1981	Nov 1982	16	12	28	18
July 1990	March 1991	8	92	100	108
March 2001	Nov 2001	8	120	128	128
Dec 2007	June 2009	18	73	91	81
Average		11.1	58.4	69.5	68.5

Source: US National Bureau of Economic Research

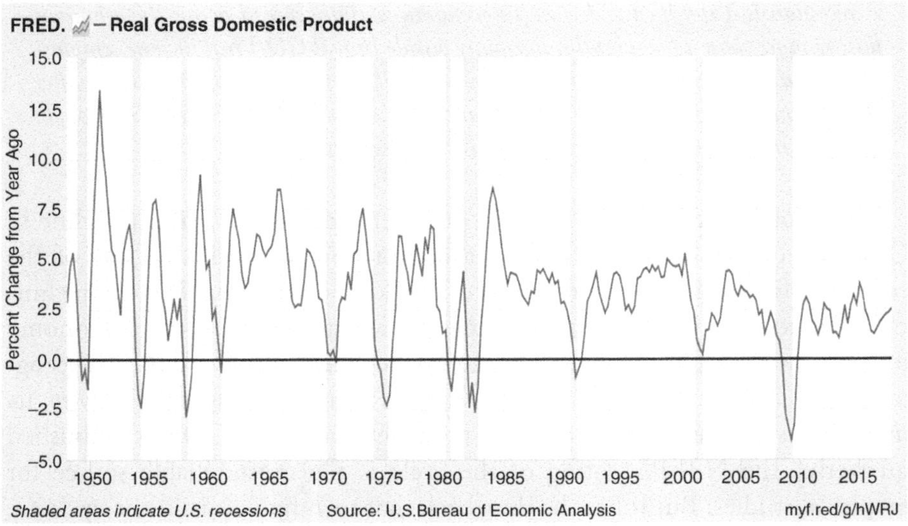

Fig. 8.1 US real GDP, year-on-year change. (Source: The Federal Reserve of Saint Louis)

considerably since the mid-1980. Expansions have become more long-drawn while recessions have become less frequent, albeit no less severe (the latest one being a case in point). This is illustrated in Fig. 8.1 which shows year-on-year growth in real GDP where the shaded areas indicate periods of recession.

The possible reasons for the longer expansions include:

- Better inventory and supply-chain management
- The shift toward a greater weight of less cyclical service-producing sectors
- The growth in the size of the public sector which, by its nature, is less cyclical
- An increased role of built-in stabilizers such as unemployment insurance and features of the tax system
- The greater use of counter-cyclical policies

Some Salient Features of Business Cycles

All components of the GDP, except public consumption, tend to track the general business cycle. But their degree of cyclicality varies considerably. The short-term growth in *household consumption* tends to track short-term GDP very closely, as shown in Fig. 8.2, which is unsurprising given its weight in the GDP (approx. 70%). But this stability applies only to consumption of *non-durable goods* (approx. 15% of GDP) and *services* (approx. 45% of GDP).

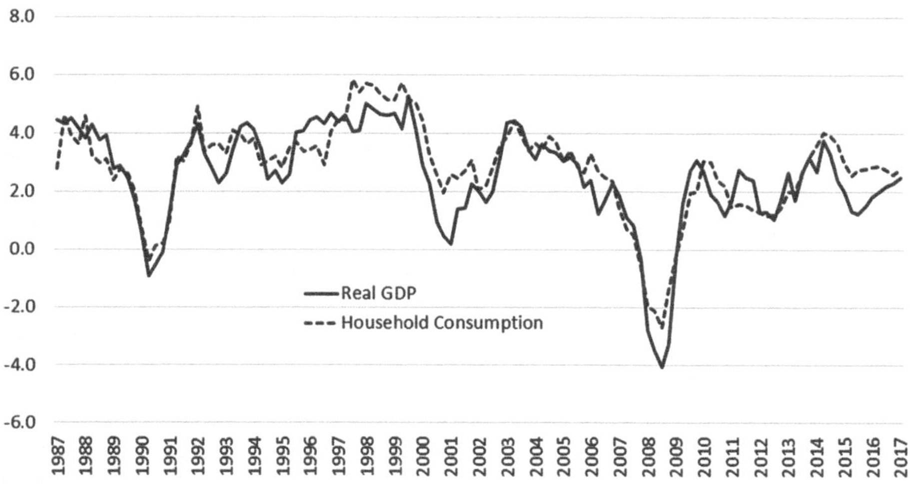

Fig. 8.2 US real GDP versus household consumption, year-on-year change. (Source: US Bureau of Economic Analysis)

Consumption of *durable goods* (approx. 10% of GDP) exhibits considerably greater variation than overall GDP.

The same applies to *Fixed investment* (approx. 17% of GDP), encompassing both non-residential investment in structures, equipment and software (approx. 14% of GDP) and residential investment (approx. 3.5% of GDP), which exhibits even greater variation than durables consumption. Changes in *business inventories* often net out over shorter periods, but can reinforce more significant cyclical changes. Sustained upswings leading to expectations of higher further sales can increase desired levels of inventories, boosting production levels. Shortfalls in sales during downturns, on the other hand, often lead to involuntary inventory accumulation, prompting greater reductions in production levels than would otherwise have occurred. Finally, the international business cycle can clearly exert an influence through net exports. This can be very pronounced for small open economies, but tends to be more muted for a large economy such as the US where net exports take up a limited weight. Still, the sovereign debt crisis in the euro area, which followed the Great Recession in the US in relatively short order, arguably contributed to slowing the US recovery and added to deflationary pressures.

These differences in variability are illustrated in Fig. 8.3 which contrasts the growth in overall GDP with the growth in durables consumption and fixed investment. A consequence of this pattern is that the most volatile components of GDP often account for a major part of the swings in activity, even though their relative weight in overall GDP is smaller than that of the more stable components.

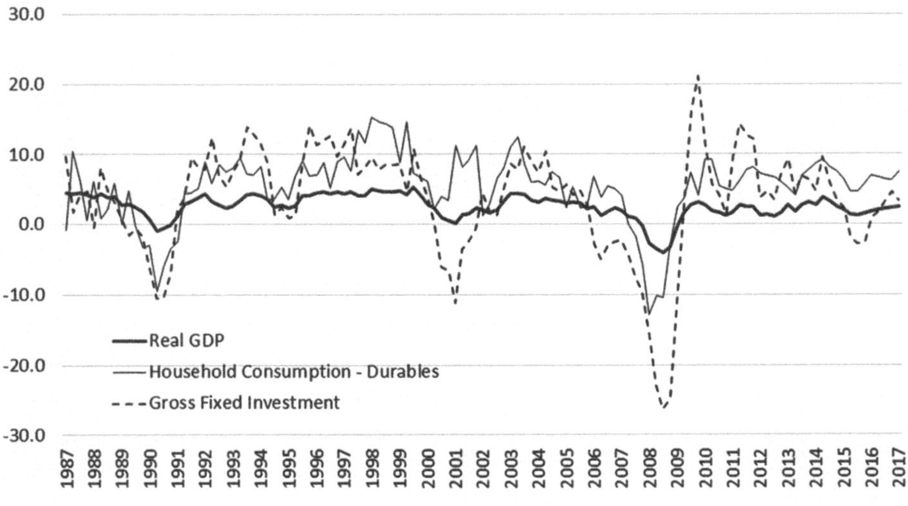

Fig. 8.3 US real GDP versus volatile components, year-on-year change. (Source: US Bureau of Economic Analysis)

Corporate Profits

Corporate profits exhibit a cyclical variation several times higher than that of overall GDP, and this tends to be particularly pronounced around turning points in the cycle. This is illustrated in Fig. 8.4 which plots the annual change in nominal GDP on the left axis against the annual change in corporate profits on the right axis. Note that the scales have been manipulated so as to better discern the cyclicality of profits.

One factor behind this is *operating leverage*, the ratio of fixed to variable costs. Depending on the industry, the firm's plant and machinery may be so specific to its production that no secondary market for its capital exists. At the same time, management may judge that the cyclical downturn will prove temporary and decide to keep hard-to-replace capital intact. When a high proportion of cost is effectively fixed in the short run, a pronounced downturn will reduce operating margins, an effect which is then reversed in a subsequent upturn. Operating margins tend to track *capacity utilization* (see below), shrinking when it decreases and expanding when it increases.

Another general observation is that corporate profits often lead the general business cycle during downturns, a phenomenon which was especially visible in the period immediately before the Great Recession from December 2007 to June 2009. A drop in sales will show up in profits immediately, but order backlogs still need to be filled and investment plans finalized before firms will proceed to reduce their overall business activity.

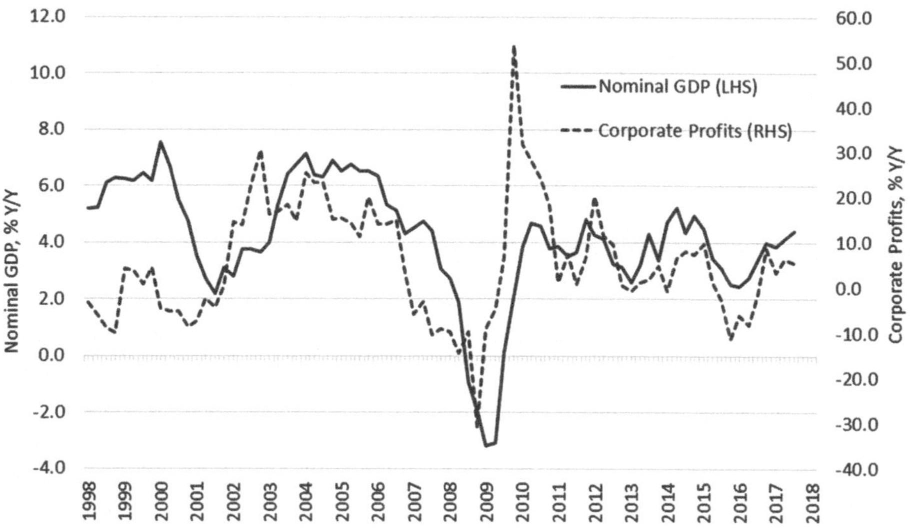

Fig. 8.4 Nominal GDP and corporate profits after tax, including inventory valuation adjustment (IVA) and capital consumption adjustment (CCAdj), forwarded one quarter. (Source: US Bureau of Economic Analysis)

The Output Gap

We noted in Chap. 4 that longer-term growth in the economy is governed primarily by the supply side. *Potential GDP* can be defined as the level of output consistent with a full, but not excessive, use of the economy's factors of production. *Actual GDP*, on the other hand, is driven primarily by aggregate demand, and both its level and growth rate at any given time can vary from that of potential GDP. The *output gap* is defined as the percentage difference between actual and potential GDP.

When actual GDP is below its potential, the output gap is negative, which implies that the economy has slack resources and is not using its full potential. When actual GDP is above its potential, on the other hand, the output gap is positive, and the economy's factors of production are being overutilized. The general notion is that neither situation can be chronic. A situation of underutilization of resources should eventually prompt a cheapening of the factors of production and induce renewed activity, whereas a situation of overutilization should eventually prompt a slowdown as capacity constraints set in and upward pressure on the price of resources impedes further expansion. The dominant view, however, is that such adjustments may take longer than what is acceptable. Protracted downturns might become self-reinforcing, especially if they lead to deflation, whereas excessive rates of inflation can become difficult to revert. This is the key justification for stabilization policies, aimed at avoiding both extremes. Nowadays, not least in the US, stabilization policies have become the domain of the central bank, the Federal Reserve, while changes to fiscal and other macroeconomic policies are often motivated by other than cyclical factors.[2] We will return to monetary policy in Sect. 8.3.

Estimating Potential GDP

In the US, the most prominent provider of output gap estimates is the Congressional Budget Office (CBO). The CBO uses a *production function approach* which relates input (or "supply") to potential output (i.e. potential GDP). The input is potential supply of labor, which is combined with estimates of the capital stock and of total factor productivity[3] to estimate potential GDP. Sectors vary in their dependency on capital and labor and estimates are therefore made separately for non-farm business, farm sector, the federal government, state and local governments, households and non-profit institutions.

The potential supply of labor is estimated on the basis of trends in participation rates in different segments of the population. This is then combined with estimates of the natural rate of unemployment to create estimates of potential employment for each sector. The natural rate of unemployment is also known as the NAIRU, that is, the non-accelerating inflation rate of unemployment. A rate of unemployment equal to the natural rate is generally considered to be consistent with a level of actual GDP at the same level as potential GDP, that is, with an output gap of zero. The difference between the actual rate of unemployment and the natural rate is referred to as the *unemployment gap*, which is a close cousin of the output gap. A negative unemployment gap tends to coincide with a positive output gap and vice versa, as shown in Fig. 8.5. The two measures therefore convey similar cyclical information.

An alternative approach to that of the CBO is to model the growth in potential GDP as a *trend growth*. The most widely used technique is the so-called Hodrick-Prescott[4] filter which is designed to remove the cyclical component (in this case, the business cycle) from a time series.

---

[2] This, of course, does not imply that the Fed will ignore the cyclical impact of such policies. At the time of writing, a key question is whether the tax cuts implemented by the Trump administration will imply a boost to growth which might accelerate the path toward normalization of the Fed's policy rates.

[3] As mentioned in Chap. 4, total factor productivity is associated with technological progress, improvements in efficiency and so on. Technically, it is the residual output which is not explained by the labor and capital input. The CBO estimates that labor and capital account for only about 60% of the growth in real non-farm business GDP since 1950. See further Shackleton (2018).

[4] See further Hodrick and Prescott (1997).

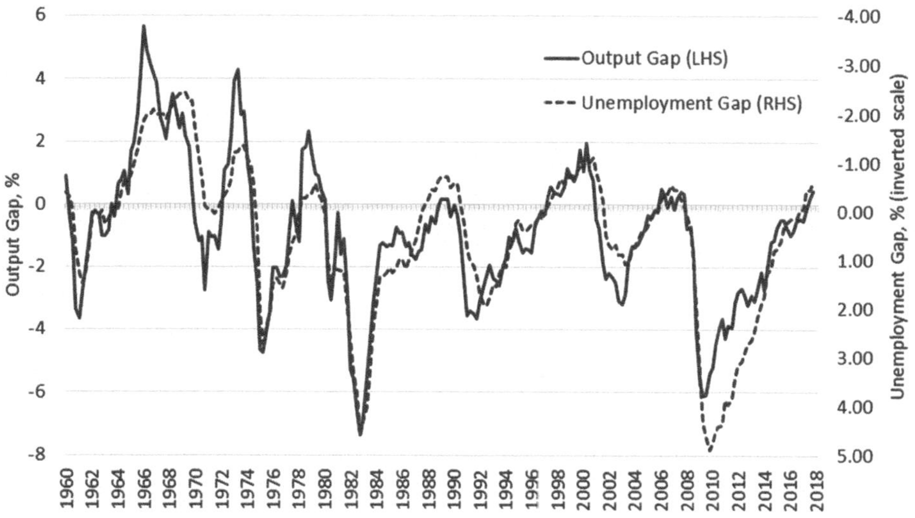

Fig. 8.5 Output gap versus unemployment gap. (Source: US Congressional Budget Office and Bureau of Labor Statistics)

Both approaches have their advantages and drawbacks. The production function approach sometimes captures structural changes in the economy too slowly. As an example, the CBO has been criticized for underestimating the growth in productivity in the late 1990s, leading to overly pessimistic estimates of potential GDP. Because the trend method will follow movements in actual GDP more closely, it has a better chance of capturing such changes. The flipside of this, however, is that large cyclical fluctuations might lead to changes in estimates of potential GDP using the trend approach, without any true structural changes having taken place. Imbalances in the economy might then be underestimated. The production factor approach has the appeal that it is based on observable economic drivers rather than merely statistical trends.

Whereas the level of unemployment provides an indication of slack in the labor market, capacity utilization provides an indication of spare capacity with respect to capital. It is measured as the ratio of current output to a maximum sustainable level of output. This is most meaningful, and measurable, for goods producing industries, and the Fed publishes this statistic on a monthly basis covering industries in manufacturing, mining and utilities. Capacity utilization is never 100%, and the maximum level since 1980 has been 85. To get to a comparable index for the labor market, the current unemployment rate can be subtracted from 100. An average of this and the level of capacity utilization provides an overall measure of resource utilization, a practical proxy for the output gap (Fig. 8.6).

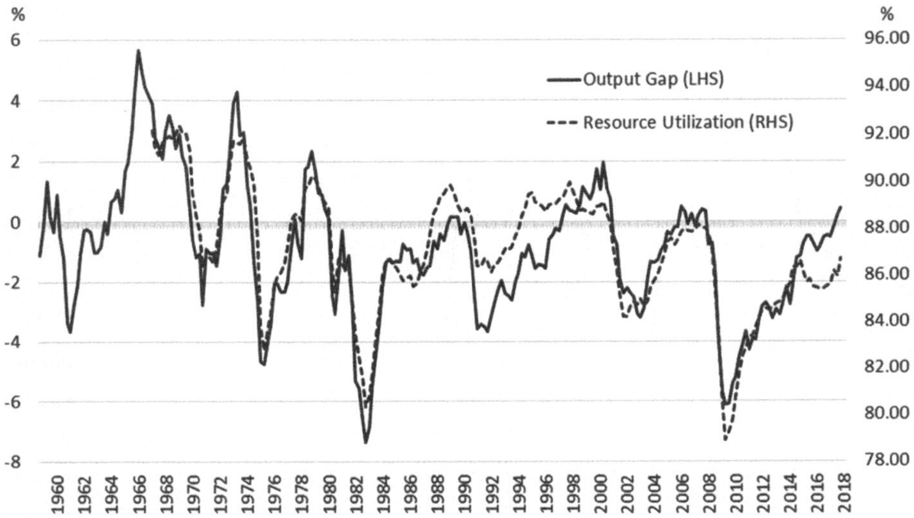

Fig. 8.6 Output gap versus resource utilization. (Source: Bureau of Labor Statistics and the Federal Reserve)

The output gap, as well as the NAIRU, is based on the notion that the economy has an upper capacity limit beyond which inflationary pressures will, sooner or later, set in. This does not imply, however, that any precise relationship between the output gap and inflation can be established. This has led some observers to discard the concept altogether. We referred to the Great Moderation in Chap. 4, the observation that inflation in developed economies has generally been exceptionally low since the early 1980s. This probably reflects both the effects of globalization and inflation expectations that have been held in check by the generally low level of economic growth and the greater credibility of central banks. More recently, the severity of the Great Recession may have instilled caution among wage-earners and a reluctance to press employers for higher compensation. These are the likely reasons why the "Phillips curve", the relationship between unemployment and inflation (or wage growth), has been practically "flattened out of existence".

A study by economists from the Federal Reserve (Peach et al. 2011) puts this into perspective. The authors note that the linkage between resource utilization and inflation was indeed supported by the data from WWII to around the mid-1980s, but gets weak thereafter. Using the unemployment gap as a measure of labor market slack, they show that its impact on inflation is significant only when it moves beyond a threshold of +/−1.56 percentage points.

This threshold has barely broken to the upside in recent decades but was passed significantly to the downside in the recent crisis, when inflation moved duly lower. Figure 8.7 shows this in terms of the output gap, labor costs and

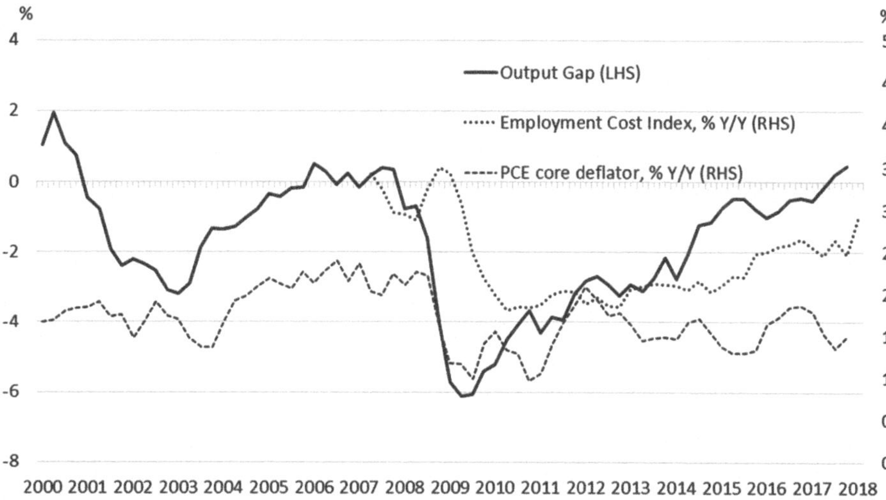

Fig. 8.7 Output gap and labor costs. (Source: The Congressional Budget Office and the Bureau of Labor Statistics)

the Personal Consumption Expenditure (PCE) core deflator. Labor costs do indeed appear to exhibit mild upward pressures, but there are so far few signs that this has been passed on to core inflation. A more significantly positive output gap would likely change this. The Phillips curve might still be dormant. But, to quote Mark Twain, rumors of its death have been exaggerated.

The Business Cycle and the Output Gap

While the general observation is that expansions have become more protracted, Table 8.1 also illustrates that there are clearly no hard and fast rules as to their duration.[5] Comparing the length of a given expansion to the historical average therefore provides only limited guidance. The level of the output gap, and its change over time, allows us to think in terms of different phases in the economic cycle which go beyond the simple observation of whether it is expanding or contracting at any given time.

To conceptualize, in order to move from a zero to a negative output gap over a given period, the growth in actual GDP must have been lower than the growth in potential GDP; to move from a zero to a positive output gap, actual growth must have been higher than potential. Starting from either a negative or positive output gap, we can generalize as indicated in Fig. 8.8:

[5] In the words of former Fed Chair, Janet Yellen, *"Expansions don't die of old age"*. See further https://www.federalreserve.gov/mediacenter/files/FOMCpresconf20151216.pdf

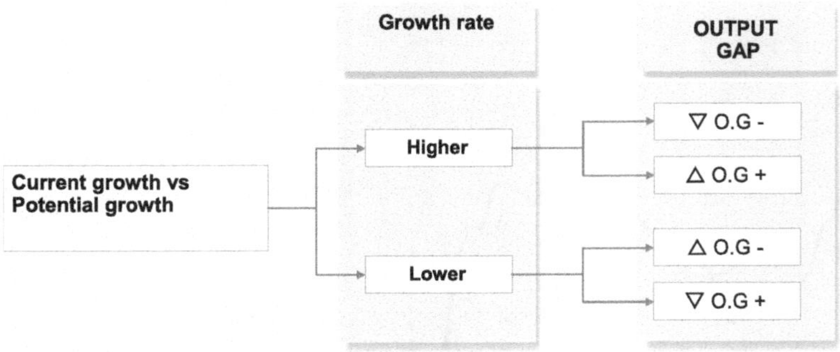

Fig. 8.8 Actual versus potential growth and the output gap

When the economy grows at a rate above its longer-term potential, it either diminishes a negative output gap or adds to a positive output gap. When it grows below its potential rate, it either increases a negative output gap or reduces a positive one.

A practical illustration of such growth cycles is given in Fig. 8.9, which contrasts the output gap with the difference between annual growth in actual and potential GDP over the past 30 years. Higher actual than potential growth throughout the first half of the 1990s gradually eliminated the negative output gap and created a positive gap in the second half of the decade. The low growth, and the recession, that followed in the early 2000s created a new negative gap which was gradually reduced up until around 2005. The Great Recession from December 2007 to June 2009 created a new (and giant) negative output gap which has now finally been eliminated after about eight years of actual GDP growth above its potential rate.

Using the concept of the output gap, we can think of the economy as going through different phases. This is illustrated in stylized form in Fig. 8.10. Beginning in Phase I, the level of actual GDP is below that of potential GDP, so the output gap is negative. But the growth in actual GDP is above that of potential GDP, so this negative output gap is diminishing. If the higher than potential growth continues, the negative output gap will turn positive and will grow more positive the longer this growth outperformance lasts. This is referred to as Phase II. Sometime into Phase II, growth again falls below potential and the economy transitions to Phase III where the positive output gap is gradually reduced. If this lower than potential growth continues, the economy will eventually reach Phase IV where the output gap gets increasingly negative. At some point into Phase IV, actual growth again exceeds potential growth, and the economy is back in Phase I.

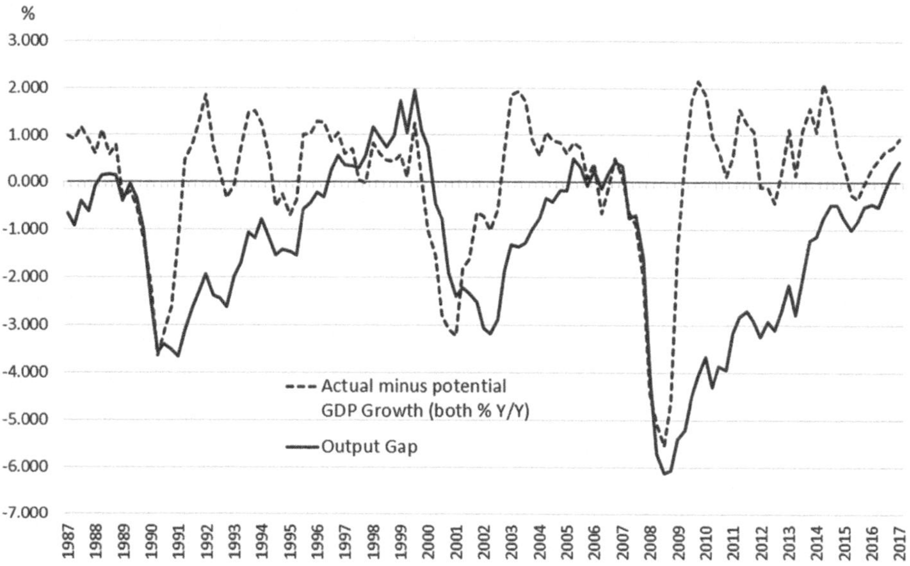

Fig. 8.9 Actual versus potential GDP growth, 1987–2017. (Source: US Bureau of Economic Analysis)

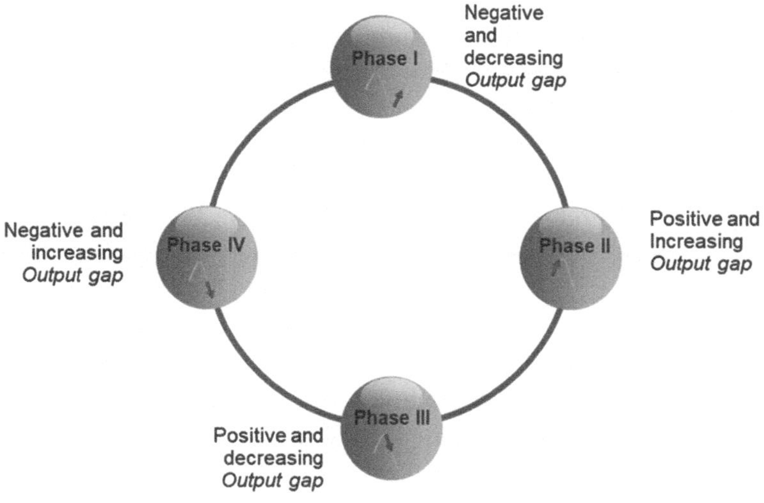

Fig. 8.10 The economy in four phases

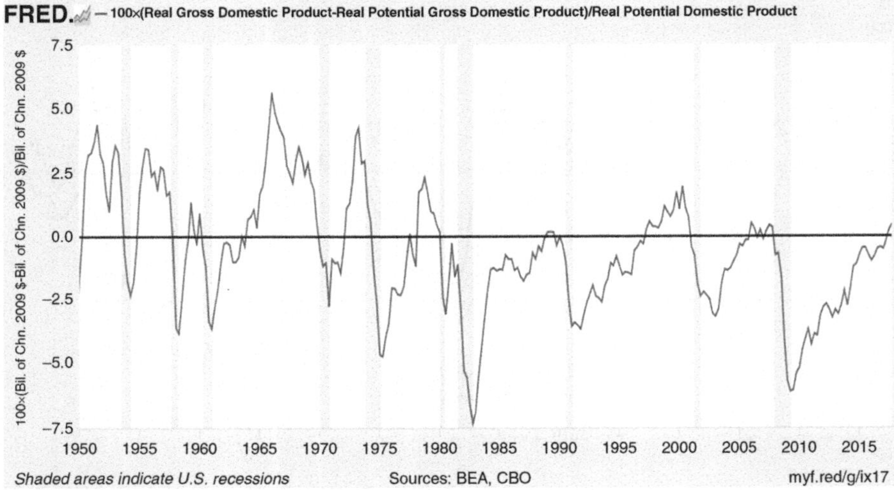

Fig. 8.11 The output gap over the business cycle. (Source: The Federal Reserve of Saint Louis)

How well does this describe actual experience? Figure 8.11 shows the cycle of the output gap since 1950 with recessions indicated by the shaded areas. Two observations are worth noting:

- The I through IV sequence does not always apply. Over the shorter term (typically two to six quarters), both Phases I and III have occasionally been followed by reversals back to a previous phase.[6] This highlights the importance of *growth cycles* within periods of expansion.
- Recessions have practically always been preceded by periods with a positive output gap, and tend to occur either in Phase III or IV. The main exception to this was the second part of the "double dip" recession in the early 1980s.

Although reversals to a previous phase constitute a complication, as we shall see in the next chapter, identifying which phase the economy is *currently* in can serve as a useful basis for baseline TAA strategies, whereas the probability of transitions to a different phase is relevant to building risk scenarios. We will look closely at the characteristics of each phase in the next chapter.

[6] Note that only these two reversals are technically possible. The economy can revert back to Phase IV from Phase I on a slowdown in growth. But it cannot move from Phase IV to Phase III without first having been in Phases I and II. Similarly, an increase in growth during a Phase III can move the economy back to Phase II, but it cannot move from Phase II to Phase I without first having been in Phases III and IV.

8.3 Monetary Policy and the Output Gap

The Federal Reserve has the dual mandate of promoting maximum employment and price stability. In the spirit of the Taylor rule discussed in Chap. 4, we might rephrase this to imply an output gap of zero and a rate of inflation of 2% (the latter being the official target of the Fed). Inspecting the historical record, it is clear that a level of zero for the output gap has been more the exception than the rule, highlighting the significant challenges to monetary policy. Price stability, on the other hand, has certainly been the rule in recent years, and the concerns of policy-makers have mainly been risks to the downside.

How relevant is the output gap for actual monetary policy? Figure 8.12 shows the output gap and the effective Fed funds rate since the mid-1980s. As can be seen, turning points in monetary policy have tended to coincide with reversals in the output gap from either positive or negative levels. The record since 2009, however, constitutes a clear exception. The most obvious reason for this has been the severity of the Great Recession and the perceived risk of outright deflation. Another possible concern has been the potentially greater sensitivity of the economy, and the financial markets, to higher interest rates. As relevant as these considerations have been, current estimates of the output gap suggest that such concerns should now have been overcome.

Some observers, however, argue that the decline in the unemployment rate in particular overstates the improvement in the labor market due to the decline in the *labor participation rate*, that is, the labor force as a percentage of the non-institutional population (above the age of 16). The participation rate stood at 66% in December of 2007 when the Great Recession began. By January of 2018, it stood at 62.7%, more than 3 percentage points below the pre-crisis level. This explains part of the decrease in the unemployment rate.[7] Another relevant measure is the *prime employment rate*, that is, the number of workers between the ages of 25 and 54 currently employed, as a percentage of the total population. This rate stood at 79.8% by December of 2007 and was 78.9% by the end of 2017, or nearly a full percentage point below the pre-crisis level. Is the US then truly at "full employment"?

---

[7] To illustrate the mechanics of this, suppose that the number of potential workers is 100 and that 60 are currently employed while 5 are unemployed. The labor force (sum of employed and unemployed) is therefore 65 and the unemployment rate (unemployed as a percentage of the labor force) is 7.7%. If one person moves from being unemployed to being employed, the unemployment rate will drop from 7.7% to 6.1%. But if that person instead leaves the labor force, it will decrease from 65 to 64 but the unemployment rate will still fall, in this case from 7.7% to 6.3%, without any improvement in employment having taken place.

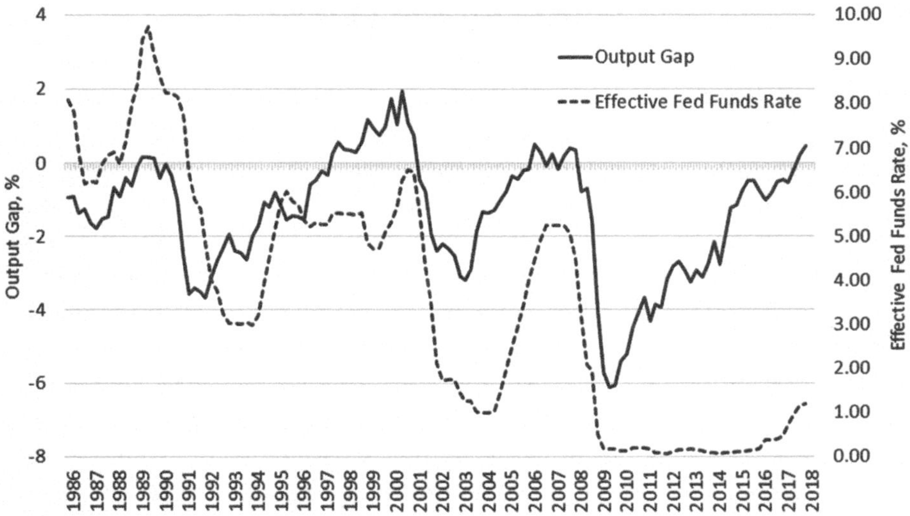

Fig. 8.12 The output gap and the Fed funds rate. (Source: The U.S. Congressional Budget Office and the Federal Reserve)

Relevant as these observations are, the central question is how much of the decline in the participation rate is due to cyclical as opposed to structural (demographic) factors. The cyclical factors refer to the observation that severe recessions often lead some workers to give up on finding work and leave the workforce altogether. Some of these workers might arguably decide to re-enter the workforce if labor demand gets sufficiently strong.

Against this, however, stands the observation that the decline in labor participation began well before the recent crisis and has identifiable demographic roots. This is illustrated in Fig. 8.13 which shows both the participation rate and the employment rate. Labor participation began decreasing already around the year 2000 reflecting in part the entry into retirement of the first part of the cohort known as the baby boomers, born between 1946 and 1964.

Table 8.2 shows the current and projected age distribution of the non-institutional population along with the participation rate in each age segment. As the table shows, the percentage weight of people in the highest age categories and their participation rate have been increasing in recent years, and the Bureau of Labor Statistics (BLS) projects that this trend will continue. In contrast, the participation rate of the youngest segment of the population has been decreasing, reflecting a greater proportion of the young seeking college education (which might auger well for longer-term productivity).

Even though the participation rate in the highest age categories is on the rise, it is still significantly below that of the rest of the workforce. The net

Fig. 8.13 Participation rate and prime-age employment rate. (Source: US Bureau of Labor Statistics)

Table 8.2 Age distribution and the participation rate

Group	Civilian noninstitutional population							
	Percent distribution				Participation rate			
	1996	2006	2016	2026	1996	2006	2016	2026
Total, 16 years and older	100	100	100	100	66.8	66.2	62.8	61
16 to 24	16.1	16.1	15.2	13.6	65.5	60.6	55.2	52.5
25 to 54	57.6	54.6	49.6	47.4	83.8	82.9	81.3	81.6
55 to 64	10.5	13.7	16.3	14.9	57.9	63.7	64.1	66.6
65 to 74	9.1	8.2	11.2	13.6	17.5	23.6	26.8	30.2
75 and older	6.7	7.4	7.7	10.5	4.7	6.4	8.4	10.8

Source: Data from the US Bureau of Labor Statistics

result of the projections is therefore a continued decrease in the overall participation rate as the average age of the population continues to increase. From this perspective, the level of the unemployment does arguably imply full employment and a limit on the growth in labor supply going forward.

Given that inflationary pressures still look muted, the Fed is probably not "behind the curve", but the case for normalizing monetary policy will get stronger the deeper the economy moves into Phase II. The key question for markets is at what pace, and to what extent, this will happen. In the next section, we will examine how changes in Fed policy rates tend to influence the yield curve.

8.4 Monetary Policy and Yield Curve Dynamics

Figure 8.14 depicts the *slope of the yield curve*, represented by the yield spread between ten-year and two-year US Treasury bonds, against the level of the *Fed funds rate* (inverted right-hand scale) over the past 30 years. The slope of the yield curve is a useful proxy for the *perceived stance* of *monetary policy*. As discussed in Chap. 4, the steeper is the yield curve the more upward sloping is the structure of forward rates, and a steep curve is therefore consistent with the view that monetary policy is currently lax, and that future monetary tightening will follow once excess capacity in the economy and disinflationary pressures have been reduced. Conversely, a flat or inverted curve signals that monetary policy is perceived to be tight. Steep curves have therefore tended to coincide with low levels of policy rates and vice versa.

The slope of the curve has exhibited significant volatility in the years following the Great Recession, mostly driven by the long end of the market. This is shown in Fig. 8.15. The increase in the slope from early May 2013 is associated with the so-called taper tantrum, following a speech by former Fed Chair Ben Bernanke in which he hinted at the eventual unwinding of the program of Quantitative Easing, which is widely perceived to have contributed to the low level of long-bond yields. The short end of the market was relatively unaffected by this but the long end of the market sold off, leading to a steepening of the yield curve. Long-dated yields, however, came down again in subsequent months and the curve commenced a longer-term trend toward flattening.

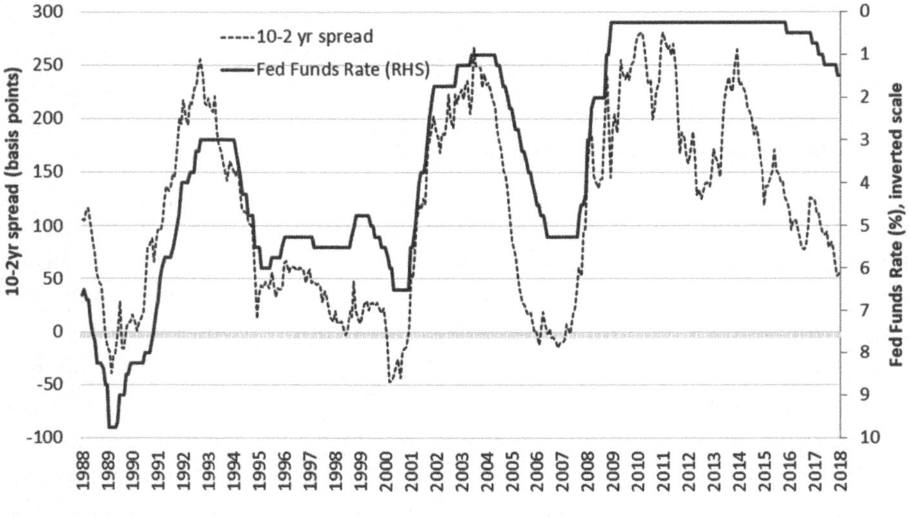

Fig. 8.14 Policy rates and the slope of the yield curve

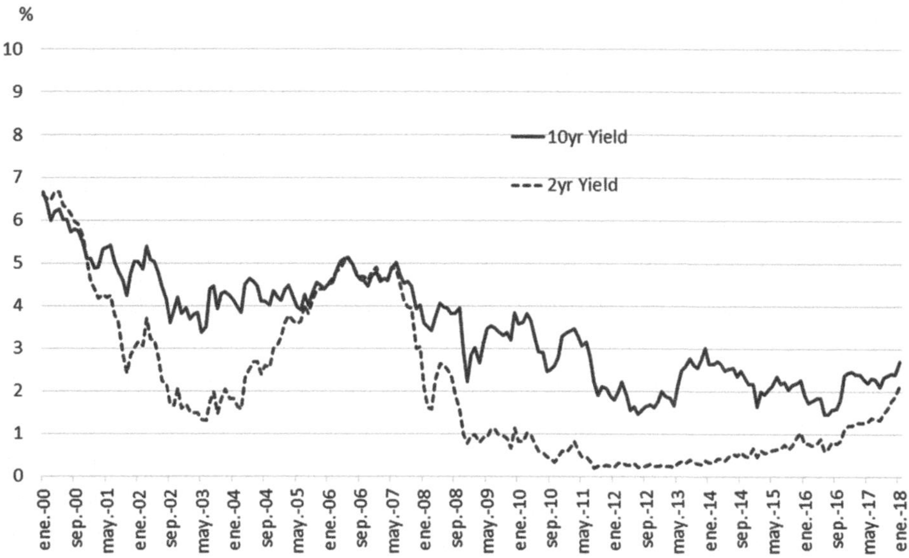

Fig. 8.15 Ten-year and two-year Treasury bond yields

This flattening is now driven by the short end of the curve and has accelerated since the Fed began increasing rates from December of 2015. Will this flattening process continue? It most likely will. To see why, we turn to Table 8.3.

We can define a *bear market flattening* as a scenario in which bond yields are generally rising (bear market) but where short-dated yields are rising by more than long-dated yields (flattening). Similarly, we can define a *bull market steepening* as a scenario with yields generally falling (bull market) but with short-dated yields falling by more than long-dated yields. The yield curve has predominantly followed one of these two dynamics.

Table 8.3 shows changes in the yield curve from a maximum level of Fed policy rates to a subsequent low and from that low to a subsequent high over the past 30 years. Decreases in policy rates have almost invariably led to a bull market steepening of the curve with short-dated bond yields falling by more than long-dated yields. A single exception to this was seen in the period from March 1997 to November 1998, in which longer-dated bond yields fell the most. Increases in policy rates, on the other hand, tend to lead to a bear market flattening with the largest increase in yields at the short end of the curve. Note that even though long-dated bond yields have tended to rise by less than short-dated bond yields in this scenario, they are still subject to upward pressure. Another reading of this is that even the long end of the bond market is ultimately driven by actual and expected short-term rates, as argued in Chap. 4.

Table 8.3 Fed funds rates and the yield curve

	Fed Funds	Chg, bps	2yr yield	Chg, bps	10yr yield	Chg, bps	Yield Curve
May-89	9.75		8.80		8.60		
Sep-92	3.00	-675	3.80	-501	6.35	-225	Bull Market Steepening
Feb-95	6.00	300	6.76	297	7.20	85	Bear Market Flattening
Jan-96	5.25	-75	4.93	-184	5.58	-162	Bull Market Steepening
Mar-97	5.50	25	6.42	150	6.90	132	Bear Market Flattening
Nov-98	4.75	-75	4.51	-192	4.71	-219	*Bull Market Flattening*
May-00	6.50	175	6.67	217	6.27	156	Bear Market Flattening
Jun-03	1.00	-550	1.30	-537	3.51	-276	Bull Market Steepening
Jun-06	5.25	425	5.15	385	5.14	162	Bear Market Flattening
Dec-08	0.25	-500	0.76	-439	2.21	-292	Bull Market Steepening
Jan-18	1.50	125	2.14	138	2.71	49	Bear Market Flattening

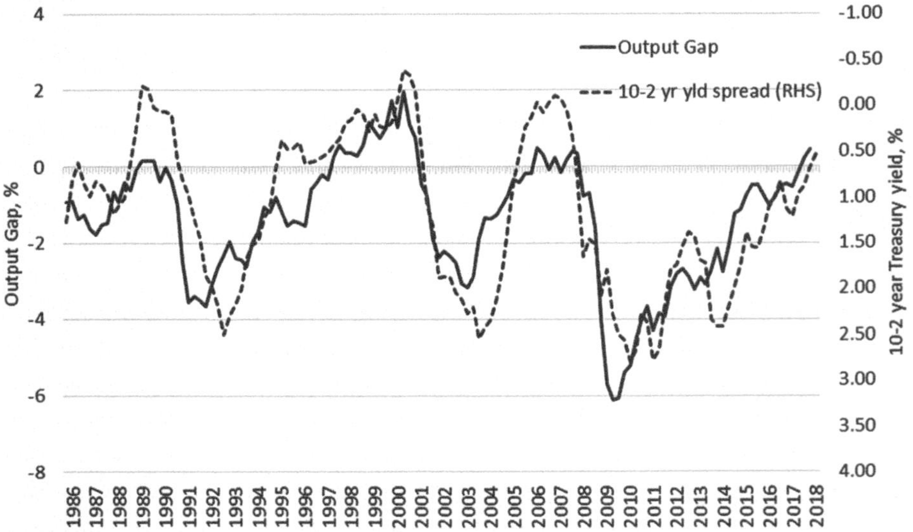

Fig. 8.16 Output gap and the slope of the yield curve

Figure 8.16 puts the yield curve into the context of the output gap. Curve flattening tends to begin in Phase I of the cycle and continue as the economy enters Phase II. If actual GDP growth continues to outstrip potential growth, the curve will likely flatten further.

The ultimate consequence of this flattening process would be an inversion of the yield curve. As Fig. 8.17 illustrates, inverted curves tend to signal an upcoming recession, even if the curve tends to provide this warning somewhat prematurely. As noted earlier, recessions normally happen after the economy has first entered Phase III or IV, and Phase II is often of relatively long duration. As we shall see in the subsequent chapter, Phase II scenarios are typically positive for equities, even if this is conditioned by the degree to which monetary policy is tightened.

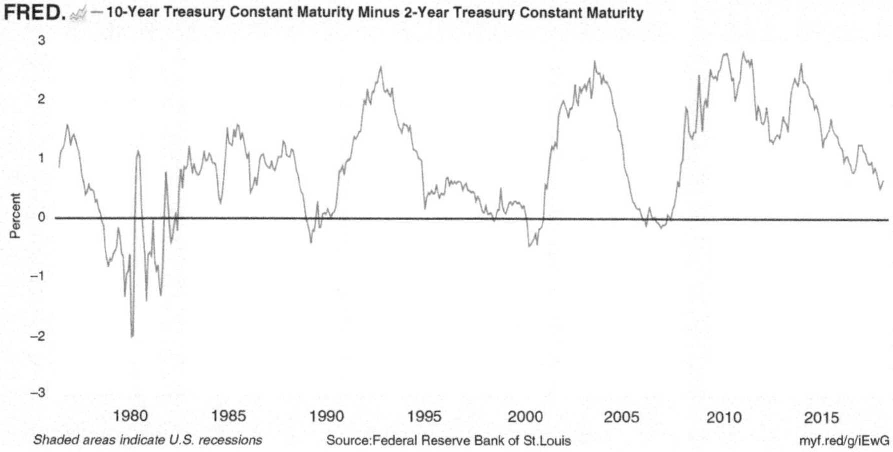

Fig. 8.17 Recessions and the slope of the yield curve

References

Hodrick, Robert J., and Edward C. Prescott. 1997. "Postwar U.S. Business Cycles: An Empirical Investigation", *Journal of Money, Credit and Banking*, 29(1), 1–16.

Peach, Richard, Robert Rich, and Anna Cororaton. 2011. "How Does Slack Influence Inflation?", Federal Reserve of New York, *Current Issues in Economics and Finance*, 17(3).

Shackleton, Robert. 2018. "Estimating and Projecting Potential Output Using CBO's Forecasting Growth Model", Congressional Budget Office, Working Paper 2018-03, February.

9

The Four Phases Framework

"Bull markets are born on pessimism, grow on skepticism, mature on optimism, and die on euphoria."
—Sir John Templeton

In the previous chapter, we demonstrated the importance of the business cycle and argued in favor of understanding it in terms of the *output gap*. But we said only a little about asset class returns over the cycle. This is where macro meets the markets and is the focus of this chapter.

Section 9.1 looks at markets in different states of the world, what is often referred to as "regimes" or "scenarios". This is done from three different angles: relative asset class performance, correlations between asset classes and general performance dependent on the output gap. Section 9.2 converts these photos into a movie, so to speak, by examining asset class performance as the economy goes through the four phases described in Chap. 8. Performance data for each phase are presented, followed by general comments on the phase. Section 9.3 makes an overall assessment of the Four Phases framework and concludes.

9.1 Macro-Sensitivities

Asset Class Performance in Different States of the World

Sheikh and Sun (2012) analyze the performance of five asset classes under different economic regimes over the period from Q4 of 1973 to Q4 of 2010. To make this directly comparable to what comes next, we will limit

H. Lumholdt, *Strategic and Tactical Asset Allocation*,
https://doi.org/10.1007/978-3-319-89554-3_9

ourselves to their findings with respect to *commodities*, represented by the Commodity Research Bureau Future Price Index, *US Treasuries*, represented by the Barclays Capital All Treasury Index, and *US equities*, represented by the S&P500 Price Index.[1]

The authors model the return of these asset classes in multiple regressions to capture their sensitivity to changes in GDP growth and inflation (for commodities and Treasuries) and to growth, inflation and unemployment (for US equities). Isolating the two factors of growth and inflation, they find the relationship between average annual returns and different regimes which is summarized in Table 9.1.

The table lends itself to the following observations:

- *Rising growth/rising inflation:* works best for commodities and is the worst regime for bonds. Equity performance is low-to-average under this regime.
- *Rising growth/falling inflation*: the best regime for equities which exhibit highly positive performance. This is the next best regime for bonds and a bad regime for commodities which exhibit close to no performance.
- *Falling growth/rising inflation:* the best regime for commodities and a generally positive regime for bonds. Equities exhibit significant underperformance under this regime.
- *Falling growth/falling inflation:* the best regime for bonds and the worst for commodities. Equities exhibit a close to average performance in this regime.

Sheikh and Sun note that the relevant information is published with a delay and discuss the importance of economic foresight. They define *perfect foresight* as being able to forecast both the *direction* and the *magnitude* of the changes in economic factors correctly, and *imperfect foresight* as being able to

Table 9.1 Average annual return (%) under different regimes, from Q4 1973 to Q4 2010

	Regime 1	Regime 2	Regime 3	Regime 4
	Growth: rising Inflation: rising	Growth: rising Inflation: falling	Growth: falling Inflation: rising	Growth: falling Inflation: falling
	32 periods	34 periods	36 periods	47 periods
Commodity	9.1	1.5	11.7	-6.3
Treasury	3.9	8.7	5.5	11.5
U.S. Equities	4.5	14.7	1.0	5.5

Source: Based on Sheikh and Sun (2012)

[1] The two asset classes not included here are the US dollar, represented by a dollar index future, and credit, represented by the Barclays Capital Baa Credit Index. See further, Sheikh and Sun (2012).

forecast only half of the magnitude of changes correctly. To gauge the importance of foresight, they construct a portfolio of the assets analyzed with given relative weights, comparing a static approach which no changes in weights (the equivalent of a pure SAA) to a regime-based approach where the weights are allowed to vary within a given band. Unsurprisingly, they find that perfect foresight gives rise to significant outperformance. More interestingly, imperfect foresight adds value too, and the authors find that this applies especially to extreme periods such as recessions, severe recessions and stagflation. In more stable periods with moderate and strong recovery, on the other hand, the static approach produces results similar to that of the regime-based approach. The authors conclude that CIOs with good insight into economic conditions can generally benefit from using a regime-based approach to asset allocation.

Ilmanen et al. (2014) examine the sensitivities to growth and inflation of *global stocks*, *global bonds* and *commodities* over the period from 1972 to 2013.[2] Global stocks are represented by the MSCI World Index in US dollars, bonds are represented by a GDP-weighted composite of six 10-year government bonds, and commodities are represented by an equal dollar-weighted composite of 24 commodities, respectively. Growth is classified according to the Chicago Fed National Activity Index and a surprise index for US industrial production. Inflation is classified according to the US CPI and a surprise index for inflation.[3] Sub-periods within the sample period are classified as "up" or "down" scenarios for growth and inflation by comparing the estimated value for each macro factor to its median value.

The authors examine the performance of the three assets classes in terms of their Sharpe ratio. This is done both independently for each growth and inflation scenario and for combinations of growth and inflation. The results are summarized in Table 9.2.

Inspecting the table, we see that *equities* depend critically on growth being positive but also tend to benefit from falling inflation. The best scenario for this asset class is therefore rising growth and falling inflation, which coincides with the findings of Sheikh and Sun. Conversely, *bonds* perform badly under high growth but equally benefit from falling inflation, and their best scenario is therefore one in which both growth and inflation are falling, which also

[2] The study goes beyond the macro-factors reported here to include asset class and risk factor sensitivities to real yields, volatility and illiquidity. Since they are of particular interest in our context, we limit ourselves to their findings with respect to the influence of the macro-factors on the asset classes.

[3] Each of the two macro-factors, growth and inflation, is thus a composite of two series which are first normalized to z-scores by subtracting historical means from each observation and dividing by historical volatility. For further details, see Ilmanen et al. (2014).

Table 9.2 Sharpe ratios of asset classes in different macro-scenarios

	All	Sub-periods			
		Gwth. Up	Gwth. Down	Inflat. Up	Inflat. Down
Global Equities	0.31	0.85	0.09	0.14	0.47
Global Bonds	0.46	0.28	0.63	0.00	0.96
Commodities	0.32	0.47	0.17	0.60	-0.03
		Gwth. Up + Infl. Up	Gwth. Up + Infl. Down	Gwth. Down + Infl. Down	Gwth. Down + Infl. Down
Global Equities		0.71	1.03	-0.18	0.29
Global Bonds		-0.09	0.71	0.10	1.22
Commodities		0.73	0.06	0.43	-0.09

Source: Based on Ilmanen et al. (2014)

coincides with the findings in the previous study. Finally, *commodities* depend positively on both growth and inflation and, according to Ilmanen et al., perform the best with both rising. This is somewhat different from the findings of Sheikh and Sun which see this asset class performing the best with growth rising but inflation falling. Generally, however, the patterns are quite similar even though different yardsticks for performance have been applied. This begs the question of when in the economic cycle the different regimes tend to apply. We will return to this in Sect. 9.2.

We round off with some empirical studies on the significance of the output gap to the return on equities. Cooper and Priestley (2009) examine the relationship between the output gap and stock market returns in the G-7 countries. The authors note the particular advantage of the output gap that it is a classic business cycle variable, related to production data, which is independent of any asset price information. Four separate measures for the output gap are used: the Congressional Budget Office or CBO estimates (for the US) and three different estimates based on trend models for industrial production. Stock market data are for the period from 1948 to 2005. The authors find that a negative gap tends to predict positive stock returns and vice versa, consistent with the idea that returns vary over the business cycle. This relationship is more significant in some markets than in others but is generally found to hold across the G-7 countries examined. The ability of the output gap to predict subsequent stock returns is found to become more significant as the time horizon is increased from 1 to 3 months and from 3 to 12 months. Focusing on the US market over the period from 1948 to 2010, Biswas (2014) reaches conclusions similar to those of Cooper and Priestley, but finds that the relationship is more significant using a weighted average output gap than one based on trend fitting. While the relationship between the output gap and market returns is found to be generally strong, it tends to weaken during periods of economic stability.

Asset Class Correlations

How do these findings of macro-sensitivities equate with the correlations of returns between the main asset classes? Focusing on bonds versus equities, Ilmanen (2003) makes the following general observations:

- *Discount rate effects.* A general notion is that of *discount rate effects* from bonds to stocks. Lower bond yields increase the value of future discounted earnings and tend to increase the P/E ratio—and vice versa. This is consistent with a *positive correlation* between the returns on the two asset classes.
- *Cash flow effects.* "Flight to quality" will typically dominate during output shocks such as recessions, creating a *negative correlation* as capital flows move out of equities and into bonds.
- *Changes in growth rates.* The "G" of stock market valuations rises in an economic upswing but higher growth will typically push bond yields higher, giving rise to a *negative correlation.*
- *Inflation.* Higher inflation raises expected future short rates (because of expectations regarding monetary policy) and raises the risk premium on bond yields. But equities are not neutral to inflation. *Expected future monetary tightening*, affecting earnings, and an *increased risk premium,* both follow from (significant) increases in inflation giving rise to a *positive correlation.*

Using data for average stock and bond returns over the period from 1952 to 2001, Ilmanen finds the following general patterns:

- *Growth.* High or low growth tends to give rise to a negative correlation.
- *Inflation.* High inflation tends to give rise to a high and positive correlation, low inflation gives rise to a low and positive correlation, whereas deflation leads to a negative correlation.
- *Monetary policy.* Periods of monetary easing and of monetary tightening tend to affect both asset classes in a similar way, giving rise to a *positive correlation.* Stocks tend to outperform bonds during periods of easing.

This is generally consistent with the findings regarding macro-sensitivities. A related question is the direction of *causation* between the two main asset classes. We suggest a framework for analysis in Fig. 9.1. The key question here is which of the two factors of growth and inflation is the dominant driver in a given scenario. We therefore assume that expectations regarding one of the two factors change in a significant way while the other remains relatively constant. Higher real economic growth tends to increase real interest rates and, by implication, nominal rates. This increases the discount factor for future stock earnings but the

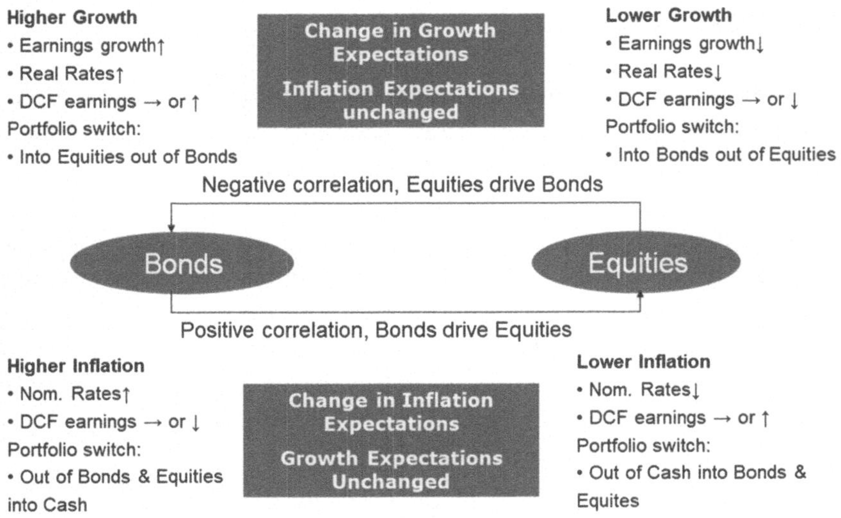

Fig. 9.1 Drivers of asset class correlations

effect of operating leverage on earnings will typically overpower this effect. The value of stocks, therefore, rises and investors will tend to switch into equities and out of bonds. Conversely, lower growth reduces real and nominal rates to the benefit of bonds but has a net negative effect on future earnings, to the detriment of stocks. Investors tend to switch out of stocks and into bonds in this scenario. In both cases, the direction of causation arguably goes from stocks to bonds, and the changes in growth imply a negative correlation between the two asset classes.

Significant changes in inflation with growth unchanged drive nominal bond yields higher or lower, in principle leaving real yields unchanged. Expectations of higher inflation work to the detriment of bonds, increasing the discount rate on future stock earnings. Since growth expectations are unchanged, the discounted cash flow from future earnings falls. The portfolio switch is therefore out of both asset classes and into cash. Lower inflation works in the opposite way, benefitting both asset classes. In these scenarios what is going on in the bond market is arguably the key question to investors, and the direction of causation tends to go from bonds to stocks, which will exhibit a positive correlation.

9.2 The Four Phases Framework

The following study[4] examines the performance of US equities, US bonds and commodities in different phases of the economic cycle, as measured by the *level* and *change* in the output gap. As discussed in Chap. 8, the position of the

[4] The author thanks Ignacio Chacon for doing the hard work of crunching the numbers when this study was undertaken.

output gap bears an overall relation to monetary policy. But different phases I through IV have nevertheless seen cases of both easing and tightening by the Fed. We therefore show returns for each phase with both higher and lower policy rates.

Some comments on data and methodology:

- The study covers the period from Q4 of 1971 to Q4 of 2009.
- The output gap is based on quarterly data from the OECD.
- The markets examined comprise equities, represented by a total return index for the S&P500, 7–10-year US Treasury bonds, represented by a total return index, and commodities, represented by the GSCI total return index.
- To reduce the element of "noise", the data for the output gap have been filtered using a centered moving average[5]. This average is based on data for five quarters, comprising the present quarter, two previous and two subsequent quarters. This determines the value for the output gap, and its variation from the previous quarter is then calculated to determine the phase of the economy.
- "Rates up" and "rates down" refer to whether the Fed increased or decreased the Fed Funds Target Rate in a given phase. In the few cases when no rate change took place in a given phase, this classification refers to the latest rate change observed.

The charts for each phase show annualized excess returns over three-month T-bills for each asset class on the y-axes and the standard deviation of the excess returns on the x-axes. Also shown in the charts is the number of quarters from the whole sample period belonging to each phase, the number of times a given phase occurred and its average duration in quarters. This is shown for both "rates up" and "rates down" scenarios. The amount of easing or tightening for each quarter is also indicated.

The standard deviations are calculated on the basis of all return data observed in the same phase over the whole sample period. It is therefore a measure of the *reliability* of the return data rather than of the volatility of the markets within a given phase. The box below each chart provides data in *absolute terms*. Note that Inflation Trend refers to the average change in inflation. This is measured as the annualized percentage change per quarter in the year-on-year change in the CPI.

---

[5] This methodology assigns the highest weight to the central data point. Using five data points, the weights become, respectively, 11%, 22%, 33%, 22% and 11%. Because of this structure, the centered moving average is also referred to as a triangular moving average.

Phase I: Negative and Narrowing Output Gap

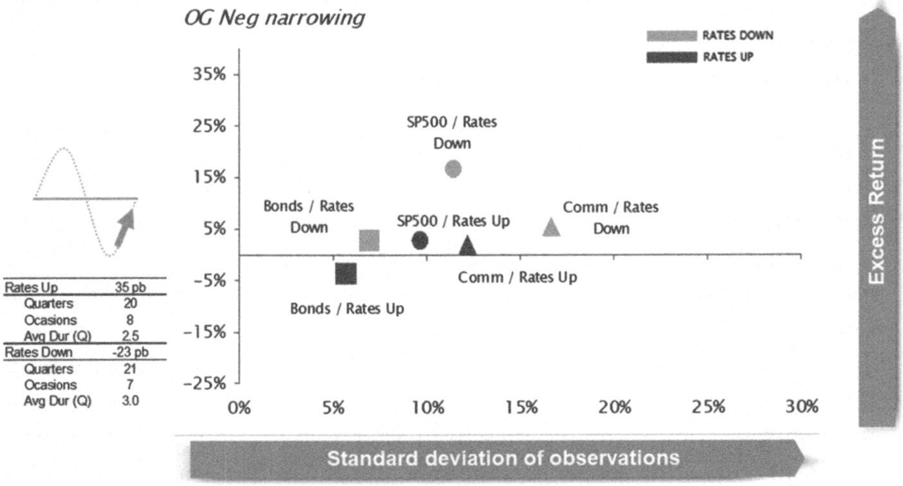

Phase I	Inflat. Trend	%GDP QoQ	%Earn. QoQ	%PE QoQ	%SP500 QoQ	% Bonds QoQ
Rates Up	-0.2%	5.4%	15.4%	-9.4%	5.3%	-5.5%
Rates Down	-0.7%	4.8%	8.9%	9.5%	18.5%	0.6%

Fig. 9.2 Phase I

Comments on Phase I

- This is a phase with the economy recovering from a low point in the cycle.
- Phase I is typically of shorter than average duration (2.5 to 3 quarters). Inventory accumulation often boosts production, and housing construction and consumer durables demand tend to increase.
- Corporate margins expand and earnings growth picks up, helped by operating leverage.
- Inflationary pressures normally remain absent and monetary policy, even when tightened, typically remains lax.
- The standard deviation of observations is relatively low.
- The stock market generally performs well but especially so with short-term rates decreasing.
- Bonds hold up in this phase when rates are falling but tend to underperform cash when they are rising.
- Commodities tend to do best in this phase when rates are falling.

Phase II: Positive and Widening Output Gap

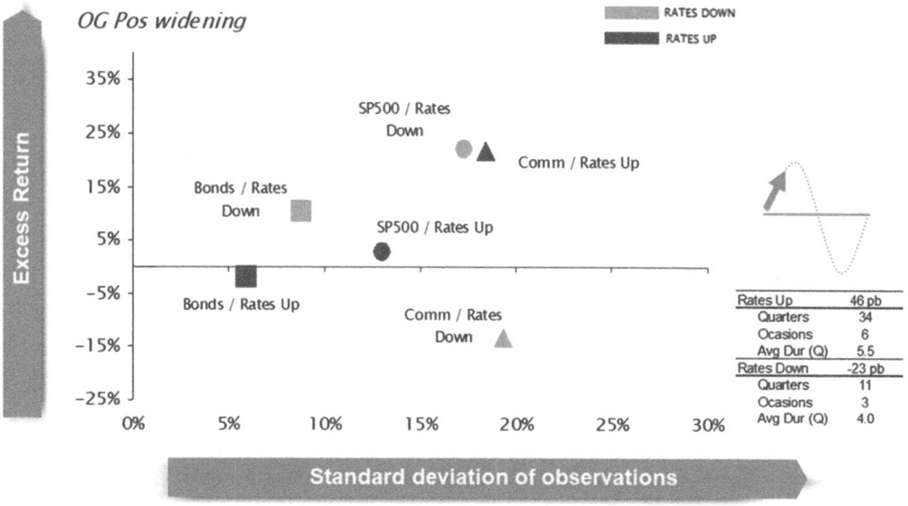

Phase II	Inflat. Trend	%GDP QoQ	%Earn. QoQ	%PE QoQ	%SP500 QoQ	% Bonds QoQ
Rates Up	1.2%	4.5%	16.4%	-10.5%	5.3%	-2.5%
Rates Down	-0.3%	4.2%	2.0%	24.0%	25.6%	9.3%

Fig. 9.3 Phase II

Comments on Phase II

- This is a phase where the economy has fully recovered, but where growth continues to be higher than potential.
- This phase is typically of longer than average duration (4 to 5.5 quarters) and normally sees healthy earnings growth.
- The standard deviation of observations is about average.
- Capacity constraints and labor shortages begin to appear; inflation begins to pick up at some time during this phase, but the timing of this can vary significantly.
- In inflationary periods, commodities tend to do well.
- Periods with the Fed still easing to get growth under way have seen stocks do very well, whereas commodities underperform in this scenario. But this is more the exception than the rule. Higher rates are more often seen, which tends to give rise to multiple contraction and a more moderate, but still positive, performance of the stock market.
- Bonds typically underperform cash, the exception being periods with falling rates

Phase III: Positive and Narrowing Output Gap

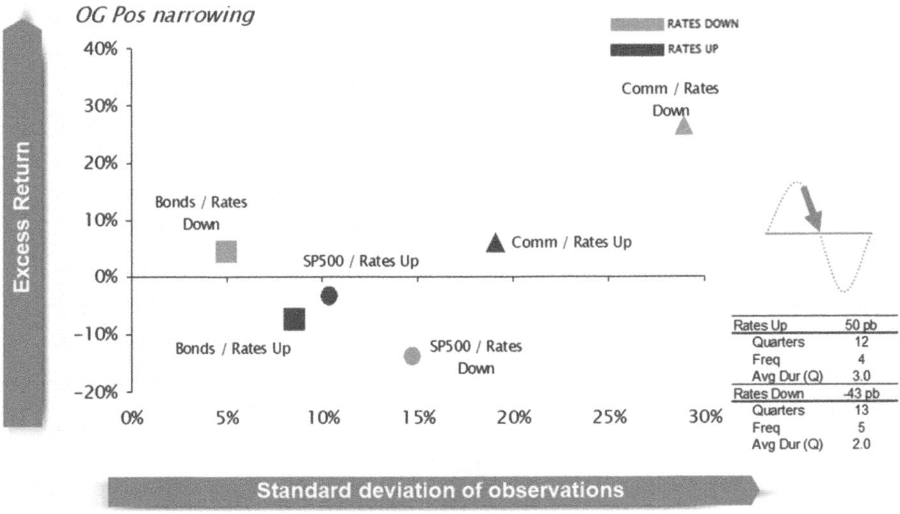

Phase III	Inflat. Trend	%GDP QoQ	%Earn. QoQ	%PE QoQ	%SP500 QoQ	% Bonds QoQ
Rates Up	2.7%	0.8%	16.5%	-14.8%	1.1%	-5.8%
Rates Down	0.2%	1.6%	-3.4%	-6.8%	-10.4%	3.6%

Fig. 9.4 Phase III

Comments on Phase III

- Growth in the economy is slowing to below potential, often induced by previous monetary tightening.
- This phase is typically of shorter than average duration (2 to 3 quarters).
- The standard deviation of observations is about average.
- Earnings growth sometimes holds up for a while but eventually slows.
- Inflation pressures often remain from the previous upswing and occasionally intensify. When this applies, monetary authorities are often reluctant to ease policy immediately.
- This is generally the worst phase for stocks. It is empirically worse with falling rates which has tended to coincide with more pronounced downturns. Multiples tend to contract in this period, both with rates falling and rising.
- Bonds perform well with falling rates but underperform when the central bank is still fighting inflation through higher rates.
- Commodities tend to do well in this phase, but especially when rates are falling.

Phase IV: Negative and Widening Output Gap

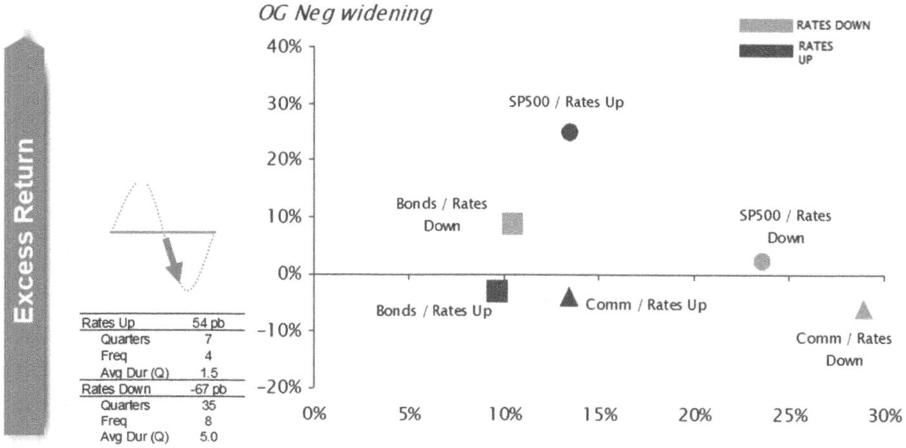

Phase IV	Inflat. Trend	%GDP QoQ	%Earn. QoQ	%PE QoQ	%SP500 QoQ	% Bonds QoQ
Rates Up	-1.3%	1.7%	9.8%	19.5%	29.3%	-4.4%
Rates Down	-1.6%	-0.3%	-8.8%	14.6%	4.6%	7.4%

Fig. 9.5 Phase IV

Comments on Phase IV

- The lower than average growth has continued and may turn into a recession.
- This phase is typically of longer than average duration (up to 5 quarters).
- The standard deviation of observations is at a maximum, making this phase the most uncertain scenario for asset returns.
- Earnings growth typically slows and frequently becomes negative.
- Inflationary pressures abate and monetary policy is typically eased in this phase. The opposite has occasionally happened, which has coincided with a high performance of stocks, typically coming from a low level of valuations. Multiple expansion has then been the main driver of returns.
- Bonds tend to perform well in this phase with falling rates as both real rates and inflation expectations are reduced. But they have tended to underperform in the less typical cases of rates going higher.
- Commodities generally do badly in this phase.

9.3 Assessment and Conclusion

How do these results compare with what we saw in the previous studies? We generally see a similar pattern and make the following observations:

- *Rising growth/falling inflation* generally corresponds to *Phase I*. This phase tends to be most reliably positive for equities and moderately positive for commodities, but positive for bonds only in a scenario of rates moving lower.
- *Rising growth/rising inflation* generally corresponds to *Phase II*. Rates are more likely to move higher in this phase, giving rise to moderately positive performance for equities, a strongly positive scenario for commodities, but a negative performance for bonds. The less typical scenario of rates moving lower in this phase tends to boost equity performance considerably, but still leaves bond performance mediocre. Commodities, however, tend to underperform considerably with rates down in Phase II.
- *Falling growth /rising inflation* generally corresponds to *Phase III*. This is the phase most reliably negative for stocks and generally looks like the mirror image of Phase I. We equally find this scenario to be positive for commodities, both with rates up and down, whereas bond performance is only positive in scenarios with rates moving lower.
- *Falling growth/falling inflation* generally corresponds to *Phase IV*. Rates moving lower have been the most typical pattern in this phase, which tends to produce only mediocre equity performance, a clearly negative performance of commodities and a clearly positive performance of bonds. The less likely scenario of rates moving higher has produced a significantly positive performance for stocks but commodities still underperform, whereas bonds see modest underperformance. This is the least reliable phase in terms of performance which is particularly relevant for equities. Phase IV does not always see recessions, but when it does equities tend to rebound significantly from their minimum levels. Timing this correctly is beyond difficult.

This is clearly not a framework for trading decisions, even though it is still useful for understanding the general backdrop to such decisions. The more relevant question is whether it can improve decisions on TAA. We believe it can. Information on the output gap is clearly not available on a timely basis, but several proxies can be used, such as the resource gap, the slope of the yield curve and leading indicators such as the CLI, as illustrated in the appendix to Chap. 7. Finessing the exact position of the output is clearly next to impossible, but in cases where it is likely to be significantly negative or positive, having a view on whether it is likely narrowing or widening will often suffice. This can be assessed on the basis of more timely growth indicators.

More generally, having a view of the position of the output gap allows us to ask the relevant questions. A large negative output gap clearly places the emphasis on tracking growth whereas inflation readings are likely to take a backstage. A likely transitioning from a Phase I to a Phase II prompts very different questions. What are the readings on inflation and which are the signals coming from the Fed? This is not determined solely on the basis of the most recent indicators.

Generally, macro-information is by nature more piecemeal than, for example, company-specific information. Incoming information is fitted into a more general perception of the current scenario. A given data point may coincide entirely with market expectations, but if it reinforces a perception that, say, growth is buoyant, it is still relevant. This is why we agree with the notion of Sheikh and Sun that being able to forecast precisely is not required. Identifying the current scenario correctly and having a good idea of what the direction of change is will often suffice to formulate a TAA strategy which does not depend critically on, say, the next payrolls report.

Generally, we favor formulating a base-line TAA strategy on the basis of an assessment of which phase the economy is *currently* in, without necessarily trying to forecast when the economy will transition to a new phase. Such considerations are relevant to developing risk scenarios, however, and deciding beforehand how this would modify the TAA. TAA decisions based on an assessment of the current phase do not need to be aggressive from the outset but can be modified with incoming information. If most indicators suggest that we are in, say, Phase I, and we decide to overweight stocks on this basis, such an overweight might be increased if incoming information reaffirms the notion that growth is currently above potential. Or it might be reduced on the basis of contradictory incoming information.

As discussed in Chap. 4, valuations are clearly relevant to SAA decision and, as we saw, have some claims to predictive power for long-term asset returns. In the shorter-term context, however, valuations are often more the effect of market moves than the cause of them. This does not exempt valuations of relevance. Markets which are either particularly cheap or particularly expensive will often move more decidedly in a new direction when sentiment changes, as was seen when, for example, the tech bubble burst in the early 2000s. But the turning points are more likely to be determined by the cycle than by valuations.

To round off, we direct the reader's attention to Sir John Templeton's wise words quoted above. Market scenarios apply to a logic which is not immediately intuitive. Having a general framework for understanding where we are, or more precisely in which phase, is therefore essential to successful TAA decisions.

References

Biswas, A. 2014. "The Output Gap and Expected Security Returns", *Review of Financial Economics*, 23(3), 131–140.

Cooper, I., and R. Priestley. 2009. "Time-Varying Risk Premiums and the Output Gap", *Review of Financial Studies*, 22, 2801–2833.

Ilmanen, A. 2003. "Stock-bond correlations", *Journal of Fixed Income* 13(2), 55–66.

Ilmanen, Antti., Thomas Maloney and Adrienne Ross. 2014. "Exploring Macroeconomic Sensitivities: How Investments Respond to Different Economic Environments", *The Journal of Portfolio Management*, 40(3), Spring.

Sheikh, A., and J. Sun. 2012. "Regime Change: Implications of Macroeconomic Shifts on Asset Class and Portfolio Performance", *The Journal of Investing*, 21(3), 36–54.

Appendix: The Mechanics of Mean-Variance Optimization[1]

In the following, we will assume that investment returns are completely described by the two moments of mean and variance. To think in terms of asset allocation, we will refer to the elements in the portfolio as "assets" rather than "securities". We will begin this review with the Markowitz model[2] and round off with the capital asset pricing model (CAPM). Throughout, risk will be understood to mean the standard deviation of the return, or volatility. We will begin with a portfolio consisting of two risky assets and later generalize to n assets.

Two Risky Assets

Notation R_a: Return on asset *a*

R_b: Return on asset *b*

$\bar{R}_a$: Expected (mean) return on asset *a*

$\bar{R}_b$: Expected (mean) return on asset *b*

$\bar{R}_p$: Expected (mean) return on portfolio

w_a: Weight in the portfolio of asset *a*

w_b: Weight in the portfolio of asset *b* ($=1 - w_a$)

σ_a^2: The variance of the return on asset 1

[1] This Appendix is meant as a quick refresher. For a more complete coverage, see, for example, Elton et al. (2014) or Bodie et al. (2014).
[2] Markowitz (1952, 1959).

H. Lumholdt, *Strategic and Tactical Asset Allocation*,
https://doi.org/10.1007/978-3-319-89554-3

σ_b^2: The variance of the return on asset 2
σ_{ab}: The covariance between the returns on assets *a* and *b*
σ_p^2: The variance of the return on the portfolio

All wealth is invested in the two assets, implying that $w_a + w_b = 1$. The *expected return* of the portfolio is a linear combination of the expected return on each asset:

$$\bar{R}_p = w_a \bar{R}_a + (1 - w_a)\bar{R}_b \tag{A.1}$$

The *variance* of the returns on the portfolio is given by:

$$\sigma_p^2 = E\left[R_p - \bar{R}_p\right]^2$$

Expanding this expression, we get:

$$\begin{aligned}
\sigma_p^2 &= E\left[w_a R_a + (1 - w_a)R_b - \left(w_a \bar{R}_a + (1 - w_a)\bar{R}_b\right)\right]^2 \\
&= E\left[w_a\left(R_a - \bar{R}_a\right) + (1 - w_a)\left(R_b - \bar{R}_b\right)\right]^2 \\
&= E\left[w_a^2\left(R_a - \bar{R}_a\right)^2 + (1 - w_a)^2\left(R_b - \bar{R}_b\right)^2 + 2w_a(1 - w_a)\left(R_a - \bar{R}_a\right)\left(R_b - \bar{R}_b\right)\right]
\end{aligned}$$

Note that $E\left(R_a - \bar{R}_a\right)^2$ and $E\left(R_b - \bar{R}_b\right)^2$ are the *variances* of the returns on assets a and b, respectively, while $E\left[\left(R_a - \bar{R}_a\right)\left(\left(R_a - \bar{R}_b\right)\right]\right.$ is their *covariance*. We can therefore write:

$$\sigma_p^2 = w_a^2\sigma_a^2 + (1 - w_a)^2\sigma_b^2 + 2w_a(1 - w_a)\sigma_{ab} \tag{A.2}$$

and

$$\sigma_p = \left[w_a^2\sigma_a^2 + (1 - w_a)^2\sigma_b^2 + 2w_a(1 - w_a)\sigma_{ab}\right]^{1/2} \tag{A.3}$$

The covariance can be expressed as the product of the standard deviation of each asset and the correlation coefficient between the assets (ρ_{ab}) i.e. $\sigma_{ab} = \sigma_a\sigma_b\rho_{ab}$. We can therefore write (A.2) as

$$\sigma_p^2 = w_a^2\sigma_a^2 + (1-w_a)^2\sigma_b^2 + 2w_a(1-w_a)\sigma_a\sigma_b\rho_{ab} \tag{A.4}$$

and

$$\sigma_p = \left[w_a^2\sigma_a^2 + (1-w_a)^2\sigma_b^2 + 2w_a(1-w_a)\sigma_a\sigma_b\rho_{ab}\right]^{1/2} \tag{A.5}$$

We see that portfolio risk depends both on the risk of the individual assets and on the correlation of their returns. This is what gives rise to a diversification effect. To examine this more closely, we begin with the case of *perfect positive correlation*. Substitute $\rho_{ab} = 1$ into (A.4) to get:

$$\sigma_p^2 = w_a^2\sigma_a^2 + (1-w_a)^2\sigma_b^2 + 2w_a(1-w_a)\sigma_a\sigma_b \tag{A.6}$$

which corresponds to

$$\sigma_p^2 = \left[w_a\sigma_a + (1-w_a)\sigma_b\right]^2$$

hence

$$\sigma_p = w_a\sigma_a + (1-w_a)\sigma_b \tag{A.7}$$

The standard deviation of the portfolio is now a simple weighted average of the standard deviation of each asset, and there is no diversification effect. However, only in this extreme case of a perfect positive correlation does that apply. We see this from the fact that any $\rho_{ab} < 1$ would make the right hand side of Eq. (A.4) smaller than (A.6).

Consider now a *zero correlation* between the two assets ($\rho_{ab} = 0$). Equation (A.4) reduces to

$$\sigma_p^2 = w_a^2\sigma_a^2 + (1-w_a)^2\sigma_b^2 \tag{A.8}$$

and

$$\sigma_p = \left[w_a^2\sigma_a^2 + (1-w_a)^2\sigma_b^2\right]^{1/2} \tag{A.9}$$

σ_p is now smaller than $w_a\sigma_a + (1 - w_a)\sigma_b$ unless $w_a = 1$ *or* 0, in which case the portfolio would be concentrated in either asset a or asset b, which would obviously exclude any diversification effect.

Finally, let's consider the case of a *perfect negative correlation* ($\rho_{ab} = -1$). As discussed previously, negative correlations between any two assets are hard to find over long time horizons, but frequently occur over shorter periods of time (e.g. in "flight to quality" situations). Substituting $\rho_{ab} = -1$ into Eq. (A.4) we get

$$\sigma_p^2 = w_a^2\sigma_a^2 + (1-w_a)^2\sigma_b^2 - 2w_a(1-w_a)\sigma_a\sigma_b$$

which corresponds to

$$\sigma_p^2 = \left[w_a\sigma_a - (1-w_a)\sigma_b\right]^2 \quad \text{(A.10)}$$

or to

$$\sigma_p^2 = \left[-w_a\sigma_a + (1-w_a)\sigma_b\right]^2 \quad \text{(A.11)}$$

hence

$$\sigma_p = w_a\sigma_a - (1-w_a)\sigma_b \quad \text{(A.12)}$$

or

$$\sigma_p = -w_a\sigma_a + (1-w_a)\sigma_b \quad \text{(A.13)}$$

Either (A.12) or (A.13) is valid depending on which of the two is positive. In this case, it is (in principle) possible to entirely eliminate the risk of the portfolio. To find the w_a (and, by implication, w_b) necessary for this, set (A.13) equal to zero and solve for w_a to get

$$w_a = \frac{\sigma_b}{\sigma_a + \sigma_b} \quad \text{(A.14)}$$

The effect of diversification in the two assets case is illustrated in Fig. A.1, in stylized form.

We saw that with a perfect positive correlation, both the risk and the return of the portfolio become linear combinations of the two assets in the portfolio.

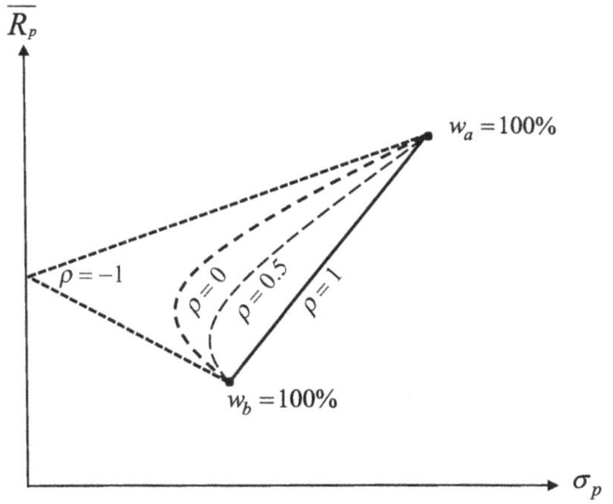

Fig. A.1 Correlation and diversification

For correlations lower than one, however, the diversification effect is represented by the non-linear combinations of assets a and b in Fig. A.1 and, in the extreme case of $\rho_{ab} = -1$, by the straight lines to the vertical axis. Comparing the linear combination of $\rho_{ab} = 1$ with all the others, we see that diversification reduces the level of risk of the portfolio for a given level of return or, which is the equivalent, increases the level of return for a given level of risk.

To find the minimum variance portfolio in the two-asset case, we differentiate (A.4), that is, $\sigma_p^2 = w_a^2\sigma_a^2 + (1-w_a)^2\sigma_b^2 + 2w_a(1-w_a)\sigma_a\sigma_b\rho_{ab}$, with respect to w_a and set it equal to zero:

$$\frac{\partial \sigma_p^2}{\partial w_a} = 2w_a\sigma_a^2 - 2\sigma_b^2 + 2w_a\sigma_b^2 + 2\sigma_a\sigma_b\rho_{ab} - 4w_a\sigma_a\sigma_b\rho_{ab} = 0$$

Solving for w_a, we get:

$$w_a = \frac{\sigma_b^2 - \sigma_a\sigma_b\rho_{ab}}{\sigma_a^2 + \sigma_b^2 - 2\sigma_a\sigma_b\rho_{ab}} \qquad \text{(A.15)}$$

This is the general formula which, as we saw, becomes $\dfrac{\sigma_b}{\sigma_a + \sigma_b}$ when $\rho_{ab} = -1$. We see directly that for uncorrelated assets ($\rho_{ab} = 0$), (A.15) is reduced to

$$w_a = \frac{\sigma_b^2}{\sigma_a^2 + \sigma_b^2} \qquad \text{(A.16)}$$

A Numerical Example

A portfolio consists of an equity fund (asset a) and a high-yielding fixed income fund (asset b). The expected return of the equity fund is 12.5%, while that of the bond fund is 7.5%. The standard deviations of their returns are 18.0% and 12.5%, respectively. Table A.1 below shows the expected return and standard deviation of the portfolio in decimal form, using formulas (A.7), (A.9) and (A.15). As can be seen, the standard deviation of the portfolio falls the lower is the correlation, but this has no cost in terms of the return of the portfolio, which depends exclusively on the weighting of the two assets. Figure A.2 gives a graphical illustration.

To calculate the weighting of each asset class required to minimize the standard deviation of the portfolio we use formulas (A.14) and (A.15) to get the results set out in Table A.2.

Table A.1 Standard deviation of portfolio returns with different levels of correlation

			Standard deviation of portfolio return			
w_a	w_b	$\bar{R}_p$	$\rho = 1$	$\rho = 0.5$	$\rho = 0$	$\rho = -0.5$
0.0	1.0	0.0750	0.1250	0.1250	0.1250	0.1250
0.1	0.9	0.0800	0.1305	0.1225	0.1139	0.1047
0.2	0.8	0.0850	0.1360	0.1220	0.1063	0.0878
0.3	0.7	0.0900	0.1415	0.1237	0.1028	0.0765
0.4	0.6	0.0950	0.1470	0.1273	0.1040	0.0735
0.5	0.5	0.1000	0.1525	0.1328	0.1096	0.0799
0.6	0.4	0.1050	0.1580	0.1399	0.1190	0.0936
0.7	0.3	0.1100	0.1635	0.1483	0.1315	0.1121
0.8	0.2	0.1150	0.1690	0.1580	0.1462	0.1333
0.9	0.1	0.1200	0.1745	0.1686	0.1625	0.1561
1.0	0.0	0.1250	0.1800	0.1800	0.1800	0.1800

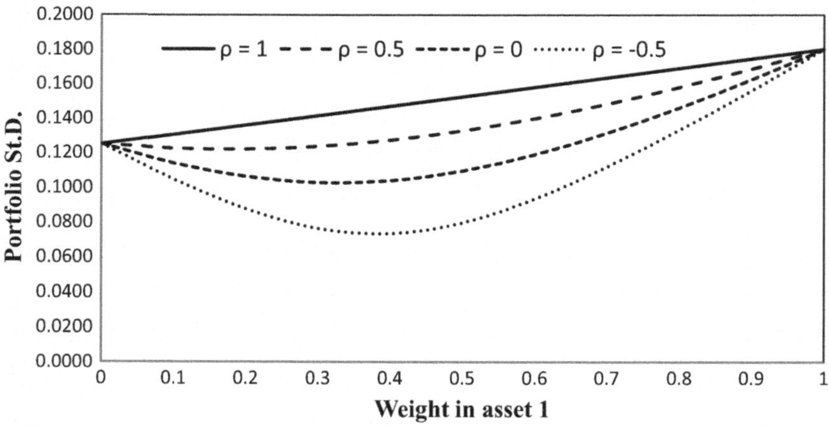

Fig. A.2 Portfolio volatility and asset correlation

Table A.2 Minimum standard deviation portfolio

	Minimum St.D portfolio		
	$\rho = 0.5$	$\rho = 0$	$\rho = -0.5$
w_a	0.1714	0.3254	0.3811
w_b	0.8286	0.6746	0.6189
$\bar{R}_p$	0.0836	0.1028	0.1098
σ_p	0.122	0.1027	0.0734

Portfolios of n Risky Assets

Generalizing to n assets, we can express the *expected return* on the portfolio as:

$$\bar{R}_p = \sum_{i=1}^{n} w_i \bar{R}_i \tag{A.17}$$

which is a simple weighted average of the return on each asset with $\sum_{i=1}^{n} w_i = 1$.

Portfolio *variance* equals

$$\sigma_p^2 = \sum_{i=1}^{n}\sum_{j=1}^{n} w_i w_j \sigma_{ij} \tag{A.18}$$

The double summation implies that we are adding up n^2 numbers. Each number corresponds to a pair of values for i and j in the equation. The variance of the portfolio corresponds to the weighted average covariance of these pairs. Writing this in matrix form we get:

$$\sigma_p^2 = \begin{bmatrix} w_1 w_1 \sigma_{11} & w_1 w_2 \sigma_{12} & \cdots & w_1 w_n \sigma_{1n} \\ w_2 w_1 \sigma_{21} & w_2 w_2 \sigma_{22} & \cdots & w_2 w_n \sigma_{2n} \\ \vdots & \vdots & \ddots & \vdots \\ w_n w_1 \sigma_{n1} & w_n w_2 \sigma_{n2} & \cdots & w_n w_n \sigma_{nn} \end{bmatrix} \tag{A.19}$$

Because the covariance of each asset with itself is equal to its variance, that is, $\sigma_{ii=}\sigma_i^2$, we can decompose (A.18) into

$$\sigma_p^2 = \sum_{i=1}^{n} w_i^2 \sigma_i^2 + \sum_{\substack{i=1 \\ i \neq j}}^{n} \sum_{j=1}^{n} w_i w_j \sigma_{ij} \tag{A.20}$$

The first term corresponds to the sum of the *n variances*, while the second term corresponds to the sum of the $n^2 - n$ covariances. Accordingly, our matrix will now read:

$$\sigma_p^2 = \begin{bmatrix} w_1^2\sigma_2^2 & w_1w_2\sigma_{12} & \cdots & w_1w_n\sigma_{1n} \\ w_2w_1\sigma_{21} & w_2^2\sigma_2^2 & \cdots & w_2w_n\sigma_{2n} \\ \vdots & \vdots & \ddots & \vdots \\ w_nw_1\sigma_{n1} & w_nw_2\sigma_{n2} & \cdots & w_n^2\sigma_n^2 \end{bmatrix} \tag{A.21}$$

The diagonal from the upper left to the bottom right represents the weighted variances, while the off-diagonals represent the weighted covariances. Note that since $w_iw_j\sigma_{ij} = w_jw_i\sigma_{ji}$ the matrix is symmetric and each weighted covariance appears twice. The number of computations is therefore limited to $n\,variances + \frac{n^2 - n}{2}\,covariances$. Maintaining the matrix notation, we can rewrite (A.21) as the following product:

$$\sigma_p^2 = w'\Sigma w \tag{A.22}$$

where w'= the transpose of the weight vector, Σ= the variance-covariance matrix and w= the weight vector. In expanded form this gives us:

$$\sigma_p^2 = \begin{bmatrix} w_1 & w_2 & \cdots & w_n \end{bmatrix} \begin{bmatrix} \sigma_1^2 & \sigma_{12} & \cdots & \sigma_{1n} \\ \sigma_{21} & \sigma_2^2 & \cdots & \sigma_{2n} \\ \vdots & \vdots & \ddots & \vdots \\ \sigma_{n1} & \sigma_{n2} & \cdots & \sigma_n^2 \end{bmatrix} \begin{bmatrix} w_1 \\ w_2 \\ \vdots \\ w_n \end{bmatrix}$$

The Limits to Diversification

Our previous analysis suggests that including more assets in the portfolio would increase the scope for diversification, if the assets involved are not perfectly positively correlated. This is generally true, but note that the diversification effect will eventually be exhausted. To illustrate, suppose that the n assets are equally weighted in the portfolio, so that $w_i = \frac{1}{n}$. We can now rewrite (A.20) as

$$\sigma_p^2 = \sum_{i=1}^{n} \left(\frac{1}{n}\right)^2 \sigma_i^2 + \sum_{i=1}^{n}\sum_{j=1}^{n} \left(\frac{1}{n}\right)\left(\frac{1}{n}\right)\sigma_{ij} \tag{A.23}$$

Factoring out $\frac{1}{n}$ from the first term of the equation and $\frac{n-1}{n}$ from the second, we get:

$$\sigma_p^2 = \frac{1}{n}\sum_{i=1}^{n}\left[\frac{\sigma^2}{n}\right] + \frac{n-1}{n}\sum_{i=1}^{n}\sum_{j=1}^{n}\left[\frac{1}{n(n-1)}\sigma_{ij}\right] \tag{A.24}$$

The first and second term in the square brackets represent the average of the n variances and the average of the $\frac{n-1}{n}$ covariances, respectively. As $n \to \infty$, the first term in (A.24) approaches zero, implying that all asset specific, or unsystematic, risk has been diversified away. Hence, in the unlikely case of entirely independent assets ($\sigma_{ij} = 0$), the variance of the overall portfolio would eventually be reduced to zero. In the more realistic case of a positive covariance, the variance of the portfolio approaches the *average covariance* of the assets. The interpretation is that given a sufficiently high n, all asset specific risk can be diversified away. However, the non-specific or systematic risk, which affects all assets, will remain. This is referred to as *market risk.*

The Efficient Frontier

We can plot all individual assets and combinations of assets in $\left(\bar{R}, \sigma^2\right)$ space, represented by the points either on or within the boundary in Fig. A.3. We call this the *feasible set* of portfolios. Only portfolios on the upward sloping part of the boundary (the part in bold connecting points MVP through A, B and C) are efficient. We call this part the *efficient frontier* (EF). The EF *dominates* all portfolios below it, both those off the boundary and those on its downward sloping part, since it offers either a lower risk for a given level of expected return or a higher expected return for a given level of risk. To illustrate, the point A' has the same level of risk as point A but offers a lower expected return and can therefore be excluded out of hand as inefficient.

Where on the EF would an investor choose to be? The answer is that this depends on her attitude to risk. This is illustrated in the figure by the two different indifference curves, I_1 and I_2. The points of tangency between the indifference curves and the EF (A and B) represent the optimum portfolios. But investors represented by I_2 have a greater tolerance for risk than those

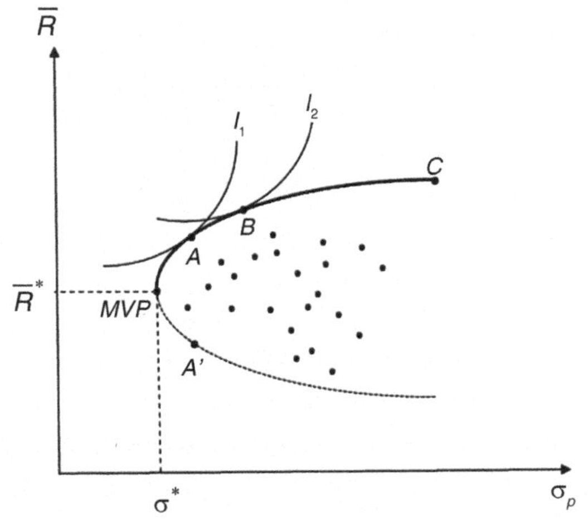

Fig. A.3 The efficient frontier

represented by I_1 and will therefore have more "aggressive" portfolios with both a higher expected return and a higher volatility.

The point MVP represents the portfolio with the minimum variance with a return of $\overline{R}^*$. If we solve (A.18) for the portfolio weights $(w_1, \ldots, w_n)$ that will minimize its variance for each and every level of expected return equal to and higher than $\overline{R}^*$, we can trace out the efficient frontier. Our optimization problem will therefore have two constraints. The first one is that the expected return of the portfolio must be equal to some attainable target, $\overline{R}_p$. The second constraint is that the portfolio must be fully invested[3]:

$$\min_{\{w_1,\ldots,w_n\}} \sigma_p^2 = \sum_{i=1}^{n}\sum_{j=1}^{n} w_i w_j \sigma_{ij}$$

subject to:

$$\sum_{i=1}^{n} w_i \overline{R}_i = \overline{R}_p$$

and

$$\sum_{i=1}^{n} w_i = 1$$

[3]Technically, our second constraint will allow for short sales, that is, assets weights <0. We will look aside from this in the following.

Forming the Lagrangian, we get:

$$L=\sum_{i=1}^{n}\sum_{j=1}^{n}w_i w_j \sigma_{ij}+\lambda_2\left(\sum_{i=1}^{n}w_i\bar{R}_i-\bar{R}_p\right)+\lambda_1\left(\sum_{i=1}^{n}w_i-1\right) \quad \text{(A.25)}$$

Our equation has $n+2$ unknowns. Taking the partial derivatives of L with respect to w_i, λ_1 and λ_2 and setting the first derivatives equal to zero, we can solve for the $n+2$ unknowns.

A Portfolio of Three Risky Assets

To illustrate, consider a portfolio with three risky assets. The *expected return* of the portfolio is:

$$w_a\bar{R}_a+w_b\bar{R}_b+w_c\bar{R}_c=\bar{R}_p$$

and

$$w_a+w_b+w_c=1.$$

The *variance* of the return on the portfolio in this case is:

$$\sigma_p^2=w_a^2\sigma_a^2+w_b^2\sigma_b^2+w_c^2\sigma_c^2+2w_a w_b\sigma_{ab}+2w_a w_c\sigma_{ac}+2w_b w_c\sigma_{bc} \quad \text{(A.26)}$$

We wish to minimize (A.26) subject to the same constraints we applied before. Forming the Lagrangian, we get:

$$\begin{aligned}L=&\,w_a^2\sigma_a^2+w_b^2\sigma_b^2+w_c^2\sigma_c^2+2w_a w_b\sigma_{ab}+2w_a w_c\sigma_{ac}+2w_b w_c\sigma_{bc}\\&+\lambda_1\left(w_a\bar{R}_a+w_b\bar{R}_b+w_c\bar{R}_c-\bar{R}_p\right)+\lambda_2\left(w_a+w_b+w_c-1\right)\end{aligned}$$

Taking the partial derivatives of L with respect to w_a, w_b, w_c, λ_1 and λ_2 and setting them equal to zero yields the following system of equations:

$$\frac{\partial L}{\partial w_a}=2w_a\sigma_a^2+2w_b\sigma_{ab}+2w_c\sigma_{ac}+\lambda_1\bar{R}_a+\lambda_2=0$$

$$\frac{\partial L}{\partial w_b}=2w_b\sigma_b^2+2w_a\sigma_{ab}+2w_c\sigma_{bc}+\lambda_1\bar{R}_b+\lambda_2=0$$

$$\frac{\partial L}{\partial w_c} = 2w_c\sigma_c^2 + 2w_a\sigma_{ac} + 2w_b\sigma_{ac} + \lambda_1\bar{R}_c + \lambda_2 = 0$$

$$\frac{\partial L}{\partial \lambda_1} = w_a\bar{R}_a + w_b\bar{R}_b + w_c\bar{R}_c - \bar{R}_p = 0$$

$$\frac{\partial L}{\partial \lambda_2} = w_a + w_b + w_c - 1 = 0$$

We can express this system of linear equations in matrix format as: $CX = K$.

$$\overset{C}{\begin{bmatrix} 2\sigma_a^2 & 2\sigma_{ab} & 2\sigma_{ac} & \bar{R}_a & 1 \\ 2\sigma_{ab} & 2\sigma_b^2 & 2\sigma_{bc} & \bar{R}_b & 1 \\ 2\sigma_{ac} & 2\sigma_{bc} & 2\sigma_c^2 & \bar{R}_c & 1 \\ \bar{R}_a & \bar{R}_b & \bar{R}_c & 0 & 0 \\ 1 & 1 & 1 & 0 & 0 \end{bmatrix}} \overset{X}{\begin{bmatrix} w_a \\ w_b \\ w_c \\ \lambda_1 \\ \lambda_2 \end{bmatrix}} = \overset{K}{\begin{bmatrix} 0 \\ 0 \\ 0 \\ \bar{R}_p \\ 1 \end{bmatrix}} \tag{A.27}$$

A solution to this system is $X = C^{-1}K$, where C^{-1} is the inverse of the matrix of coefficients.[4]

A Numerical Example

We have added a third risk asset to our previous numerical example: a commodity fund. Our target for the return on the portfolio is 9.5% (0.095). Table A.3 sums up the relevant information:

To find the weights of the three asset classes, substitute this information into C in (A.27), calculate the inverse of C, and multiply it by K.

$$C = \begin{bmatrix} 0.0648 & 0.0216 & 0.0288 & 0.1250 & 1 \\ 0.0216 & 0.0288 & 0.0024 & 0.0750 & 1 \\ 0.0288 & 0.0024 & 0.0800 & 0.0600 & 1 \\ 0.1250 & 0.0750 & 0.0600 & 0 & 0 \\ 1 & 1 & 1 & 0 & 0 \end{bmatrix}$$

[4] Multiply $CX = K$ by C^{-1} on either side to get $C^{-1}CX = C^{-1}K$ or $IX = C^{-1}K$, where I is the identity matrix. Hence, $X = C^{-1}K$.

Table A.3 Returns, volatility, correlations and covariances, three assets

Returns and vol.			Correlations				Covariances			
Asset	Returns	Volatility		Stocks	Bonds	Comm.		Stocks	Bonds	Comm.
Stocks	0.125	0.180	Stocks	1.00	0.50	0.40	Stocks	0.0324	0.0108	0.0144
Bonds	0.075	0.120	Bonds	0.50	1.00	0.05	Bonds	0.0108	0.0144	0.0012
Comm.	0.060	0.200	Comm.	0.40	0.05	1.00	Comm.	0.0144	0.0012	0.0400

$$C^{-1} = \begin{bmatrix} 0.699 & -3.030 & 2.331 & 17.729 & -1.263 \\ -3.030 & 13.132 & -10.101 & -10.157 & 1.473 \\ 2.331 & -10.101 & 7.770 & -7.571 & 0.790 \\ 17.729 & -10.157 & -7.571 & -12.782 & 0.886 \\ -1.263 & 1.473 & 0.790 & 0.886 & -0.084 \end{bmatrix}$$

$$X = \begin{bmatrix} 0.699 & -3.030 & 2.331 & 17.729 & -1.263 \\ -3.030 & 13.132 & -10.101 & -10.157 & 1.473 \\ 2.331 & -10.101 & 7.770 & -7.571 & 0.790 \\ 17.729 & -10.157 & -7.571 & -12.782 & 0.886 \\ -1.263 & 1.473 & 0.790 & 0.886 & -0.084 \end{bmatrix} \begin{bmatrix} 0 \\ 0 \\ 0 \\ 0.095 \\ 1 \end{bmatrix} = \begin{bmatrix} 0.4212 \\ 0.5084 \\ 0.0705 \\ -0.3279 \\ 0.0007 \end{bmatrix}$$

The first three entries in the last vector represent the portfolio weights. Stocks take up 42.1%, bonds 50.8% and commodities 7.1% (rounded). The expected return of the portfolio is $0.421 \times 12.5\ \% + 0.508 \times 7.5\ \% + 0.071 \times 6.0\ \% = 9.5\%$. Its standard deviation (square root of Eq. (A.26)) is 12.3% (rounded). Note that commodities have both a lower return and a higher volatility than stocks and bond, and thus look unattractive as a stand-alone asset. However, they still get a role in the optimal portfolio due to their low correlation with the other two assets.

Introducing a Risk-Free Asset

Our previous analysis concerned only risky assets. We now introduce a risk-free asset, f. Investors can borrow or lend at its level of interest, R_f.[5] Lending would correspond to, for example, making a deposit in a bank with an adequate deposit insurance or investing in T-bills. Given its risk-free nature, the variance and the standard deviation of its return, σ_f^2 and σ_f, are zero. Let r be a portfolio of risky assets with an expected return of $\overline{R}_r$. Using Eq. (A.1), we can express the expected return of a portfolio consisting of the risky and the risk-free asset as:

[5] This variation of the model is due to Tobin (1958).

$$\bar{R}_p = w_r \bar{R}_r + (1 - w_r) R_f \tag{A.28}$$

where w_r is the weight of the risky asset in the portfolio and $(1 - w_r)$ is the weight of the risk-free asset. Using Eq. (A.2), we can calculate the variance of the return of this portfolio as:

$$\sigma_p^2 = w_r^2 \sigma_r^2 + (1 - w_r)^2 \sigma_f^2 + 2w_r (1 - w_r) \sigma_{rf} \tag{A.29}$$

Since σ_f^2 and σ_f are zero, the covariance between the risk-fee and the risky asset, $\sigma_{rf} = \sigma_r \sigma_f \rho_{rf}$, is also zero. (A.29) therefore reduces to

$$\sigma_p^2 = w_r^2 \sigma_r^2$$

and

$$\sigma_p = \left[w_r^2 \sigma_r^2 \right]^{1/2} = w_r \sigma_r \tag{A.30}$$

Solving (A.30) for w_r we get $\frac{\sigma_p}{\sigma_r}$. Inserting this into (A.28) gives us the following expression:

$$\bar{R}_p = \frac{\sigma_p}{\sigma_r} \bar{R}_r + \left(1 - \frac{\sigma_p}{\sigma_r} \right) R_f$$

or

$$\bar{R}_p = R_f + \frac{(\bar{R}_r - R_f)}{\sigma_r} \sigma_p \tag{A.31}$$

$\bar{R}_p$ is a straight line, called the *capital allocation line* (CAL), depicting expected return and risk from different combinations of the risk-free asset and the risky assets. The intercept of $\bar{R}_p$ is R_f and its slope is $\frac{(\bar{R}_r - R_f)}{\sigma_r}$, representing the excess return for assuming an extra unit of risk. Figure A.4 provides an illustration. An investor might consider three different risky portfolios, A, B and C, the risk-free asset alone, or some combination of R_f and these portfolios. Or she might borrow at R_f and invest 150% of her wealth in a

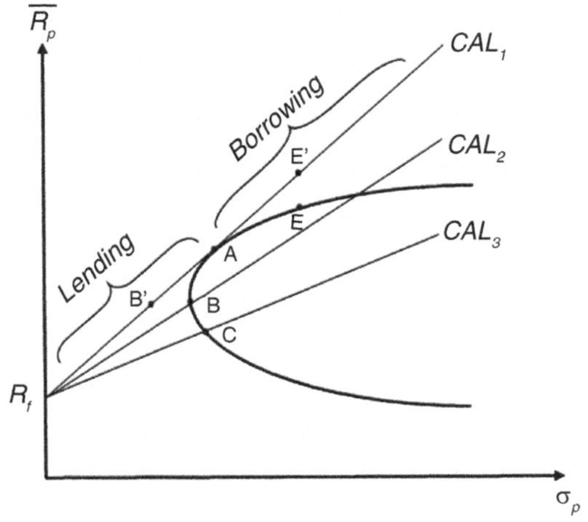

Fig. A.4 Efficient frontier with borrowing

portfolio of risky assets such as E'. To illustrate the last case, suppose that the risk-free rate is 4% and that the expected return on portfolio A is 11% (0.11). Assuming that point E' represents 150% of our investor's wealth, we use (A.28) to calculate the expected return:

$$\overline{R}_p = w_r\overline{R}_r + (1 - w_r)R_f = 1.5 \times 0.11 + (1 - 0.5) \times 0.04 = 0.145 \text{ or } 14.5\%$$

Note, that borrowing at the risk-free rate is the equivalent of having a negative weight in this asset. Suppose that the standard deviation of the return on A is 15%. Using (A.30), the standard deviation of this leveraged portfolio is:

$$\sigma_p = w_r\sigma_r = 1.5 \times 0.15 = 0.225 \text{ or } 22.5\%$$

We see that the three portfolios are all represented by straight lines emanating from R_f and going through either A, B or C. Of these three lines, CAL_1 is preferable because it has the highest slope (the highest Sharpe ratio). This is also the line which is tangent to the efficient frontier at point A. So the efficient frontier has now effectively become CAL_1. Except at the point of tangency (A), the new efficient frontier dominates the original one. To illustrate, portfolio B′ offers the same expected return as point B, but has a lower risk. Portfolio E', on the other hand, has the same risk as portfolio E, but a higher expected return. The inclusion of the risk-free asset alters the efficient frontier in a meaningful way.

The CAPM

The capital asset pricing model (CAPM)[6] extends the Markowitz mean-variance efficient framework, asking what the implications would be if all investors compose their portfolios according to this model. This equilibrium model offers an explanation of how risky assets are priced, that is, it's a descriptive model, as opposed to the Markowitz model which is prescriptive. It is based on a series of simplifying assumptions:

(i) All investors are risk-averse and compose their portfolios based on expected returns and standard deviation of returns.
(ii) Investors have the same one-period time horizon and the same estimates of expected returns and risk for this period.
(iii) All assets are perfectly divisible; investors can buy or sell any fraction of assets.
(iv) Investors can lend or borrow unlimited amounts at the same risk-free rate.
(v) There are no taxes and no transaction costs.
(vi) All relevant information is freely and simultaneously available to investors.

The Capital Market Line

On these assumptions, all investors will hold the same tangency portfolio of risky assets, even if they will differ with respect to lending or borrowing at the risk-free rate. The CAL is therefore the same for *all* investors and is referred to as the *capital market line* (CML). The CML is a straight line emanating from the risk-free rate R_f to the tangency portfolio, referred to as the *Market Portfolio*, M.

$$\bar{R}_p = R_f + \frac{\left(\bar{R}_M - R_f\right)}{\sigma_M^2}\sigma_p \tag{A.32}$$

The slope of the CML, $\frac{\left(\bar{R}_M - R_f\right)}{\sigma_M^2}$, represents the *market price of risk*, that is, the extra return obtained by increasing the level of risk by one unit. This is more commonly known as the *Sharpe ratio.* Since all investors will hold the market portfolio, in equilibrium it must contain all risky assets according to their market weight. If a given asset were not included, its demand would be effectively be

[6] Treynor (1962), Sharpe (1964), Lintner (1965a, b) and Mossin (1966).

zero, and its price would fall until its expected return rose sufficiently to induce inclusion into the market portfolio. We saw that when two assets are perfectly positively correlated, the set of portfolio possibilities becomes a straight line. Hence, all the portfolios on the CML are perfectly positively correlated, and their Sharpe ratio is the same of that of the market portfolio.

The Security Market Line and Beta

Given the assumption that investors hold only mean-variance efficient portfolios, all asset specific or unsystematic risk has been diversified away, and is therefore unrewarded. This implies that the only relevant risk measure for an individual asset, or portfolio, becomes its covariance with the market portfolio, σ_{iM}, which exhibits *systematic risk* only. Consistent with this, the return on individual assets can be expressed as:

$$\bar{R}_i = R_f + \frac{\left(\bar{R}_M - R_f\right)}{\sigma_M^2}\sigma_{iM} = \left(\bar{R}_M - R_f\right)\frac{\sigma_{iM}}{\sigma_M^2} \tag{A.33}$$

This equation is called the *security market line* (SML). The risk of the market as a whole becomes its covariance with itself which, as mentioned previously, is equal to its variance, that is, $\sigma_{MM} = \sigma_M^2$.

If we define $\frac{\sigma_{iM}}{\sigma_M^2}$ as β_i, (A.33) can now be written:

$$\bar{R}_i = R_f + \left(\bar{R}_M - R_f\right)\beta_i \tag{A.34}$$

which is the CAPM as it is commonly known.

β_i is central to the model. It is a *standardized measure* because it relates the covariance of an asset's return to the variance of the market portfolio. The slope of the SML is $\left(\bar{R}_M - R_f\right) / \beta_M$ where β_M denotes the beta of the market portfolio. Figure A.5 provides an illustration.

The beta of the market portfolio itself, $\beta_M = \frac{\sigma_{MM}}{\sigma_M^2}$ is 1, since $\sigma_{MM} = \sigma_M^2$. The slope of the SML therefore reduces to $\left(\bar{R}_M - \bar{R}_f\right)$ which is referred to as the *market risk premium* "Defensive" assets, such as A, with $\beta_i < 1$ have a lower than average systematic risk, "aggressive" assets, such as B, $\beta_i > 1$ have a higher than average systematic risk, while average assets $\beta_i = 1$ have the same risk as the market portfolio. In the first case, the expected return of the asset will be lower than that of the market portfolio, in the second case it will be higher, and in the

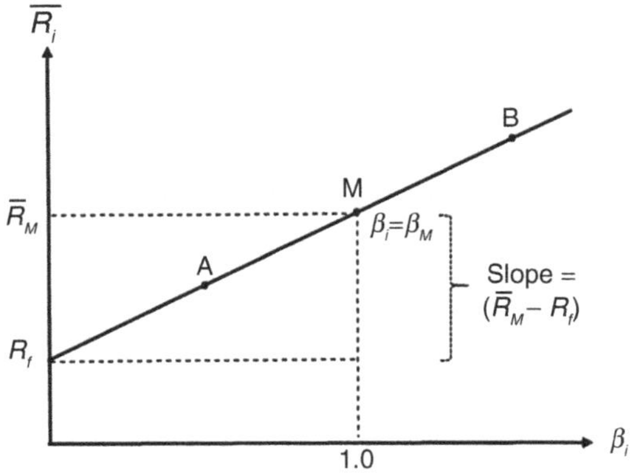

Fig. A.5 The security market line

third case it will be the same. The beta of a portfolio is simply the weighted average of the betas of its components securities, that is, $\beta_p = \sum_{i=1}^{n} \beta_i w_i$.

As an example, suppose the risk-free rate is 4% and the return on the market portfolio is 12%. To estimate the *required return* on an asset with β_i = 1.5, we insert into (A.34) to get:

$$\overline{R}_i = \left(\overline{R}_M - R_f\right)\beta_i = 0.04 + \left(0.12 - 0.04\right) \times 1.5 = 0.16 \text{ or } 16\%.$$

References

Acharya, V. V., and L. H. Pedersen 2005. "Asset Pricing with Liquidity Risk", *Journal of Financial Economics*, 77, 375–410.

Acharya, V. V., Y. Amihud, and S. Bharath. 2013. "Liquidity Risk of Corporate Bond Returns: A Conditional Approach", *Journal of Financial Economics*, 110, 358–386.

Altman, E. I. 1989. "Measuring Corporate Bond Mortality and Performance", *Journal of Finance*, 44(4), 909–922.

Amene, Noël, and Veronique Lesourd. 2003. "Portfolio Theory and Performance Analysis", Hoboken, NJ: John Wiley & Sons.

Amihud, Yakov, and Haim Mendelson. 1986. "Asset Pricing and the Bid–Ask Spread", *Journal of Financial Economics*, December, 17(2), 223–249.

Amihud, Yakov. 2002. "Illiquidity and Stock Returns: Cross-Section and Time-Series Effects", *Journal of Financial Markets*, January, 5(1), 31–56.

Anderson, R., S. Bianchi, and L. Goldberg. 2012. "Will My Risk Parity Strategy Outperform?", *Financial Analysts Journal*, 75–93.

Ang, Andrew, and J. Chen. 2002. "Asymmetric Correlations of Equity Portfolios", *Journal of Financial Economics*, 63(3), 443–494.

Ang, Andrew, Robert J. Hodrick, Yuhang Xing, and Xiaoyan Zhang. 2006. "The Cross-Section of Volatility and Expected Returns", *Journal of Finance*, 61, 259–299.

Ang, Andrew, Robert J. Hodrick, Yuhang Xing, and Xiaoyan Zhang. 2009a. "High Idiosyncratic Volatility and Low Returns: International and Further U.S. Evidence", *Journal of Financial Economics*, 91, 1–23.

Ang, Andrew, W. Goetzmann, and S. Schaefer. 2009b. "Evaluation of Active Management of the Norwegian Government Pension Fund–Global", Norwegian Government Pension Fund.

Arnott, Robert D., Jason Hsu, and Philip Moore. 2005. "Fundamental Indexation", *Financial Analysts Journal*, March/April, 61(2), 83–99.

H. Lumholdt, *Strategic and Tactical Asset Allocation*,
https://doi.org/10.1007/978-3-319-89554-3

Arnott, Robert D. 2006. "An Overwrought Orthodoxy", *Institutional Investor*, 18 December, 36–41.
Arnott, Rob, Noah Beck, Vitali Kalesnik, and John West. 2016a. "How Can 'Smart Beta' Go Horribly Wrong?", Research Affiliates, February.
Arnott, Robert D., Noah Beck, and Vitali Kalesnik. 2016b. "To Win with 'Smart Beta' Ask If the Price Is Right", Research Affiliates, June.
Arnott, Robert D., Noah Beck, and Vitali Kalesnik. 2016c. "Timing 'Smart Beta' Strategies? Of Course! Buy Low, Sell High!" Research Affiliates, September.
Artzner, P., F. Delbaen, J.-M. Eber, and D. Heath. 1999. "Coherent Measures of Risk", *Mathematical Finance*, 9, 203–228.
Asness, Clifford S. 2003. "Fight the Fed Model: The Relationship Between Future Returns and Stock and Bond Market Yields", *Journal of Portfolio Management*, Fall, 11–24.
Asness, Clifford S. 2006. "The Value of Fundamental Indexing", *Institutional Investor*, October, 40(10), 94–99.
Asness, Clifford S., Andrea Frazzini, and Lasse H. Pedersen. 2012. "Leverage Aversion and Risk Parity", *Financial Analysts Journal*, January/February, 68(1), 47–59.
Asness, Clifford S. 2012. "An Old Friend: The Stock Market's Shiller P/E". AQR Capital.
Asness, Clifford S., Andrea Frazzini, Ronen Israel, Tobias J. Moskowitz, and Lasse Heje Pedersen. 2015. "Size Matters, If You Control Your Junk", Fama-Miller Working Paper, January 22.
Asness, Clifford S., Swati Chandra, Antti Ilmanen, and Ronen Israel. 2017. "Contrarian Factor Timing Is Deceptively Difficult", *The Journal of Portfolio Management*, 43, 72–87.
Bae, K. H., G. A. Karolyi, and R. M. Stulz. 2003. "A New Approach to Measuring Financial Market Contagion", *Review of Financial Studies*, 16, 717–64.
Bailey, J. V., T. M. Richards, and D. E. Tierney. 1990. "Benchmarks, Portfolios and the Manager/Plan Sponsor Relationship", in Current Topics in Investment Management, ed. Frank J. Fabozzi and T. Dessa Fabozzi, 349–363. New York: Harper Collins.
Bailey, J. V. 1992. "Are Manager Universes Acceptable Performance Benchmarks?", *Journal of Portfolio Management*, Spring, 9–13.
Bailey, Jeffery V., Thomas M. Richards, and David E. Tierney. 2007. "Evaluating Portfolio Performance", in Managing Investment Portfolios: A Dynamic Approach, 3rd edition, ed. John Maginn, Donald Tuttle, Dennis McLeavey and Jerald Pinto. Hoboken, NJ: John Wiley & Sons.
Baker, Malcolm, Brendan Bradley, and Jeffrey Wurgler. 2011. "Benchmarks as Limits to Arbitrage: Understanding the Low-Volatility Anomaly", *Financial Analysts Journal*, 67(1), 40–54.
Baker, N. L., and R. A. Haugen. 2012. "Low Risk Stocks Outperform Within All Observable Markets of the World". Available at SSRN 2055431.
Banz, R. 1981. "The Relationship Between Return and Market Value of Common Stock", *Journal of Financial Economics*, 9, 3–18.

Barberis, Nicholas, Andrei Shleifer, and Robert Vishny. 1998. "A Model of Investor Sentiment", *Journal of Financial Economics*, 49(3), 307–343.

Barberis N., and M. Huang. 2001. "Mental Accounting, Loss Aversion, and Individual Stock Returns", *Journal of Finance*, 56, 1247–1292.

Basu, S. 1977. "Investment Performance of Common Stocks in Relation to Their Price-Earnings Ratios: A Test of the Efficient Market Hypothesis", *The Journal of Finance*, 663–682.

Bauman, S. W., M. C. Conover, and R. E. Miller. 1998. "Growth Versus Value and Large-Cap Versus Small-Cap Stocks in International Markets", *Financial Analysts Journal*, 75–89.

Bekaert, G., and E. Engstrom. 2010. "Inflation and the Stock Market: Understanding the 'FED Model", *Journal of Monetary Economics*, 57(3), 278–294.

Bender, Jennifer, and Taie Wang. 2016. "Can the Whole Be More than the Sum of the Parts? Bottom-Up Versus Top-Down Multifactor Portfolio Construction", *The Journal of Portfolio Management*, 42(5), 39–50

Bernstein, William J., and Robert D. Arnott. 2003. "Earnings Growth: The Two Percent Dilution", *Financial Analysts Journal*, 59(5), 47–55.

Best, Michael J., and Robert G. Grauer. 1991. "On the Sensitivity of Mean-Variance-Efficient Portfolios to Changes in Asset Means: Some Analytical and Computational Results", *Review of Financial Studies*, 4(2), 315. 28p.

Biswas, A. 2014. "The Output Gap and Expected Security Returns", *Review of Financial Economics*, 23(3), 131–140.

Black, Angela J., Bin Mao, and David G. McMillan. 2009. "The Value Premium and Economic Activity: Long-Run Evidence from the United States", *Journal of Asset Management*, 10(5), 305–317.

Blitz, David, and Pim Van Vliet. 2007. "The Volatility Effect: Lower Risk Without Lower Return", *Journal of Portfolio Management*, 102–113.

Blitz, D., J. Pang, and P. van Vliet. 2013. "The Volatility Effect in Emerging Markets", *Emerging Markets Review*, 16, 31–45.

Bodie, Zvi, Alex Kane, and Alan J. Marcus. 2014. "Investments", 10th edition. New York: McGraw-Hill-Irwin.

Bogle, John C. 1991a. "Investing in the 1990s", *The Journal of Portfolio Management*, 17, 5–14.

Bogle, John C. 1991b. "Investing in the 1990s: Occam's Razor Revisited", *The Journal of Portfolio Management*, 18, 88–91.

Bogle, John C., and Michael W. Nolan. 2015. "Occam's Razor Redux: Establishing Reasonable Expectations for Financial Market Returns", *The Journal of Portfolio Management*, 42, 119–134.

Brennan, Michael J., and Avanidhar Subrahmanyam. 1996. "Market Microstructure and Asset Pricing: On the Compensation for Illiquidity in Stock Returns", *Journal of Financial Economics*, July, 41(3), 441–464.

Britten-Jones, Mark. 1999. "The Sampling Error in Estimates of Mean-Variance Efficient Portfolio Weights", *The Journal of Finance*, 54(2), 655–671.

Brzenk, Phillip, and Aye Soe. 2015. "A Tale of Two Benchmarks: Five Years Later", S&P Dow Jones Indices, March.
Brinson, Gary P., and Nimrod Fachler. 1985. "Measuring Non-US Equity Portfolio Performance", *Journal of Portfolio Management*, Spring, 73–76.
Brinson, Gary P., L. Randolph Hood, and Gilbert L. Beebower. 1986. "Determinants of Portfolio Performance", *Financial Analysts Journal*, July/August, 42(4), 39–44.
Brinson, Gary P., Brian D. Singer, and Gilbert L. Beebower. 1991. "Determinants of Portfolio Performance II: An Update", *Financial Analysts Journal*, 47(3), 40–8.
Broadie, M. 1993. "Computing Efficient Frontiers Using Estimated Parameters", *Annals of Operations Research*: Special Issue on Financial Engineering, 45, 21–58.
Burmeister, Edwin, Richard Roll, and Stephen A. Ross. 1994. "A Practitioner's Guide to Arbitrage Pricing Theory", in A Practitioner's Guide to Factor Models, ed. John W. Peavy III, 1–30. Charlottesville: The Research Foundation of The Institute of Chartered Financial Analysts.
Cahan, Rochester, and Yin Luo. 2013. "Standing Out from the Crowd: Measuring Crowding in Quantitative Strategies", *Journal of Portfolio Management*, 39, 14–23.
Campbell, J. Y., and R. J. Shiller. 1991. "Yield Spreads and Interest Rate Movements: A Bird's Eye View", *Review of Economic Studies*, 58(3), 495–514.
Campbell, J. Y., and R. J. Shiller. 1998. "Valuation Ratios and the Long-Run Stock Market Outlook", *Journal of Portfolio Management*, Winter, 11–26.
Capaul, C., I. Rowley, and W. F. Sharpe. 1993. "International Value and Growth Stock Returns", *Financial Analysts Journal*, 27–36.
Carhart, Mark M. 1997. "On Persistence in Mutual Fund Performance", *The Journal of Finance*, March, 52(1), 57–82.
Chan, Kalok, A. Hameed, and W. Tong. 2000a. "Profitability of Momentum Strategies in International Equity Markets", *Journal of Financial and Quantitative Analysis*, 35, 153–172.
Chan, Louis K. C., Y. Hamao, and J. Lakonishok. 1991. "Fundamentals and Stock Returns in Japan", *The Journal of Finance*, 1739–1764.
Chan, Louis K. C., J. Karceski, and J. Lakonishok. 2000b. "New Paradigm or Same Old Hype in Equity Investing?", *Financial Analysts Journal*, 56(4), 23–36.
Chan, K. C., and Nai-Fu Chen. 1991. "Structural and Return Characteristics of Small and Large Firms", *The Journal of Finance*, 46.
Chen, Nai-Fu, Richard Roll, and Stephen A. Ross. 1986. "Economic Forces and the Stock Market", *Journal of Business*, 59(3), 383–403
Chen, Nai-fu. 1991. "Financial Investment Opportunities and the Macroeconomy", *Journal of Finance*, June, 529–554.
Chen, Nai-fu, and Feng Zhang. 1998. "Risk and Return of Value Stocks", *Journal of Business*, 71(4).
Chen, Honghui, Greg Noronha, and Vijay Singal. 2006. "Index Changes and Losses to Investors in S&P 500 and Russell 2000 Index Funds", *Financial Analysts Journal*, July/August.
Chen, L., D. Lesmond, and J. Wei. 2007. "Corporate Yield Spreads and Bond Liquidity", *Journal of Finance*, 62, 119–149.

Cheung, Y. Wong, and L. K. Ng. 1998. "International Evidence on the Stock Market and Aggregate Economic Activity", *Journal of Empirical Finance*, 5, 281–296.

Chordia, T., and L. Shivakumar. 2002. "Momentum, Business Cycle and Time-Varying Expected Returns", *Journal of Finance*, 57, 985–1019.

Chow, G., E. Jacquier, M. Kritzman, and K. Lowry. 1999. "Optimal Portfolios in Good Times and Bad", *Financial Analysts Journal*, 55(3), 65–73.

Christopherson, J. A. 1998. "Normal Portfolios: Construction of Customized Benchmarks", in Active Equity Portfolio Management, ed. F. J. Fabozzi. Frank J. Fabozzi Associates.

Collin-Dufresne, P., R. S. Goldstein, and J. S. Martin. 2001. "The Determinants of Credit Spread Changes", *Journal of Finance*, 56, 2177–2207.

Cooper, I., and R. Priestley. 2009. "Time-Varying Risk Premiums and the Output Gap", *Review of Financial Studies*, 22, 2801–2833.

Cutler, D. M., J. M. Poterba, and L. H. Summers. 1989. "What Moves Stock Prices?", *Journal of Portfolio Management*, 15, 4–12.

Daniel, Kent, David Hirshleifer, and Avanidhar Subrahmanyam. 1998. "Investor Psychology and Security Market Under- and Overreactions", *Journal of Finance*, 53, 1839–1886.

Dasgupta, Amil, Andrea Prat, and Michela Verardo. 2011. "The Price Impact of Institutional Herding", *Review of Financial Studies*, 24(3), 892–925.

Datar, Vinay, Narayanan Naik, and Robert Radcliffe. 1998. "Liquidity and Stock Returns: An Alternative Test", *Journal of Financial Markets*, August, 1(2), 203–219.

De Bondt, W., and R. Thaler. 1985. "Does the Stock Market Overreact?", *Journal of Finance*, 40, 793–805.

De Long, J. B., A. Shleifer, L. Summers, and R. Waldmann. 1990. "Noise Trader Risk in Financial Markets", *Journal of Political Economy*, 98, 703–738.

DeMiguel, Victor, Lorenzo Garlappi, and Raman Uppal. 2009. "Optimal Versus Naive Diversification: How Inefficient Is the 1/N Portfolio Strategy?", *Review of Financial Studies*, 22, 1915–1953.

Dichev, I. D. 1998. "Is the Risk of Bankruptcy a Systematic Risk?", *The Journal of Finance*, 53(3), 1131–1147.

Dick-Nielsen, J., P. Feldhütter, and D. Lando 2012. "Corporate Bond Liquidity Before and After the Onset of the Subprime Crisis", *Journal of Financial Economics*, 103, 471–492.

Dimson, Elroy, Paul Marsh, and Mike Staunton. 2002. "Triumph of the Optimists: 101 Years of Global Investment Returns". New Jersey: Princeton University Press.

Dimson, E., P. Marsh, and M. Stuanton. 2011. "Investment Style: Size, Value and Momentum", in Credit Suisse Global Investment Returns Sourcebook 2011, Credit Suisse Research Institute, Zurich, 41–54.

Driessen, J. 2005. "Is Default Event Risk Priced in Corporate Bonds?", *Review of Financial Studies*, 18, 165–195.

Duval, Jack. 2006. "The Myth of Time Diversification: Analysis, Application, and Incorrect New Account Forms", *PIABA Bar Journal*, Spring edition.

Elton, E. J., M. J. Gruber, D. Agrawal, and C. Mann 2001. "Explaining the Rate Spread on Corporate Bonds", *Journal of Finance*, 56, 427–465.

Elton, Edward J., Martin J. Gruber, Stephen J. Brown, and William N. Goetzmann, 2014. "Modern Portfolio Theory and Investment Analysis", 9th Ed., Wiley.

Estrada, J. 2009. "The Fed Model: The Bad, the Worse and the Ugly", *Quarterly Review of Economics and Finance*, 49, 214–238.

Estrada, J. 2007. "Investing in the Twenty-First Century: With Occam's Razor and Bogle's Wit", *Corporate Finance Review*, May/June.

Fama, E. F. 1965. "The Behaviour of Stock-Market Prices", *Journal of Business*, 38, 34–105.

Fama, E., and R. Bliss. 1987. "The Information in Long-Maturity Forward Rates", *American Economic Review*, 77, 680–692.

Fama, E. F., and K. R. French. 1992. "The Cross-Section of Expected Stock Returns", *Journal of Finance*, 47(2), 427–465.

Fama, E. F., and K. R. French. 1995. "Size and Book-to-Market Factors in Earnings and Returns", *Journal of Finance*, 50(1), 131–155.

Fama, E. F., and K. R. French. 1998. "Value Versus Growth: The International Evidence", *The Journal of Finance*, 1975–1999.

Feibel, Bruce J. 2003. "Investment Performance Analysis". Hoboken, NJ: John Wiley & Sons.

Feinman, J. 2005. "Inflation Illusion and the (Mis)pricing of Assets and Liabilities", *Journal of Investing*, Summer, 29–36.

Ferreira, M. A., and P. Santa-Clara. 2011. "Forecasting Stock Market Returns: The Sum of the Parts Is More than the Whole", *Journal of Financial Economics*, 100(3), 514–537.

Flannery, M. J., and A. A. Protopapadakis 2002. "Macroeconomic Factors Do Influence Aggregate Stock Returns", *The Review of Financial Studies*, 15(3), 751–782.

Fons, J. S. 1987. "The Default Premium and Corporate Bond Experience", *Journal of Finance*, 42(1), 81–97.

Forner, C., and J. Marhuenda 2003. "Contrarian and Momentum Strategies in the Spanish Stock Market", *European Financial Management*, 9(1), 67–88.

Francis, J. C., and D. Kim. 2013. "Modern Portfolio Theory: Foundations, Analysis, and New Developments". Hoboken, NJ: John Wiley & Sons, Inc.

Frazzini, A., and L. Pedersen. 2014. "Betting Against Beta", *Journal of Financial Economics*, 111, 1–25.

George, Thomas, and Chuan-Yang Hwang. 2004. "The 52-Week High and Momentum Investing", *Journal of Finance*, 59, 2145–2176.

Glaser, M., and M. Weber. 2003. "Momentum and Turnover: Evidence from the German Stock Market", *Schmalenbach Business Review*, 55, 108–135.

Goetzmann, William N., Stephen J. Brown, Martin J. Gruber, and Edwin J. Elton. 2014. "Modern Portfolio Theory and Investment Analysis", 9th edition, John Wiley & Sons.

Grossman, S. J., and J. E. Stiglitz. 1980. "On the Impossibility of Informationally Efficient Markets", *American Economic Review*, 70(3), 393–408.

Hameed, A., and Y. Kusnadi. 2002. "Momentum Strategies: Evidence from Pacific Basin Stock Markets", *Journal of Financial Research*, 25(3), 383–397.

Harvey, C. R., Y. Liu, and H. Zhu. 2016. "… and the Cross-Section of Expected Returns", *The Review of Financial Studies*, 29(1), 5–68.

Haugen, Robert A., and A. James Heins. 1972. "On the Evidence Supporting the Existence of Risk Premiums in the Capital Markets", Wisconsin Working Paper, December.

Haugen, Robert A., and A. James Heins. 1975. "Risk and the Rate of Return on Financial Assets: Some Old Wine in New Bottles", *Journal of Financial and Quantitative Analysis*, 10, 775–784.

Haugen, Robert A., and Nardin L. Baker. 1991. "The Efficient Market Inefficiency of Capitalization-Weighted Stock Portfolios", *The Journal of Portfolio Management*, 35–40.

Hodrick, Robert J., and Edward C. Prescott. 1997. "Postwar U.S. Business Cycles: An Empirical Investigation", *Journal of Money, Credit and Banking*, 29(1), 1–16.

Holston, Kathryn, Thomas Laubach, and John C. Williams. 2016. "Measuring the Natural Rate of Interest: International Trends and Determinants", FRB San Francisco Working Paper, December.

Hon, M. T., and I. Tonks. 2003. "Momentum in the United Kingdom Stock Market", *Journal of Multinational Financial Management*, 13(1), 43–70.

Hong, Harrison, and Jeremy C. Stein. 1999. "A Unified Theory of Underreaction, Momentum Trading and Overreaction in Asset Markets", *Journal of Finance*, 54, 2143–2184.

Horowitz, J. L., Loughran Tim, N. E. Savin. 2000. "The Disappearing Size Effect", *Research in Economics*, 54.

Hou, Kewei, Chen Xue, and Lu Zhang. 2017. "Replicating Anomalies", NBER Working Paper No. 23394.

Houweling, P., A. Mentink, and T. Vorst. 2005. "Comparing Possible Proxies of Corporate Bond Liquidity", *Journal of Banking & Finance*, 29(6), 1331–1358.

Houweling, Patrick, and Jeroen van Zundert. 2017. "Factor Investing in the Corporate Bond Market", *Financial Analyst Journal*, 73(2), 100–115.

Huang, J., and M. Huang. 2012. "How Much of the Corporate-Treasury Yield Spread Is Due to Credit Risk?", *Review of Asset Pricing Studies*, 2(2), 153–202.

Hsu, J. C., H. Kudoh, T. Yamada. 2013. "When Sell-Side Analysts Meet High-Volatility Stocks: An Alternative Explanation for the Low-Volatility Puzzle", *Journal of Investment Management*, 11(2), 28–46.

Ibbotson, Roger G., and Paul D. Kaplan. 2000. "Does Asset Allocation Policy Explain 40, 90, or 100 Percent of Performance?", *Financial Analysts Journal*, January/February, 56(1), 26–33.

Ibbotson, Roger G. 2010. "The Importance of Asset Allocation", *Financial Analysts Journal*, March/April, 66, 18–20.

Ibbotson, R., Z. Chen, D. Kim, and W. Hu. 2013. "Liquidity as an Investment Style", *Financial Analysts Journal*, 69(3), 30–44.

Ibbotson, Roger, Roger J. Harrington, and James P. Harrington. 2017. "Stocks, Bonds, Bills and Inflation (SBBI) Yearbook". Wiley.

Ilmanen, Antti. 2011. "Expected Returns: An Investor's Guide to Harvesting Market Rewards". Chichester, UK: John Wiley & Sons.

Ilmanen, Antti, and Jared Kizer. 2012. "The Death of Diversification Has Been Greatly Exaggerated", *Journal of Portfolio Management*, Spring, 38(3), 15–27.

Ilmanen, Antti, and Thomas Maloney. 2015. "Portfolio Rebalancing, Part 1 of 2: Strategic Asset Allocation", AQR Portfolio Solutions Group.

Israel, R., D. Palhares, and S. A. Richardson. 2016. "Common Factors in Corporate Bond and Bond Fund Returns", AQR Working Paper.

Israel, Ronen, and Adrienne Ross. 2017. "Measuring Factor Exposures: Uses and Abuses", *The Journal of Alternative Investments*, 20(1), 10–25.

Jegadeesh, N., and S. Titman. 1993. "Returns to Buying Winners and Selling Losers: Implications for Stock Market Efficiency", *Journal of Finance*, 48(1), 65–91.

Jegadeesh, N., and S. Titman. 2001. "Profitability of Momentum Strategies: An Evaluation of Alternative Explanations", *Journal of Finance*, 56(2), 699–720.

Jensen, Michael. 1968. "The Performance of Mutual Funds in the Period 1945–1964", *Journal of Finance*, 23(2), 389–416.

Jensen, Gerald, and Jeffrey Mercer. 2002. "Monetary Policy and the Cross-Section of Expected Stock Returns", *Journal of Financial Research*, Spring, 55, 125–139.

Jung, Jeeman, and Robert Shiller. 2005. "Samuelson's Dictum and the Stock Market", *Economic Inquiry*, 43(2), 221–228.

Kaplan, Paul D. 2008. "Why Fundamental Indexation Might—or Might Not—Work", *Financial Analysts Journal*, January/February, 64(1), 32–39.

Kaplan, Paul D. 2009. "Déjà Vu All Over Again", Morningstar Advisor, (February/March): 29–33.

Keim, D. B. 1983. "Size-Related Anomalies and Stock Return Seasonality: Further Empirical Evidence", *Journal of Financial Economics*, 12, 13–32.

Klement, Joachim. 2015. "What's Growth Got to Do with It? Equity Returns and Economic Growth", *Journal of Investing*, 24(2), 74–78.

Kritzman, Mark. 1987. "How to Build a Normal Portfolio in Three Easy Steps", *The Journal of Portfolio Management*, Summer, 13(21–23).

Kritzman, Mark. 1994. "What Practitioners Need to Know … About Time Diversification", *Financial Analysts Journal*, January/February, 14–18.

Kritzman, M., and D. Rich. 2002. "The Mismeasurement of Risk", *Financial Analysts Journal*, 58, 91–99.

Kritzman, M., and Y. Li. 2010. "Skulls, Financial Turbulence, and Risk Management", *Financial Analysts Journal*, 66, 30–41.

Kritzman, M., S. Page, and D. Turkington. 2010. "In Defense of Optimization: The Fallacy of 1/N", *Financial Analysts Journal*, 66(2), 31–39.

Kumar, Alok. 2009. "Who Gambles in the Stock Market?", *Journal of Finance*, August, 64(4), 1889–1933.

Kuenzi, David E. 2008. "Strategy Benchmarks", *Journal of Portfolio Management*, 29(2), 46–56.

Lakonishok, Josef, Andrei Shleifer, and Robert W. Vishny. 1992a. "The Impact of Institutional Trading on Stock Prices", *Journal of Financial Economics*, 32, 23–43.

Lakonishok, Josef, Andrei Shleifer, and Robert W. Vishny. 1992b. "The Structure and Performance of the Money Management Industry", *Brookings Papers on Economic Activity: Microeconomics.*

Lakonishok, J., A. Shleifer, and R. W. Vishny. 1994. "Contrarian Investment, Extrapolation, and Risk", *Journal of Finance*, 49, 1541–1578.

La Porta, Rafael, Josef Lakonishok, Andrei Shleifer, and Robert Vishny. 1997. "Good News for Value Stocks: Further Evidence on Market Efficiency", *Journal of Finance*, 52, 859–874.

Ledoit, Olivier, and Michael Wolf. 2003. "Improved Estimation of the Covariance Matrix of Stock Returns with an Application to Portfolio Selection", *Journal of Empirical Finance*, 10, 603–621.

Ledoit, Olivier, and Michael Wolf. 2004. "Honey, I Shrunk the Sample Covariance Matrix – Problems in Mean-Variance Optimization", *Journal of Portfolio Management*, 30(4), 110–119.

Lin, H., J. Wang, and C. Wu. 2011. "Liquidity Risk and Expected Corporate Bond Returns", *Journal of Financial Economics*, 99, 628–650.

Lintner, John. 1965a. "The Valuation of Risk Assets and the Selection of Risky Investments in Stock Portfolios and Capital Budgets", *Review of Economics and Statistics*, February, 47, 13–37.

Lintner, John. 1965b. "Security Prices, Risk and Maximal Gains from Diversification", *Journal of Finance*, December, 20, 587–615.

Litterman, R., and J. Scheinkman 1991. "Common Factors Affecting Bond Returns", *Journal of Fixed Income*, 1, 51–61.

Liu, W. 2006. "A Liquidity-Augmented Capital Asset Pricing Model", *Journal of Financial Economics*, 82(3), 631–671.

Liu, X., and L. Zhang. 2008. "Momentum Profits, Factor Pricing, and Macroeconomic Risk", *Review of Financial Studies*, 21, 2417–2448.

Lo, A., and A. MacKinlay. 1990. "Data-Snooping Biases in Tests of Financial Asset Pricing Models", *Review of Financial Studies*, 3, 431–467.

Lo, Andrew W. 2016. "What Is an Index?", *The Journal of Portfolio Management*, 42(2), 21–36.

Longin, F., and B. Solnik. 2001. "Extreme Correlation of International Equity Markets", *Journal of Finance*, 56(2), 649–676.

Longstaff, F., S. Mithal, and E. Neis. 2005. "Corporate Yield Spreads: Default Risk or Liquidity? New Evidence from the Credit-Default-Swap Market", *Journal of Finance*, 60, 2213–2253.

Mandelbrot, B. B. 1963a. "New Methods in Statistical Economics", *Journal of Political Economy*, 71, 421–40.

Mandelbrot, B. B. 1963b. "The Variation of Certain Speculative Prices", *Journal of Business*, 36, 394–419.

Markowitz, Harry. 1952. "Portfolio Selection", *Journal of Finance*, March, 7, 77–91.

Markowitz, Harry. 1959. Portfolio Selection: Efficient Diversifications of Investments. Cowles Foundation. Monograph No. 16. New York: John Wiley & Sons, Inc.

Michaud, R. 1989. "The Markowitz Optimization Enigma: Is Optimization Optimal?" *Financial Analysts Journal*, 45(1), 31–42.

Modigliani, Franco, and Leah Modigliani. 1997. "Risk-Adjusted Performance", *Journal of Portfolio Management*, Winter, 23(2), 45–54.

Mossin, Jan. 1966. "Equilibrium in a Capital Asset Market", *Econometrica*, October, 35, 768–83.

Muga, L., and R. Santamaria. 2007. "The Momentum Effect in Latin American Emerging Markets", *Emerging Markets Finance and Trade*, 43(4), 24–45.

Pástor, Ĺuboš, and Robert Stambaugh. 2003. "Liquidity Risk and Expected Stock Returns", *Journal of Political Economy*, June, 111(3), 642–685.

Peach, Richard, Robert Rich, and Anna Cororaton. 2011. "How Does Slack Influence Inflation?", Federal Reserve of New York, *Current Issues in Economics and Finance*, 17(3).

Perold, André F., and William F. Sharpe. 1988. "Dynamic Strategies for Asset Allocation", *Financial Analyst Journal*, January, 16–27.

Perold, André F. 2007. "Fundamentally Flawed Indexing", *Financial Analysts Journal*, November/December, 63(6), 31–37.

Rachev, S. T., C. Menn, and F. J. Fabozzi. 2005. "Fat-Tailed and Skewed Asset Distributions". New York: Wiley.

Reinganum, M. R. 1981. "Misspecification of Capital Asset Pricing: Empirical Anomalies Based on Earnings' Yields and Market Values", *Journal of Financial Economics*, 9, 19–46.

Ritter, J. R. 2005. "Economic Growth and Equity Returns", *Pacific-Basin Finance Journal*, 13, 489–503.

Ritter, J. R. 2012. "Is Economic Growth Good for Investors?" *Journal of Applied Corporate Finance*, 24(3), 8–18.

Rockafellar, T. R., and S. Uryasev 2002. "Conditional Value-at-Risk for General Loss Distribution", *Journal of Banking and Finance*, 26(7), 1443–1471.

Roll, R. 1977. "A Critique of the Asset Pricing Theory's Tests", *Journal of Financial Economics*, March, 4(2), 129–176.

Roll, Richard. 1978. "Ambiguity When Performance Is Measured by the Securities Market Line", *Journal of Finance*, September, 33(4), 1051–1069.

Rosenberg, B., K. Reid, and R. Lanstein. 1985. Persuasive Evidence of Market Inefficiency, *The Journal of Portfolio Management*, Institutional Investor Journals, 11, 9–16.

Ross, Stephen. 1976. "The Arbitrage Theory of Capital Asset Pricing", *Journal of Economic Theory*, 13(3), 341–360.

Rouwenhorst, K. G. 1998. "International Momentum Strategies", *Journal of Finance*, 53(1), 267–284.

Samuelson, P. A. 1963. "Risk and Uncertainty: A Fallacy of Large Numbers", *Scientia*, April/May, 1–6.

Samuelson, Paul. 1998. "Summing Up on Business Cycles: Opening Address", in Beyond Shocks: What Causes Business Cycles, Conference Series 42, ed. J. Fuhrer and S. Schuh, 33–36. Boston: Federal Reserve Bank of Boston.

Schwert, G. W. 2003. "Anomalies and Market Efficiency", in Handbook of the Economics of Finance, ed. G. M. Constantinides, M. Harris, and R. M. Stulz, 939–974. Boston: Elsevier.

Shackleton, Robert. 2018. "Estimating and Projecting Potential Output Using CBO's Forecasting Growth Model", Congressional Budget Office, Working Paper 2018-03, February.

Shankar, S. Gowri. 2007. "Active Versus Passive Index Management: A Performance Comparison of the S&P and the Russell Indexes", *The Journal of Investing*, 16-2, 85–95.

Sharpe, William F. 1964. "Capital Asset Prices: A Theory of Market Equilibrium Under Conditions of Risk", *Journal of Finance*, September, 19, 425–442.

Sharpe, William F. 1966. "Mutual Fund Performance", *Journal of Business*, January, 39, 119–38.

Sharpe, William. 1988. "Determining a Fund's Effective Asset Mix", *Investment Management Review*, 2(6), 59–69.

Sharpe, William. 1992. "Asset Allocation, Management Style and Performance Measurement", *Journal of Portfolio Management*, 18(2), 7–19.

Sharpe, William F. 1994. "The Sharpe Ratio", *The Journal of Portfolio Management*, 21(1), 49–58.

Sharpe, William F., Peng Chen, Jerald E. Pinto, and Dennis W. McLeavey. 2007. "Asset Allocation", in Managing Investment Portfolios: A Dynamic Approach, 3rd edition, ed. John Maginn, Donald Tuttle, Dennis McLeavey and Jerald Pinto. Hoboken, N.J.: John Wiley & Sons.

Sheikh, A., and J. Sun. 2012. "Regime Change: Implications of Macroeconomic Shifts on Asset Class and Portfolio Performance", *The Journal of Investing*, 21(3), 36–54.

Shiller, Robert. 1990. "Market Volatility". Cambridge, MA: MIT Press.

Shleifer, A., and R. Vishny. 1990. "Equilibrium Short Horizons of Investors and Firms", *American Economic Review Papers and Proceedings*, 80, 148–153.

Siegel, Jeremy. 2006. "The Noisy Market' Hypothesis", *Wall Street Journal*, June 14.

Siegel, Jeremy. 2014. "Stocks for the Long Run", 5th edition. New York: McGraw Hill.

Soe, Aye, and Srikant Dash. 2009. "A Tale of Two Benchmarks". Standard & Poor's Occasional Paper, June.

Statman, M. 2000. "The 93.6 Per cent Question of Financial Advisors", *Journal of Investing*, Spring, 9(1), 16–20.

Stoll, H. R., and R. E.Whaley. 1983. "Transaction Costs and the Small Firm Effect", *Journal of Financial Economics*, 12, 57–79.

Swensen, David F. 2009. "Pioneering Portfolio Management: An Unconventional Approach to Institutional Investment". New York, NY: Free Press.

Taylor, John B. 1993. "Discretion Versus Policy Rules in Practice", *Carnegie-Rochester Conference Series on Public Policy*, 39, 195–214.

Tobin, James. 1958. "Liquidity Preference as Behavior Towards Risk", *Review of Economic Studies*, February, 25, 68–85.

Treynor, J. L. 1962. "Toward a Theory of Market Value of Risky Assets", Unpublished manuscript. Final version in Asset Pricing and Portfolio Performance, 1999, ed. Robert A. Korajczyk, 15–22. London: Risk Books.

Treynor, J. L. 1965. "How to Rate the Performance of Mutual Funds", *Harvard Business Review*, January/February, 43, 63–75.

Van Dijk, M. A. 2011. "Is Size Dead? A Review of the Size Effect in Equity Returns", *Journal of Banking & Finance*, 35(12), 3263–327.

Vazza, D., and N. Kraemer. 2017. "2016 Annual Global Corporate Default Study and Rating Transition", Standard & Poor's Rating Services, April 13.

Williams, John C. 2017. "Three Questions on R-star", FRBSF Economic Letter, February.

Xiong, James X., Roger G. Ibbotson, Thomas M. Idzorek, and Peng Chen. 2010. "The Equal Importance of Asset Allocation and Active Management", *Financial Analysts Journal*, March/April, 22–30.

Xiong, J. X., and T. M. Idzorek. 2011. "The Impact of Skewness and Fat Tails on the Asset Allocation Decision", *Financial Analysts Journal*, 67(2), 23–35.

Yee, Kenton K. 2010. "Combining Fundamental Measures for Stock Selection", in Handbook of Quantitative Finance and Risk Management, Springer.

Zhang, Lu. 2005. "The Value Premium", *The Journal of Finance*, 60(1), 67–102.

Index[1]

[1] Note: Page numbers followed by 'n' refer to notes.

H. Lumholdt, *Strategic and Tactical Asset Allocation*,
https://doi.org/10.1007/978-3-319-89554-3

N

O

P

Q

R

The manufacturer's authorised representative in the EU is Springer Nature Customer Service Centre GmbH, Europaplatz 3, 69115 Heidelberg, Germany. If you have any concerns regarding our products, please contact ProductSafety@springernature.com

Printed and bound by CPI Group (UK) Ltd, Croydon, CR0 4YY
30/09/2026
02225660-0016